P9-CAN-602

Child Studies through Fantasy

Child Studies through Fantasy

Cognitive-Affective Patterns in Development

Rosalind Gould, Ph.D.
Adjunct Professor, Postdoctoral Program
New York University

QUADRANGLE BOOKS
A New York Times Company

Copyright © 1972 by Rosalind Gould

All rights reserved,
including the right to reproduce this book
or portions thereof in any form.

For information, address: Quadrangle Books, Inc.
330 Madison Avenue,
New York, New York 10017

Manufactured in the United States of America

Library of Congress Catalog Card Number: 72–189148

For Irving, Nora, Julie, and Amy

Tell me where is fancy bred,
Or in the heart or in the head?
How begot, how nourished?
   Reply, Reply.
It is engender'd in the eyes,
With gazing fed; and fancy dies
In the cradle where it lies.
   Let us all ring fancy's knell;
   I'll begin it,—Ding, dong, bell.

—*Merchant of Venice, III, 2*

Contents

Foreword

by Barbara Biber
Bank Street College of Education

Perhaps the sheer complexity of the phenomenon of cognitive-affective interdependence explains the familiar retreat to the study of one or the other arm of the phenomenon with a lingering discontent over not being able to keep the two fundamental forces that govern behavior simultaneously in focus. Some progress toward synthesis has been made since Susan Isaacs and Jean Piaget argued the problem from their two different vantage points across the English channel. Now, dedicated exponents of the Piagetian system for understanding thought processes have noted the need for major parallel work on social-emotional development. There is also considerable coming together of views since the development of an ego-psychology as part of psychoanalytic theory, reflecting expanded interest in the cognitive aspects of dealing with reality. The study presented in this book represents a major effort at synthesis, not on an abstract theoretical level but through detailed study of fantasy behavior in the early years of childhood.

The author selected for study the fantasy expression of children three, four and five years old, who were being observed in the natural situation of a nursery school where the opportunity was provided for the expression of spontaneous fantasy as part of an educational philosophy. Taken against the background of knowledge of the psychological climate of the children's home life situations, the fantasy expressed in play has been used by the author as a reflection of "the ways affects and cognition may evolve and intertwine in interdependent patterns that advance or handicap learning and personality development." The systems of the two recognized masters of their respective fields—Piaget and Freud—are the foundation for analysis. The terms of interpretation utilize concepts of both systems fluently and naturally to bring out the less-than-obvious meanings of the manifest play content. The architecture of this study report carries successfully the implicit message of the final inseparability of thought and feeling, of the impersonal and the personal, of the objective and the subjective, reinforced by explicit statements of the dynamic processes involved. The reader is asked to move back and forth from the concrete content and imagery of children's play creations to highly abstract conceptual formulations. The impact is strong, stimulating and intellectually integrating.

That play can yield insight into the progression of cognitive powers is recognized; in fact, has become a subject of intensified study and research. The present study treats affect, as expressed in the changing representations and actions of the children's make-believe play inventions, as a systematic variable in the total growth process, which takes new forms and generates new mechanisms as children progress through early childhood.

Furthermore, the study demonstrates how the variables of cognition and affect interact toward alternative outcomes of support or interference. Here the present work offers the reader new insight. This comes through in part in the author's significant pauses—reflective, interpretive, conceptual—about successive developmental milestones that point up the cumulative interdependency of these two systematic variables. Thus, one comes to recognize not only how early representation of the self in fantasy bespeaks a cognitive achievement in self differentiation, but also how the very capacity to represent oneself, or "the other" as well as the qualitative variations in the selected representations of self have roots in the good or bad core-self feeling established in earliest experiences with need, fulfillment and denial. Or, at a later developmental period, when the child is beginning to internalize standards of behavior, the code he develops for himself is seen as the product in part of cognitive capacity to engage in objective causal thinking, to distinguish actions from intentions and to foresee consequences. It is seen simultaneously as taking its character from the quality of the child's experiences in being cared for, controlled or prohibited, and from the extent to which these have yielded him confidence in his own good impulses and controls.

There is a Rashomon quality to the book at hand. It can be read from several different perspectives and has internal consistencies for each one. It is, from one perspective, a sequential study of moral development derived from study of fantasy expression and focused on the motivational factors that enter into value-based behavior. As would be expected, the characteristics that mark cognitive growth in the young child's involvement with action and thought in reality have a similar prototype in his fantasy expression: the number and complexity of ideas increase, verbal and action forms become more elaborate, and span of content wider and more extended beyond the realm of immediate and personal experience. In this study the author deals with a very different series of dimensions applicable to the manifest content of fantasy productions which can serve as additional developmental indices and which can help to locate significant points and processes of cognitive-affective interdependency in specific, researchable terms. For some of these, the author has suggested a sequential pattern for the child population she studied. Use of more distant rather than the direct "I" forms of representation appear later. The oscillation between fantasy and reality in fantasy-play decreases between the ages of three and five. The relatively advanced differentiation of five year olds appears in the more graded shifts between love and hate in their fantasy expression and fewer assumptions of either —or shifts or reversals expected from their affects. Capacity to project one's self as an animal or person is to be expected developmentally at an early age; inability to do so after age three signals interference. The roles taken are the markers of successive or alternating identifications which describe the course of development toward one or another kind of superego functioning. It is not to be expected that cognitive advances will be parallel in all domains of functioning. Comprehension of reciprocal relations may be achieved in "impersonal" areas between four and five years of age but delayed in "personal" areas. Under six years, one may expect only the beginnings of objectified reasoning in situations real or projected that affect the child personally compared to more advanced capacity in impersonal situations.

From another perspective the author develops a series of constructs that deal with the directional impact of the child's life experience on the nature of the code that emerges. Contrary to some formulations in psychoanalytic theory about the "archaic" superego, she offers evidence for regarding the earliest experiences in being provided for and taken care of as seeding and governing distinctive courses of superego evolution. Under positive circumstances, having his first basic demands met generates what the author calls a "sense of entitlement," a feeling of goodness which, in her opinion, will be maintained as a vital "affect organizer" of thought and intentionality and serves as the substratum for a later "sense of autonomy" and "sense of competence." The emergence of the wish-to-please and the identification with the provider figures in the child's life are dynamic processes that support development of ego resources. Optimally, in the author's opinion, the child's affective orientation toward adults as provider-caretakers should be established *before* they emerge as authority figures active in guiding controls of aggressive impulses. At a later stage, when the child is gradually developing his own conscience, the quality of his real life experiences with authority—how severely repressive or how moderated—is reflected in at least two ways in fantasy expression: first, in the tendency to use self representations that indicate identification with an aggressor or a provider-figure and second, in the tendency to engage in a pervasive, global self-condemnation in contrast to a limited, differentiated self-denigration. Ideally, if the child has a balance of patterns of libidinal-aggressive experiences of his world, the inevitable conflicts associated with aggressive impulses will be progressively dissolved as part of the growth process. He will be developing viable internalized controls and a sense of self-esteem connected with being able to act on these guidelines and being identified with the ideal representations which underly them. The author calls this achievement in the evolution of morality "superego constancy," and posits the interrelated development of object constancy and affective superego constancy. She regards such superego constancy as the basic ground for "internalized morality-evaluative directives in young children . . . that will lead them to choose to be good, not simply fear to be bad."

The reader can take a third perspective in which the sequential ordering of milestones in the evolution of morality serves as background and the center of attention becomes the records of the individual children and their interpretations by the author. The characteristics of fantasy expression that were used as dimensions on which to thread the developmental sequence can serve as cues for arriving at a coherent image of how an individual child is working through the inevitable dilemmas and conflicts of growing up, especially those connected with management of aggressive impulses.

From material presented on the individual children it is possible to derive a tool useful both to educational and research programs, namely, a series of questions that can be asked and answered by teachers or others taking the position of discriminating observers. Can the child engage in fantasy expression? Does he use himself as the direct "I" or does he find ways of distancing himself from being the direct agent of aggressive fantasy? In the roles he takes does he have a stable identification? Is his self-representation aligned with a provider, aggressor, or victim figure? Does he maintain a steady stance of "pretending" or does he show uncertainty about the distinction between the real and the fantasied? Do his fantasy productions show integration of knowledge of the real world with affect dynamics? Are his fantasies predominated by aggressive themes? Does he engage in unmitigated self-condemnation?

The potential value of "reading" fantasy expression in these terms becomes clear in the author's presentation of the widely contrasting patterns of the fantasy of the children in the study group and the contrasting prognostic pictures which they present. On the positive side, there is a child like Rondi who could use her knowledge of the real world as material for the elaborations of fantasied affect without becoming unsettled as to the boundaries of the real and the pretend, use distance devices to protect against anxiety associated with aggressive fantasy, find compromise solutions to aggression-conflict situations, use her imagination flexibly and place herself predominantly in the role of the provider. This child's fantasy pattern indicates a generally positive growth pattern of "progressive synchronous learning and affect experience in the real world."

By contrast, on the negative side, there is a child like Clara who is directly involved with aggressive fantasy, not having developed the possible modes of fantasy expression that protect against the anxiety generated by aggressive fantasy especially when it is directed, as it was in her case, against primary family members or other important figures such as her teachers. This kind of preoccupation with primitive aggressive-impulse imagery, devoid of the protective distance forms of more highly developed fantasy mechanisms, interferes with the synchronous development that can be predicted for children like Rondi. Even approximate mastery of the observational tools and the conceptual analysis set forth in the records of the children could lead to useful and much-needed clarification of the vague label so often applied—the "disturbed child."

At one point the author says: "The study records may be summarized in the manner of the paleontologist who recreates entire creatures from a few essential bones," an apt reflection that nevertheless understates an important characteristic of the data. As a fourth perspective, these records have certain special characteristics. Teachers' records in another kind of school would not have served the psychologist-paleontologist so well. The particular quality of these children's school experience makes a difference in the kind of fantasy material that was available for observation and analysis. This becomes plain to the reader who reads with attention to the role of the teachers and the changes in the children which are attributed, though not exclusively, to their influence.

These teachers acted as they did, and became primary figures in the children's development, as part of a basic orientation—namely, their interest and concern for the affect underlying behavior, the motivations, the fears, the wishes that are its wellsprings and the internalized feelings that accompany behavioral outcomes, whether in the form of productive achievement or conflict resolution. This is what makes it possible to say about them that they responded more to needs than to disruptiveness. Though it may distort the nicety of fit of specific teacher response to specific child need, it is possible and valuable to read from the assemblage of records some of the major components of a teacher's role that appear to contribute toward the attainment of "superego constancy" in the preschool years. The children were provided with a world of trust and dependency in which things were controllable and predictable and with teachers who could anticipate and sympathize with their demands while maintaining ground rules involving known and limited restraints and punishments. They knew how to help children find alternative ways of fulfilling wishes, how to rescue them from being overly frightened by other children's aggression or the expected reversals of their own projected aggressions, how to mitigate "loss of face" and spare them humiliation. They contributed to objective causal thinking by a pervasive means-end kind of teaching and they took responsibility for clarifying what is so important in the lives of children in groups—the distinction between accidental and intentional. They broadened the horizons of the children's competence and utilized opportunities for the children to feel good and admired for their ego achievements.

The author attributes changes in behavior, reflected in fantasy, to the children's experiences with their teachers, obviously in the role of primary figures, while recognizing that the influence of the school can only be relative to congruent or contradictory parent-child relations. I would like to recommend reading from this perspective to two groups of people whose respective views are diametrically opposed: to those who advocate dealing with children in school as though this inner world was not intrinsic to the human condition and to those others who honor it profoundly but are indifferent to or even wary of the necessity to engage in searching analysis of its components and mechanisms.

A final perspective is a practical one: what does this study of children and fantasies mean, what should it mean in the way programs of experiences are planned for three, four and five year olds in school groupings, especially since education for these young children is being increasingly accepted as part of society's responsibility? We did not need new research to inform us that fantasy is a way of thinking and feeling that is part of the warp and woof of early childhood. That knowledge has been available to us from personal recall, from the literature of biography, and from what we can see and hear if we watch and listen to children in their homes and neighborhoods. But we do need the contribution of this kind of study and others like it to sharpen our awareness of how the very condition of being young, under all circumstances, creates an impulse to "make pretend," in a child's own terminology.

In the conceptual development of the meanings of these children's play and the general principles of psychic growth inferred from them, the author has offered specific insights into how the play process serves these childhood needs. We come to see spontaneous fantasy as an intrinsic response to mental growth and activity, a unique way for expressing and resolving affective developmental dilemmas and at the same time advancing mastery of the complexities of the child's encounters with the real world. The total work gives ample support for the position that freedom for spontaneous fantasy is well-nigh indispensable to optimal integration of affects and cognition, while discouragement or failure to provide a suitable environment for its free expression may deprive the child of the path to integration that lays the foundation for social-moral development and creative ego functioning. How the whole rests on the original premise of cognitive-affective interaction is best stated in the author's words: "The child's internal wellsprings and external world experiences intermingle or oscillate in various ways in fantasy expression, to the enrichment of both sources of knowledge. The two worlds of reality and imagination need never be as far apart as is often implied."

Preface

The nursery school children's fantasy materials which form the foundation blocks for my developmental conceptualizations were recorded verbatim for me by their well-trained, perceptive teachers. I must say that when I first solicited these observational reports in 1963 I did so in a state of blissful ignorance, that is, like a happily expectant child before Christmas, knowing virtually nothing about the nature or number of "presents" I would receive or what I would do with them, but quite certain they would be wondrous to "play" with.

The setting in which the children's fantasy expressions emerged was an urban progressive school with classes through the eighth grade, where I was serving as consultant to staff and parents since 1951. The participating nursery teachers had for many years been oriented by my instruction always to include in the reports for me some verbatim descriptions of their "problem" child's behavior (verbal, affective, etc.) in a variety of episodes. I had discovered these verbatim observations to be invaluable contributions to my independent insights and evaluation. When a child's dramatic play or other spontaneous fantasy expression happened to be included in the report I was delighted, for I found these uniquely revealing of a child's feelings and ways of thinking and coping.

But I did not think to study spontaneous fantasy materials more widely and systematically until a teacher of the fours asked me to explain the prevalence of death, destruction, and violence themes in her group's dramatic play. I found her question instantly intriguing for as a "fact" it was news to me and at best I could only fumble an answer in accord with general freudian theory, and my limited experiences in child analysis. (I had by then largely restricted my private practice as a psychoanalyst to that of adults.) Her question mobilized my request to all nursery teachers in the school to record any and all "fantasy" expressions they heard and saw in their respective groups. Over the next several years I obtained slightly over 100 verbatim observations. A selected sample of these is cited in full. Her question also led me to a focused interest, in the analysis and conceptualizing of the data, on the genesis and cognitive-affective manifestations of different levels of aggressive impulses and conflict-coping in early personality evolution. I hope what I have found out or suggest will invite others to further research in this seminal, significant aspect of human development.

My indebtedness to Irene Neurath, Director of the nursery school, and to the teachers who so generously gave of their time and their perceptiveness is clearly enormous. I wish particularly to acknowledge the recorded contributions of Mimi Fajans who was also the one who first asked the question, Barbara Antonacci, Lucille Candea, and Wayne Rae—and also to thank for their valuable participation, Esther Conrad, Louise Crowe, G. K. Fishlin, Linda Geller, Lorraine Harner, and Selma Knobler.

The early drafts received sustenance and stimulation especially from the generous time and commentaries of Isidore Chein, from the suggestions of Joseph Sandler of the Hampstead Child-Therapy Clinic, and from the vital psychology staff participants in my seminars at the Jewish Board of Guardians, among whom were Carol Eagle, Lillian Schwartz, and Irving Steingart. Barbara Biber's sensitive reading of a later draft did much to shape the final emergent form.

Critical comments on different drafts along the way propelled me to more focused revisions; the accompanying positive reactions emboldened me in the process to expand my conceptual ideas. I am indebted particularly for such help to Leopold Bellak, Marianne Kris, Helen Block Lewis, Lois B. Murphy, and Evelyn Raskin. Finally, I am appreciative that the present version gained much from the discerning editorial guidance of Martha Gillmor and Robert Meister.

R.G.
November, 1971

Child Studies through Fantasy

1

Overview: Key Findings and Concepts

A young child's fantasy expressions are like crystals: each one is created afresh, yet each also reveals common properties in its unique form. While individual variations reflect the dynamic influence of particular external conditions in the process of formation, the basic substances and internal dynamic stresses that generate each provide the discernible consistencies or universals and set limits to an infinity of individual differences.

Spontaneous fantasy in early childhood offers freshly exciting insights into different aspects of children's feelings and thinking about things and themselves. Some of the ways of feeling and thinking revealed are individual variants, some developmental signposts. Generally, the fantasy constructions in play or soliloquy are formed under pressure of strong feelings and by defenses aimed to deal with conflicts inherent in psychological growth. But they emerge variously imprinted by the child's particular cognitive modes for dealing with these in his real world. Hence, one may find in young children's fantasy expressions, as I have, reflections of ways affects and cognition may evolve and entwine in interdependent patterns, that advance or handicap learning and personality development.

Interest in young children's fantasy expressions has varied in nature and extent since the turn of the century. Much of the early interest is represented in clinical reports where the primary orientation is towards fantasy and daydreaming as a "royal road" of access to impulse life, or is expressed by child educators who, loosely linking "fantasy and play," point to the creativity and learning opportunities evident in children's self-directed play experiences. A historical review, however informative, therefore, is not relevant as background to my discussion of young children's spontaneous fantasy.[1]

It is revelant to note, though, that few systematic studies of expressed fantasy in children or adults have been undertaken. The two large-scale quantitative investigations (Jersild *et al.* [1933], Singer [1966]) have been limited in their findings, handicapped initially by insufficient systematic knowledge to stake out the qualities in content, frequency, or cognate structure, likely to be meaningfully related to developmental, personality, or demographic correlates. In contrast, the large-scale qualitative observational studies pioneered by Susan Isaacs, Piaget, and Lois Murphy, yielded fertile hypotheses and advanced understanding of underlying meanings and psychological functions adumbrated in spontaneous manifest fantasy. Though differing considerably in overall aims and modes of analysis, each utilized young children's fantasy expressions as foundation for theory-building, or new discoveries about the intellectual, social, and emotional attributes of development in early childhood. My investigation upholds the vitality of their research viewpoint, and demonstrates the accessibility of dynamic and developmental information in young children's spontaneous fantasy through schematic analyses.

The analytic dimensions and theoretical extrapolations I propose are clearly germinated both by Freudian insights and approach to motivation, and by Piaget's work on the evolution of intelligence. A number of thoughtful papers have been written with the aim of extracting parallels and commonalities in the work of these wellsprings of influence on psychological understanding. These efforts are engaging and challenging. But I believe much less is to be gained from attempts to effect a syn-

[1] Jerome Singer's thoughtful survey, *Daydreaming* (1966), covers much of this. (See Bibliography, p. 275, for full citation of works referred to throughout this study.)

thesis of Freud and Piaget on the level of their theoretical constructs than from research design and interpretations that utilize the two searchlights on "mind" processes they have provided. Hence, though drawing on both, at few points do I specifically compare or contrast Freudian and Piagetian ideas.

The fantasy records that comprise my pivotal data are analyzed to serve a two-pronged purpose—to reveal individual differences in cognitive-affective patterns, and to derive from these more broadly applicable principles and constructs that help clarify particular interrelationships in early childhood between "experiences" (in Escalona's sense) and individual patterns which are cast by and in turn influence characteristics of developmental progression. My search for affective cognitive indicators in the relationships between the phenomenal aspects of fantasy expression, the inner processes that give rise to it, and the functions it serves, accounts for what original findings or testable hypotheses have emerged in this study.

More specifically, the modes of analysis and constructs bring into focus features of individuation and identification, modes of defense, and foundations of morality. These are presented as they are interrelated in form and function with both aspects of cognitive development in the early years and the child's relative balance of aggressive/libidinal experiences (internal and external). The language of the concepts I have introduced to describe underlying or mediating processes adhere as closely as possible to the inferred existential experiences of the child. Hence, my level of description or conceptualization tends to be closer to phenomenology than to metapsychology. There is no presumption that one level of abstraction is a replacement for the other.

One of the content features of the children's fantasy records that I found very fruitful to analyze for my purposes are their "self-representations." Clinical studies have long documented and Lois Murphy's (1956) wide ranging appraisal of personality development confirmed that in the dramatic play (or other modes of fantasy expression) of the normal young child as well, the characterizations reveal wishful or evaluative aspects of the child's "self." Murphy observed, "The child's image of himself appears . . . in his representation of the child of his fantasy, as naughty, good, independent of adults, escaping, paying back, achieving masculinity. . . ." (p. 62). The characters assumed by my nursery school children are spontaneous fantasy products, less trammeled than in most fantasy research by a present place, time, or range of props. I have dealt with their self-representation characterizations (which in these circumstances are often not that of a child) in two main ways. One distinguishes the form *in relation to* the child's self, i.e., *direct "I"* vs. *distance-from-self,* as in "I'm a witch." The other centers on the affective nature of the character in relation to the associated behavioral content. The data to be presented support the validity of my treating this aspect as reflective of the child's "identifications" and distinguishing three major types: *identification with the provider* and/or *protector, identification with the victim,* and *identification with the aggressor.*

These categories assumed significance for pattern analyses when I found that the nursery children whose fantasy products were recorded across time showed *consistency* in their use of either direct or distance forms of self-representation, and also in their predominant type of conveyed identification. To check on these findings I examined Piaget's comparable recordings (1945), and upon re-ordering them in chronological sequence I both confirmed the presence of individual consistency and deepened my understanding of the developmental leads given me in the nursery data. The developmental leads indicated that usually progress in both individuation and drive-defense is signalled initially by the child's use of direct "I" representations, followed by an extension to distance forms. This sequential progression is a particularly clear and significant marker at the times the child is caught up with aggressive drive-derivative feelings and content.

Another indicator in the fantasy materials of individual differences in the nature of children's involvement with destructive-aggressive imagery, that is also an aspect of developmental progression, is a response I call *fluctuating certainty.* I describe it as an "ego state" that manifests itself in a child's more or less frequent and transient inability to distinguish firmly between a pretend and a real danger. The ability to recognize and maintain clarity of distinction (and thereby a sense of safety) is recognizably a developmental advance. Beyond the age of four, I found fluctuating certainty to be a significant sign of anxiety-interference, the implications being different, of course, if it appears as an occasional reaction or is more characteristic of the child's response to aggressive content within a fantasy. When more characteristic, fluctuating certainty is found interrelated with some other markers of interference in synchronous progress: (1) Beyond age four, the child who tends to respond with fluctuating certainty is also likely to employ direct "I" representations, not distance forms, and to express unvarnished, not creatively elaborated, aggressive content in his fantasy. (2) At the extreme, the child who manifests pervasive unclarity in distinguishing between real and pretend dangers, is likely to be unable to engage in fantasy play at all, and instead to be inclined towards acting-out. In the nursery sample, moreover, the acting-out children give indications of a primary defensive identification-with-aggressor, suggestively pertinent for understanding some of the signs of their asynchronous development in individuation, reality-oriented reasoning, aspects of learning, and delayed internalization of conflict and superego evolution.

The analysis of the fantasy protocols also revealed experiential and behavioral features germane to the etiology and evolutionary potential of a *benign superego*. Among the indicators in the fantasy-reality records of early individual differences in the benign or harsh character of the superego formation is a child's consistent expression of *limited* or *global self-condemnation.* The latter I found in children with a predominant aggressor identification representation. On the level of clinical theory, I have discussed *internalization of conflict* as a recurrent process of affective content accruals in successive phase-crises, and introduced the concept of *superego constancy.* As suggested by the data, such constancy is generated by early provider-protector experiences and manifests itself in the child's behavior and personality by a relatively positive, stable, influential operation of a functional superego, in the midst of evolutionary changes in content accruals and developmental limitations. Inferrable is that superego constancy is intimately interrelated with the development of object constancy, and that superego maturity or relatively stable *ownership* and functional integration of evolved superego schema is possible to attain only when experiences engender in the child a sense of its self-in-alliance with its superego introject(s). Hence, individual and developmental differences may expect to be found in the digestible or intrinsically conflicted (regurgitable) constituents of the superego, and in the ease or resistance to functional oscillation in stressful circumstances.

The constructs of *sense of entitlement* and *wish to please* are introduced and discussed as early affective organizers in personality relevant for understanding individual differences in superego character. Neither is intrinsically moral or amoral in nature or operation. Their significance as mediating influences on superego formation and subsequent changes, however, will become clear in my discussion of their presumed genesis and manifestations in the study records.

The analysis of the 'death, destruction, and violence' fantasies, especially prevalent in the nursery school Fours, brings to light some vicissitudes of aggressive impulse derivatives and their interactive influence on the shape of individual cognitive-affective patterns. The findings represent only strands of evidence, but it will be seen how these are interwoven and limn a psychologically meaningful composite. Two distinctive profiles emerge when one compares a child expressing pre-eminent identification with the provider-protector with a child signalling pre-eminent identification with the aggressor, in the areas of thought, feelings, and behavior investigated in the present study.[2]

[2] The portrait that may be drawn of a child expressing identification with the provider is specifically noted in Ch. 6, p. 241.

Clearly, the interdependent aspects of synchronous progression in the functional attributes of ego, superego, and core-self systems, are brought to the fore by the modes of analysis, and the discussion of illustrative records, on the level of clinical theory. On this level of abstraction, my study offers documentation for the thesis that the timing and character of an emergent superego in a child before age three has a dynamic (circular and reciprocal) relationship to its deployment of particular ego resources, as well as selectively influencing the child's potential for developmental changes in the superego "shape" itself. More broadly, my study may be said to support the thesis that the affective experiences that in early childhood mediate or govern the character of a child's social-moral guidelines, profoundly influence his cognitive readiness for education in a general sense.

Key terms that recur in the text are *core-self image* or *me-self, affects and cognition,* and *fantasy.*

The me-self: It is virtually a truism that a child forms identifications in response to and reflective of its experiences with its primary caretaker(s). As well, in the process of early identification significant aspects of a child's core me-self image are forged in relation to and simultaneously with identification-inducing object representations. I view the me-self core as a dynamically segregated system precipitated out of the child's early impulse-life experiences along with the build-up of its body-image schemas, and evolving prior to the child's "I-self" recognizances. The evolution of a person's sense of self or self-image representations in the more usual broader sense begins, as I see it, with this core me-self infused with a basic cast of good or bad, strong or helpless, and which in the course of development may be variously integrated with the later representations of one's self as agent, achiever, or object for another. That is, while the qualities and relationship of the me-self schema to other self-representations or ideals can vary, in intimacy of connections or derivative influence, at different stages of development, the potential for relatively harmonious, discrepant, or viable interconnections between the core-self and later acquisitions of "I-self" imagery is a significant individual variant in personality. The core-image, for instance, may differ in particular respects from the view of self one strives to achieve in accord with one's (conscious or unconscious) ideal, or in the eyes of the beholder. That it may not jibe with one's "I-self" observations is recognized in the distinctions between "me" and "I" one hears in common parlance: "That's *just* like me"; "I did it, but it's *not* like me"; or "No one knows the *real* me." It is this kind of discrepancy that is often at the root of a pervasive sense of loneliness or chronic dissatisfaction with one's efforts.

Affects and Cognition: Affects denote primordial or drive-related emotions which at times are also motives, while cognition refers to active processes mediating or governing "knowingness." Both affective and cognitive reactions may be activated at any level of the consciousness-unconsciousness continuum. Conflict-anxiety is engendered by the simultaneous activation of apposite affective-cognitive constellations, and marks a later stage of development than experiences of conflict between oneself and external sources.

Affects and cognition is less a meaningful topic in psychology than the hallmark of a particular theoretical and research approach to understanding mental functioning and personality. The original atomistic view of man's psyche as divisible into three parts—conation, cognition, and emotions—has been dynamically integrated, demonstrating the interrelated aspects of cognitive-perceptual style and affective features in personality (e.g., Witkin *et al.,* 1962). Nonetheless, one can still find in some ongoing research and teaching, as in the current burning controversy about what is an optimal educational program for disadvantaged children, a tendency to treat these aspects as though each could be understood or dealt with as an isolated component.

In the context of my research the following premises will be evident: Affects and cognition are dimensionally independent aspects of experience in the sense that a given affect may be associated with a variety of cognitions, and a given cognition with a variety of affects. Cognitive and affective aspects of experience are interactive from birth; interactions and epiphenomena will differ at different developmental phases and for different individuals, in comfort and pain. The affective qualities intrinsic in the neonate's "fundamental education" (Spitz, 1970) constitute the pristine sources of its "ontological security" or ontological insecurity in Laing's (1960) terminology. Both the character of the affects aroused (intensity, globality), and the mode of interaction (circular or reciprocal), will influence the outcome in the immediate situation. Where reinforced in experience more permanent affective-cognitive schemas are created which selectively induce further reinforcing experiences, as in self-fulfilling prophecy behaviors.

An elemental example of the influence of affective experiences on horizontal language growth and apperceptions is found in a child's widening use of "No." Piaget's recordings of L. (1945) —J.'s younger sister—include an illustration of this point. At age 1;3 L. said "no" not only when refusing something "but also when she failed to find something she herself was feeling for. The transition between the two senses was the 'No' applied (first by adults) to a forbidden object . . ." (p. 217). Relatively enduring differences in children's apperceptions of, recourse to, and internalization of "No," are likely rooted both in the permitted reciprocity with adults, as well as in the frequency and nature of its experiences of "No-no."

Piaget recognizes that the child's intelligence does not continue to progress evenly in personal and impersonal areas, and that comprehension of physical causality does not automatically generalize to include psychological causality. At the same time, his formulations of mental growth rest on the debatable assumption that affects, being always an accompaniment of thought, can be treated as a constant—hence ignored as a possible systematic variable in his investigations of sequential progression in intelligence. This view of affects not only leads Piaget into an unsystematic inclusion of them at points,[3] but may be seen to limit

[3] Two subcategories of mental advances included in his TYPE III (1945) are purely motivational—"liquidation" and "compensation."

understanding of possible varied emergence of alternative mental operations.

On the other side, it is fairly evident that understanding of affective patterns in development would be expanded by precise coordination with cognate characteristics across time in early childhood. A systematic observational investigation of young children's fantasy in natural settings offers one promising media for analysis as attentive to evolutionary details as Piaget's work on early intelligence, and to dynamic details as the Freudian approach to motivation.

Descriptions of the interrelationships between affects and cognition may be seen in parallel focus on any level of abstraction. Consider Freud's classic description of the developmental sources and sequential forms of key anxieties. He describes a child's basic dreads as movements from survival or annihilation anxiety, to separation and loss of love anxiety, to castration anxiety, to social excommunication anxiety. The latter is explicitly related to the establishment of a superego, and implicitly to the expansion of cognitive and social experience beyond family, usually beginning around age five-six. These changes in anxiety forms are correspondent with cognitive growth changes, and may be described, e.g., as shifts (1) from an initial global conception of one's destruction, disappearance, and helplessness, to more limited possibilities of injury or loss and pain; (2) from an implicit, diffusely experienced dread to a more delimited experience of signal anxiety; and (3) from relative absence of temporal and spatial causality, where anything is possible, to reality-testing and distinctions between probable and improbable. The nature of these progressive changes is an evolution towards more differentiated and widening-world forms, which at the same time does not preclude dedifferentiation in duress (Gould, 1942).

The dynamic interplay of affects and cognition in the child's awareness of people and things, beyond his immediate person and immediate surrounds, has been described from different perspectives that exemplify, however, similar growth trends. For example: 1) the changes in the child's perception and experience of its own "size" and limitations, which lead it to attribute omnipotence and omniscience to the caretaking adults; 2) its growth from the urgency of a need-oriented receptivity to people, to a person-oriented need, both preliminary to a give-and-take relationship to needs and people; 3) the change from isolated impulse-driven reactions to a capacity for delay and control—or 4) from the internal global experience of urgency of need to a more differentiated scale of intensity between need and wish. The nature and fate of the affective aspects of these experiences influence the nature of the child's cognitive pursuits and thought content, and together they lead to the establishment of patterns of relationship between cognition and affects that will hinder or facilitate adaptive and creative functioning.

It is to the formal advent of ego psychology (Hartmann, Anna Freud), that systematic efforts to study the interrelationships of affects and cognitive functions in development may be ascribed. Some of the early enthusiasts of ego psychology formulations, however, tended to leave libidinal and affect features dangling out of sight, as though the latter were simply part of a mistaken past (Apfelbaum, 1965). My research orientation is in accord with a current in psychoanalytic thought moving towards studies of how feeling states are integrated with ego functions. Sandler and Joffe (1967), in their brief critique of Holt's initial neuro-anatomical-structural orientation to "ego autonomy," exemplify this position:

> Changes in feeling-states are, as we see it, the impetus to the development of psychological structures and represent the ultimate basis for the ego's regulatory functions. [Ego autonomy] . . . can be regarded as the individual's freedom to explore and to find new solutions without suffering intolerable disruption of the internal feeling-state of well-being or safety. . . . Genetically this feeling must be a derivative of the earliest experiences of tension and satisfaction. . . . The apparatus which the ego constructs during the course of its maturation and development . . . [is] prompted in [its] development by the ultimate need to control *feelings,* and [its] principal role is to widen the

tolerable range of inputs *without unduly disrupting the ego-tone* of safety, well-being or security (pp. 513–515 passim).

The one-sidedness of these statements as a description of significant feeling-states in optimal growth is evident in the emphasis on control or avoidance of disruptive anxiety and helplessness. However, it is reasonable to assume that feelings associated with function-pleasure, curiosity, pride, and such, can become essentials of a state of well-being only when the infant's experiences of anxiety and tension and satisfaction create a balance that is not unduly disruptive (cf. Brody and Axelrad, 1966).

Trends in the Study Data

The study data (1) consist of about one hundred verbatim recordings, mainly of the children's dramatic play in groups or monologues; (2) they were made for me by trained teachers in a middle-class, urban nursery school. The children were predominantly Caucasian, separated in age-group classes of Threes, Fours, and Fives (kindergarten). Some make-up stories and songs, and a few dream accounts volunteered to the teacher are also included. Most of the observations were made between 1964 and 1966, though the total period covered is 1964–8. The participating teachers were a relatively stable group, hence records of different child populations of the same age were submitted by some of the same teachers during that period.[4]

The fantasy episodes usually occurred in what can be called "key fantasy-arousal spots": doll-corner, block-corner, and yard-time. These were generally recorded verbatim as they were happening, or at a time later in the same day. The only knowledge the teachers had of my purpose was that I expected to use the materials as a means of understanding children better. The only instructions I gave them emphasized the need for precise nota-

[4] See Preface for acknowledgments.

tion of the children's actual language (as well as their own interventions) and accompanying affects and motor behavior.

In the nature of such open study design, the number of records made by individual teachers varies, depending greatly on a felicitous coincidence of time available to record when a fantasy began to be expressed, the teacher's interest, and observational sensitivities. Some teachers (particularly in one group of Threes, and one of Fours) recorded consistently enough, however, so that at the end of a school year I could find a number of children recorded at different times and in different fantasy contexts. Studying a child across records permitted appraisal of consistency in fantasy content and mode of expression; examining all the records from each teacher's age group offered a rough idea of age and sex differences. Though the sampling was essentially random, it is of interest that the group trends I found in the data are in accord with all those observed by others, suggesting a basic comparability in the respective samples and pointing to the presence of particular psychological universals—at least in child populations from white, middle-class backgrounds. Also, to check and supplement the inferences I had drawn from an intensive examination of these selected fantasy data, I reordered Piaget's materials (1945) into consecutive longitudinal sequences.[5] He quotes the first of his three children, Jacqueline ("J.") most frequently and extensively over a period from age eighteen months through five years; I have quoted from her records only in this study. Following J.'s fantasy expressions longitudinally permitted examination of the development and operation of affects within the frame of sequential cognitive growth.

Many of the fantasy illustrations in the text have been selected

[5] Susan Isaacs (1933) cites many examples of children's spontaneous fantasy expressions, but I could not utilize them for specific comparison with the nursery children's as I could Piaget's, because her reports are not presented in a form that allows independent evaluation of individual or developmental trends. Piaget not only gives vivid, verbatim accounts with background contexts but also notes the child's age in months and days. (When quoting him in the text, I have omitted specifying days and rounded the age to the nearest month.)

from a particular group of Fours, and a group of Threes, in which the teachers provided me with the most numerous and consecutive recordings during a school year. As an incidental observation, it is my impression, from reading across-teachers recordings, that teachers differ in their concerns about drive-laden talk, e.g., openly pleasurable excretory references, or a flow of aggressive themes. Accordingly they vary as a potential, subtle influence on the children's freedom to engage in fantasy in their classroom. In the midst of a tiger fantasy, for example, the teacher may intrude to ask what tigers "really" eat, or to interrupt a real or feared crescendo with, "Let's tell a story about tigers—in a circle." My implicit questioning of such intervention refers to the teacher's timing and motivation (concern), not to to the value of such reality-knowledge extensions in themselves.

Age Differences in Cognitive and Social Growth

The nursery sample[6] across ages three through five supports Piaget in finding that cognitive growth trends in fantasy materials are similar to those evident in reality-directed thought. Both generally show simultaneously a progressive increase in complexity and coherence of ideas (language), and in the veridical uses of reality information. One may note these general growth trends by comparing, e.g., the Tiger-Daddy play in the Threes (p. 203) with both "Digging for a Princess" (p. 22), and "Kill the Boys" (p. 126) in the Fours. But this does not necessarily mean a uniformly higher level of expression in every content area expressed in fantasy form. My data are only suggestive, but it is my impression that the pre-eminence of particular affective and psychosexual concerns transmuted in fantasy content differs in the three age groups, and that regressive thought expressions connected with transitions in phase-level content may be found

[6] There is little point in reporting the number of children sampled, for there was no uniform period of observation for any given child. Among the children cited in teacher recordings, some appear once or twice, others in several or many of the records submitted. Any repeated references to a given named child always refer to the same child.

as group trends, not only as individual variables in the same age group.

Realism or reality-tie manifested within a fantasy sequence, or in a child's preference for reality over fantasy involvement, is likely to reflect developmental as well as individual factors. For example, the reality-tie within a fantasy sequence in the Threes is developmentally distinctive, familiar to all who know children. As a group, they "swing" more fluidly between fantasy and reality than do the Fours and Fives: the make-believe action or object is more loosely reminiscent of its real model, but at the same time the action or object needs to be more "real" to them in functional essences. What needs to be "real" is often what is affectively meaningful to them within the realm of actual experiences. When Karen, in great excitement, "discovered" that her play-dough shape was a chocolate cake, she screeched over to the teacher, "Taste it! Taste it!" then also stood on tiptoe trying to put it to the teacher's mouth. The Fours might still make a chocolate cake in the sand box, but they are more likely to incorporate it into the ritual of a party, with more token gestures of eating taken for granted. In the Threes, while they explore new world horizons, acquire new motor skills, discover new sensations in applying old skills of patting, poking, banging, to new materials, they are also busily tying these down to the familiar. In brief, the type of realism that may be found in the Threes as a group reflects a different cognitive and motivational basis than the reality-tie noted in middle childhood. Similarly, the implications of being a relatively fluid "swinger" in the Threes are different for a six-year-old who swings as freely between fantasy and reality. Across ages, whatever aspects of home realities are distinctive for children in different social and cultural groups will also be reflected in different thematic concentrates of "realism."

The depiction of family relationships follows lines of increasing differentiation that (apart from individual variations) tend to begin with exclusive mommy-baby, occasionally mommy-baby-daddy content, to move at times into just mommy and daddy, and in the Fives to expand the relationship scope to include aunts, grandparents, babysitters, etc. Similarly, fantasy activities move out from family or "Superman" confines into those of their widening world. I have noted, too, that the children's mode of settling conflict of wishes reflects simultaneously cognitive and social advances with age. In the younger groups, the conflict is apperceived in "exclusive" terms: you *or* me; beginning to be noticeable in kindergarten is a more inclusive way: you *and* me. For example:

(*1965—Fives on the roof. As the boys approach the jungle gym to play*):
Joe: I'm boss!
Jac: No, you're not! I'm the oldest! (This assertion of age status also represents an advance in reasoning compared to the earlier usual recourse to "because.")
Joe: Well, today I am.
Jac: We're all bosses.
Joe: O.K. . . .
Sey (arrives breathless): Can I play? (And without waiting for an answer, adds): I'm boss.
Joe: You can play, but we're all bosses.

In Piaget's terms, this protocol exemplifies the developmental change expectable around age five, from "initial egocentrism to reciprocity." I may add that the earlier more exclusive egocentric form is not simply a reflection of the child's affective urgency for peremptory wish-fulfillment, nor of its need for concrete definition of "me" through "mine," but also reflects the child's general cognitive level of organizing inner and outer experiences in dichotomous form. When this is unrecognized, "egocentrism" tends to become an oversimplified and pejorative cliché.

Aggression in Fantasy

Still characteristic of the fantasy records in the Fours are fairly rapid shifts in manifest content, action, and characters. However, there is usually unity in the overall theme, as in "Digging for a Princess," or in the more frequent themes of death, destruction, and violence. The dangers depicted are real, in the sense that "anything is possible," but they are highly improbable as a rule. I was surprised to find how often the fantasy content revolved around the children's threat to eat some part of a designated person, occasionally even indications by some of a fear of being eaten up. For example, Arly, jealously guarding her "house" with Ben, saw Josh approaching and immediately yelled, "Go away!" When Josh stood his ground, Arly swiftly prompted Ben, "Chop him to pieces!"—adding after a moment's reflection, as an aside, "We don't have enough food." Josh instantly replied, "I'm Superman." "The Witches" record also tells a tale of children's impulse-imagery concerns expressed on an oral-incorporative level.

Although manifest themes of aggression are frequent at all ages, the children in the Fours appear most involved with them. On one level, this may be understood as reflecting this age-group's particular surge of drive-laden concerns and efforts to deal with them and utilize them in fantasy constructions. Piaget's illustrations of affect-laden fantasy and dreams ("secondary symbolism") are not numerous but when they are reordered in longitudinal sequence they reflect, among other things, age shifts in thematic emphasis which roughly follow the lines of psychosexual development and concerns delineated in psychoanalytic theory. In the fantasy records included in his classificatory scheme, a number (beginning at the age of two) are clearly reactively instigated by an experience of "insult" (physical injury or shame), or by feelings of jealousy and rage. The overall frequency of death, destruction, and violence themes in Piaget, however, is less prominent than in my study records.

One may speculate that the difference in our records lies simply in a sampling factor. Piaget's J. appears in the records as a child who "dissolves" or defends against aggressive feelings with dispatch (and "identification with comforter"). Perhaps the more prominent aggressive content in my records mainly reflects the teachers' unwitting selection of materials to record. But in view of the range of materials I received and the number of teachers involved over a period of years, it is likely that the influence of such a bias, if present, is minimal. I am more inclined to think that the difference, going beyond J.'s individual qualities, is related to the fact that the children in this study were observed away from their home surroundings. Aggressive fantasy expressed in (progressive) school settings may be instigated in some instances by separation-rage and concomitant frustrations intrinsic in a group situation; other children may find freedom to express aggressive fantasy more openly at school because of the safety afforded in group participation, or because of the "distance" afforded from the danger of direct connection of the expressed impulses to the family situation.

In any case, it need be emphasized that individual differences are evident in the intensity and character of involvement with aggressive fantasy, within the bounds of developmental or circumstantial trends that may be found in age groups.

Sex Differences

Sex differences in thematic interests, and a corresponding trend for the boys and girls to develop their play in same-sex groups, appear around age 4;6. Among the Fives, some boys begin to initiate aggressive fantasy play in the doll-corner, in contrast to their earlier engagement there in "family affairs." Their disruptive, excited actions can become so concentrated around this spot, one kindergarten teacher reported to me, that she found herself in the unusual position of first actively disengaging the boys when they were in it, then becoming alert to the possibility of its happening when several boys began to congregate near the doll-corner, and leaping to intervene with a "distracting" discussion of activity choices at the time. (In this manner, a child's behavior and the response of the adult to it may mutually reinforce psychocultural forms of sex differences.) In contrast, many of the kindergarten girls continue to seek the doll corner for domestic play, with more complexity of scene and extended family relationships depicted.

The divergence in behavior between boys and girls in the Fives appears in their different ways of dealing with (or experiencing) aggression. For example, in one year (1964–5) the Fives somehow became involved, as a group, in making a "war-book"—which consisted of each child drawing his own pictures, and when finished, dictating his accompanying story to the teacher. A number of the girls did not draw war-connected scenes at all. Instead, they filled their books with "nice and pretty" scenes of stereotyped flowers, smiling sun, and the like. All the boys but one drew scenes of guns, or planes, or dead people, and such. The one boy, Seth, was concerned with the topic in such a "real" way that he drew nothing at all. When it was his turn to dictate his story, he explained to the teacher why his book was blank:

> If there was a war there would be killing. They shoot! And a war is so terrible because you can get killed like President Kennedy. If you got killed, of course, you could (!) be dead.[7]

Also, one could observe at times an all-boy group engaged in some killing, shooting fantasy, suddenly moving to interact with one or a small cluster of girls. Characteristically, at such times the boys attempt to make contact with the girls only as their "victim." The boys' overtures are marked by their challenging, strutting stance, the girls' responses by their disinclination to admire it. Their retaliatory weapon of choice was a strictly verbal flight into reality—designed to wither and deflate the boys. For example: Boy, crowing, "I shot you dead!" Girl, flat-voiced, "You did not."

Individual Differences

Individual differences in different facets of fantasy expressions are evident in each age group: in frequency of creation, in affective intensity, preoccupation and conflict about declaratory

[7] Seth's relative inability to deal with aggressive content on a fantasy "distance" level appears in "The Witches" (p. 60).

aggressive or sexual talk and behavior, in defense preferences and strategy, in cognitive level, employment of realism and reality events or information, in modes of self-representation. Many of these differences highlight the individual child's affective concerns, aggressive/libidinal experiences of his world, and creative resources, but they also demonstrate more universal psychological verities in some areas of affective cognitive interrelationships in development. The records give a cross-sectional view of the range of individual differences and consistency over a limited period of time, the understanding of which is supplemented by Piaget's records of J., which provide a longitudinal view of consistencies in the midst of change.

As an illustration of my general description of the study data, let me quote a particularly delightful sample from the first batch of nursery records I received in the spring of 1964. "Digging for a Princess" appears to be light in tone, but also evident are individual differences in affective involvement and intensity of underlying conflict, reflected in levels of cognitive expression, as well as shifts in recourse to reality within the fantasy. Chris's ambivalence and anxiety (intensified by the separation of his parents at this time) arouses both early and current psychosexual levels of imagery. Jim, on the other hand, though apparently touched off by his internal resonance with Chris's involvement, is more ready and able than Chris to take flight into strictly male activities and exclusive male company. On another level, one can see that in the boys' ambivalence to real females, and in Olivia's persistent yearning efforts to get the boys to see *her* as a real princess, right at hand, lie the beginnings of the battle between the sexes.

Record I

Digging for a Princess

Fours — Yard time, May 1964

Chris: I hate women!

Teacher: Why do you say that, Chris?

Chris: Because when ya' marry them ya'hafta' get your blood tested.

Teacher: What else do you think about women, Chris?

Chris: I think they're kookie! I think I'm gonna marry a princess . . . because they're better—they're prettier.

Jim: Yeah, because they have jewels and gold—and they have crowns!

Olivia (comes over to the boys): What are you doing?

Jim & Chris: We're digging and looking for princesses.

Olivia: Well, I have a bride dress at home.

Chris: Aw, who cares about that.

Jim: Yeah. Ya'need a princess suit. (To teacher): Don't tell her we're gonna marry a princess.

Chris: Princesses have to wear their princess suits all the time or else they'll be stripped of their beauty.

Olivia (to teacher): What means "stripped of their beauty?"

Chris: Aw, go away! We hafta keep diggin'.

Teacher: Digging for what?

Chris: Digging for a princess, of course.

Jim: Yeah, ya' don't find them in New York. We're digging our way to find one.

Chris: Well, ya' just don't marry one like the regular way. Ya' hafta save one first. Princesses fall in love with princes. *Did ya' ever eat a princess?*

Jim: NO! (They dig for awhile silently.) I dream about army things.

Chris: Well, I dream about that I'm a lieutenant with a lovely princess.

Olivia: Boys! Boys! I just found a real live earring from a princess. (She hands them a piece of crumpled paper.)

Jim & Chris: Get out of here! (They chase her away.)

Chris (running around the hole he has dug): Romance! (Running full circle again.) Princesses! (Running full circle a third time.) Jewels! Let's get digging for those princesses!

Jim: No, we don't really want them. We hafta wait till we're grown up for that.

Chris: Yeah, till we're twenty-one!

Jim: Yeah.

Chris: And then we can buy a real drill and shovel and a pick.

Jim: And a whole car—and one of those things that go rrr-rrr-rrr.

Teacher: You mean a pneumatic drill?

Jim: Yeah.

Chris: But I wanna dig for princesses.

Jim: No!

Chris: Oh shucks. Josh, do you wanna' marry a princess?

Josh: Sure I do.

Olivia: Do you know where you could get a real princess? In Ireland or England or something.

Chris: Yeah, then we could find one and . . . we could see the Beatles while we're there!

Jim: I love the Beatles. Yeah! Yeah! Yeah!

Chris (running back from the group of girls in another part of the yard): I just went up to the princess' house and guess what—they scared me away.

What Is Fantasy?

As an inclusive term, fantasy covers a broader spectrum of cognitive processes, related to differing states of consciousness, than my study materials. The varieties of fantasy thinking that have been explored range from evidence of unconscious fantasies, often at the root of symptom formation, through hypnagogic and hypopompic reveries, to conscious daydreams and symbolic expressions in thought or make-believe. In a strict psychoanalytic sense, what I refer to as fantasy expressions are the representations or derivatives—i.e., the preconscious or unconscious transformation of impulses, desires, and affects, which in various ways draw on available cognitive capacities for the manifest fantasy product.

In a qualitative sense, fantasy productions occupy a position in the continuum of thought processes between mathematical-scientific reasoning, and primary process representational thought. Since fantasy formulations draw on ego functions, they embody characteristics of secondary-process thinking. That is, some awareness by the person of a distinction between the reality and unreality components is implicitly assumed. Though delusions and hallucinations may also be fantastic, in the sense described they can be clearly distinguished from fantasy. In the same sense, though fantasy in the unconscious is likely operative in acting-out behavior in a person, or may follow on a fantasy as here defined, this behavior too is distinguishable from fantasy.

As to the meaning or function of fantasy, there is conspicuous lack of agreement (Symposium, 1964). Sandler and Nagera (1963) succinctly summarize the reason as the "failure to distinguish between the function of fantasy on the one hand, and the vicissitudes of fantasy content on the other." In "Some Metapsychological Aspects of Fantasy," they help to clarify many of the theoretical considerations, and to provide a framework for conceptualizing the nature of fantasy:

> . . . the process of fantasying [is] an ego-function, resulting in organized wish-fulfilling imaginative content. . . . The fantasy may then be a derivative, a compromise constructed by the ego between that wish and the demands of the superego. Reality knowledge may be partially or completely suspended in the formation of this derivative or it may be utilized and influence the fantasy to a high degree. . . . The possibility exists that some fantasies represent wish-fulfillments, when the wish in question arises neither from the id nor from the superego, but from the ego itself (pp. 190, 191).

Analytic theorists commonly attribute the internal impetus to create a fantasy (whether expressed overtly or covertly) to the person's efforts in this way *to alter* intolerable limitations and frustrations in his reality situation, or *to defend* himself against the anxieties aroused by aggressive and sexual impulse-conflicts. Murphy and her associates (1962) ascribe the impetus to fantasy as the children's experience of a threat to their self-esteem or to their physical self. Some like Piaget, Greenacre, Murphy (1956), have emphasized active goal-striving motives (akin to Sandler and Nagera's "ego-wishes"), as operative at times, e.g., "to rehearse for adult roles," "to adapt to reality requirements," "to achieve mastery by creativity." In speaking of the function of children's (fantasy) play, Freud also mentions the goal of mastery, and of revenge when suffering pain experiences in reality (1920, p. 17). Piaget's view of the function (aim) of children's fantasy play as reality-adaptation, while a refreshing emphasis on the reality-adaptive function of children's fantasying, suffers from confounding a child's motivational aims, and the functions of fantasy, or potential outcome in reality and intrapsychically. It is clear that which motives will be considered primary instigators, and which secondary accompaniments or consequences to given fantasy expressions, is often a matter of type or level of analysis, sometimes of interpretation bias.

In the most important sense for our purposes, fantasy expressions in early childhood selectively and significantly reflect individual and developmental aspects of children's experiences of the real world, and inner psychological processes which mediate and evolve from these. On the basis of analyses of such materials, meaningful deductions and ultimately predictions may be made of some principles governing psychological growth and personality behavior. Spontaneous fantasy materials of young children invite systematic investigations across situations, across time, and across groups, of fantasy phenomenology itself, as well as in relation to the child's reality-oriented behaviors. They also invite studies with more limited focus on particular attributes of experience and psychological functioning in development, to which an intensive analysis of fantasy data may uniquely contribute. Moreover, fantasy may be utilized as an adjunct in experimental laboratory studies, to clarify and deepen understanding of the meanings of children's manifest responses in the situation. In Lustman's words (1966):

. . . the experimental behavior of the child is not the only or even the most important field of observation. We can actually tell most from observing the impact of the experiment as revealed by the subsequent [spontaneous] play of the child. One can . . . assess if an existing conflict has been touched and if so the degree and strength of it (p. 209).

2

Self-Representations in Fantasy: Clues to Identifications and Individuation

I used the term "self-representation" to refer either to a child's direct "I" or to characterizations it may project or assume. The earliest fantasy expressions (beginning around eighteen months) tend to center, as Piaget observes, on "self-imitative" reflections of its own reality behaviors, or to represent the child's "imitative" assumptions of selective attributes of others in its immediate surrounding (e.g., around age two, being Daddy reading the paper, or simply asserting to him, "I'm Mommy," before she kissed him). Piaget cites much fewer fantasy episodes of J.'s that are self-imitative than are imitative of significant others in her world. Whether this ratio is a meaningful clue to individual differences in a child's orientation to self and others, or tends to be a characteristic of children who express fantasy early, is an open question. In any case, the particular areas of reality experiences and the affective tone permeating the representations, whether imitative of self or other, reveal the meaningfulness of these experiences to the child. Moreover, the study data suggest that by age three or earlier, the representational characterizations reflect aspects of a child's self-image related to its primary (basic) identifications. Let me note here also that children who engage early in fantasy are likely to have had positive nurturant experiences and to have extracted from these for fantasy expression the pleasurable aspects of basic routines with caretakers as in eating (being fed), "sitting on pot," going to sleep.

Where early experiences include significant (but not overwhelming) adult aggression as well as factors encouraging active fantasy play, an 18–24 month old child may manifest its initial mode of sensorimotor steps toward internalizing and identifying-with-aggressor aspects of the caretaker by, say, hitting its own hand in a naughty child episode, and later perhaps by hitting a naughty doll-baby.

In keeping with a current trend in psychoanalytic thought towards humanizing its formulations,[1] Beres (1968) describes identification as a basic human tendency towards unification with others. "The child strives to be like the admired parental figures and in this way [?] establishes his first emotional ties." His description of the dynamic processes of identification is a succinct summary on the level of clinical theory: "Identification is based on a drive vicissitude (incorporation) and in many instances represents the attempt to retain a lost object. In other instances it serves as a defense . . . (as in identification with the aggressor). . . . But identification is also an ego mechanism that permits the child to learn . . . [behavior, attitudes, etc. of the admired parent] and involves other developing ego functions" (pp. 501 ff.).

Piaget uses the term identification in a descriptive, not dynamic sense, and "imitation" generically, not literally. Both refer to the manifest representations a child portrays in his fantasy play. Expectably, Piaget is interested in a child's imitation of its own or of another's behavior, and the changes observable with age, primarily as these provide evidence of the mental stepping stones from the sensorimotor shore to the other side—concrete representational thought. Thus, he notes that beginning around twenty-one months, the child engages increasingly in "imitative identification" of its own person with other persons or objects, and that the characteristics of his "modeling" behavior in fantasy play advance from the preceding cognitive level in these respects: (1) The imitative actions are more transformations of

[1] Actually, in *Mourning and Melancholia* Freud (1917) refers to identification as an expression of a person's love for the other.

the child's observations "dissociated from" its own or another's behavior; (2) the child now begins to describe its action in speech *before* any action takes place.

The changes Piaget describes represent not only a leap in thought, but in the child's experience of intentionality as well. Moreover, in the child's newly acquired ability to transform selectively what it observes "dissociated from" its earlier "copying" behavior, one may also see an indicator of its increasing "sense of a separate self." Piaget's observation of a psychological change in J.'s "impersonation," beginning around age two, points in the same direction of advance in individuation, along with steps towards internalized identifications. He comments that around age two within a fantasy context J. shifted from "attempts to copy the other while clearly continuing to be herself," to an ability "to become the other instead of herself." My record of Mike in the Threes will show how his self-representational content reveals his deficient ability to "become the other" in fantasy, which in turn reflects his developmental interferences in individuation, identification processes, and socialization. In other words, a child's ability to "become the other" in fantasy play signifies an expansion of its ego resources and *differentiated* sense of self. (This developmental advance is clearly distinct from the behavioral assumptions of "being the other" in reality, notable in some psychotic identifications.)

Individual Indicators and Variant Patterns

Piaget's J.

I may note here some distinctive features reflected in J.'s records which delineate her person and point up areas of differences between her and two nursery children, Mike and Jane, whose record analysis will follow.

Beginning with her earliest fantasy constructions, J.'s self-representations and imaginary companions are almost always human characters, almost never animal (cf. Ames and Learned, 1946), or part-object.

J.'s self-representational characters consistently point to her preeminent identification with the "provider," "protector," or "comforter." In her mother-baby play, for instance, she is usually the mother rather than the baby, and in various ways behaves as the good provider. On the significantly fewer occasions that she enacts the baby (after her baby sister was born), the "mother" is clearly good. Her fantasy expressions never involve either a bad Mommy or a bad child.[2] When a physical hurt or humiliation J. experienced in a reality situation was the impetus for a "revenge" reversal fantasy, J. not only represented herself as the comforter to an imaginary hurt child, but the designated child was only distantly known, geographically and otherwise, or entirely made up. It represents no great leap of thought to infer that these self-representational consistencies reflect the consistency of her nurturing and protective experiences with both parents. Beyond this, as later citations will illustrate, an early positive alignment (identification) with parental representations that has basis in ongoing reality may serve also as a defense against aggression towards family members and ambivalence-anxiety, as well as mitigate their arousal—hence, provide a foundation for a durable morality. Other types of identifications, as my study records will show, serve these ends differently and not as well.

In her fourth year J. created Marécage, a girl of about her own age, who appeared often in her fantasy expressions for about five months, always in some positive light. Marécage was able to carry through successfully or with impunity an achievement J. failed to herself or was enjoined from doing by parental restrictions—from taming a grasshopper to follow her around to not having ever to take naps. Sometimes Marécage was simply a consoling companion when J. was distressed. These attributes endowing Marécage contrast sharply with the type of characterizations that serve a child as projections of its failure to achieve, or that are designated as "bad" and deserving punishment. While one may observe the influence of phase-

[2] One must not assume from this that J. was never naughty, never chastised, or frustrated. Piaget's records make clear that all these took place.

level strivings for omnipotence in many children's fantasy characters, including some of Marécage's exploits (cited later), individual differences emerge equally clearly in children's resources and modes of coping with reality events that humiliate, and clip their wings of omnipotence. The overall balance of their affective experiences help create these differences.

The records of Mike and Jane are presented to illustrate in depth two different levels and concomitants of identification with the aggressor. Mike's record (II) is seen as reflecting his part-object self-representations, which are characterized by power attributes and reveal his diffuse concerns with aggression. One may infer the influence of a primitive identification-with-aggressor underlying his fragmented sense of self and of others. In Jane, the manifestations of her identification with the aggressor point to a far more circumscribed intrapsychic influence. Analysis of her records (III and IV) show that while there are personality impediments attributable to the aggressor aspects of her identifications and which persist across time, she also has experienced and internalized some ameliorating features enabling her to make developmental advances and acquire a responsiveness that Mike lacked. The analysis of their records thus offers an opportunity for expanding our understanding of identification with the aggressor on a conceptual as well as clinical level, and generally confirms the value of spontaneous fantasy as a source of insights into children's behaviors in their everyday reality world.

Mike: Inability to "Become the Other"

Mike is a bright boy in the Threes. He can be described as a child in a state of anomie with respect to his sense of self and of others. This state is reflected not only in his social relations, but also in causality conceptualizations of impersonal events such as rain. His records lend support to the thesis that the nature of a child's self-representations in fantasy expressions reflects its core-self image, as well as the character of its identifications at the time.

For a considerable time Mike's behavior showed that

he neither expected nor experienced warmth either from the teachers or the other children; it is not surprising he conveyed little regard for them. In the early months of school he could be seen stepping on or over a child who was in his path in the same unseeing, purpose-bent way as he would step on a table or a block that was in his way. His only evident "affective realities" were anxiety about consequences of his own or another's aggressive-destructive impulses or another's power to hurt him. His prevailing mode of behavior was aggressive. Though the sight of him—slight of build, wiry, small-featured—would hardly frighten anyone, he often terrified other children by his habit of suddenly and swiftly kicking over a child's building, grabbing its toys, and such. At these times he seemed pleased, though also poised for counterattack. When another child was "aggressive" towards him, he was clearly frightened; he did not discriminate between an accidental push and a deliberate assault, or between a threatened and an actual attack.

The following attributes of Mike's fantasy expressions and play distinguish him from the other children in his group: (1) His "ideal" self-representations, as conveyed in his manifest strivings, are *non-human* objects, not even animal figures. One time, when the jungle gym was set up near the tumbling mat, a group of children including Mike joined in pretending that the gym was a diving board and the mat below a pool.

Record II

A

Threes Indoor gym, March 1965

Mike: I'm ready for another trick. (Hard to wait his turn.)

Stuart: Go ahead. I'm an acrobat.

Mike: I can throw myself like a ball. I'm a basketball. (To a child who has just jumped): How about to swim, stupid! (He dives and rolls about freely.) Watch a big one! (Jumps vigorously onto mat and does somersault unaided.)

Teacher: Are you a circus clown?

Mike: No, I can jump. (Jumps and dives.) I slipped like a knife. Now I will be a jet plane.

B

(But he dove head first this time and bumped his head on the mat. He got up quickly. Not crying or looking at the teacher he started off for the room.)

Mike: I better go in the room. I have a headache. (He proceeds without her but she follows him into room. There he takes down his favorite toy, a mailbox, and pushes cards into it.) I have a headache.

Teacher: Why does your head hurt?

Mike: Mommy hit me this morning. (Why did she?) Because I hit Markie (his younger brother).

Mike: Mommy hit me because I hit Markie. . . . He was fighting with me. I don't like him. He took things away from me. (Note following sequence implicitly indicative of his readiness to be "giving" and "good" to his teachers, in contrast.) I will give you a letter. . . . I will give Mrs. Crowe a letter, a star. I will hold it for her (his favorite teacher, not in the room at the time). Markie may not take things away from me (oft-reiterated concept of justice of Mrs. C.'s, not his mother's)—or else I will hit him! (Thus old means of control and "jungle law" remain, in the midst of developing new concepts of morality.)

Excerpts from this recording (II) also illustrate two other aspects of the quality of his self-representational thought: (a) he only occasionally achieves even the level of non-human self-representation; (b) for the most part, he uses similes and metaphors to describe concrete, wishful physical attributes, not whole person characterizations.

Even when the teacher asked him, "Are you a circus clown?" his answer was, "No, I can jump." In psychoanalytic terms, his inner representational world seems still confined to the level of part-object representations. It is evident here, as in some other records, how closely tied in with each other are core me-self and object representations. His limited capacity for self representational conceptualization appears in reality-oriented situations too. For example, when another child's aggressive behavior frightens him, he does not respond as many children his age do in similar circumstances with something like "I'm Superman!" Instead, Mike "wildly" lists all the weapons he is going to get hold of.

(2) His "imaginative" actions and conceptualizations are largely in the service of his underlying anger at "humans," when not in the service of defense against fears related to his anger and "sense of unsafety." Though Mike obtains some "distance" from direct expressions of aggression against his primary human targets through symbolic representation of them in the dough episode, he has not achieved any internal distance from the concrete parental (or transference) figures he wishes to attack. He is therefore unable at this point to utilize fantasy expressions for working through his terrors, or for deepening his emotional understanding of himself or others—functions which fantasy play can serve for children whose internal world reflects more positive transactions with their parents than Mike enjoys.

> 11/64—Dough time. Mike became fascinated with the knife he found in the doll corner. He worked with it on the dough, saying aloud at one point, "This is a skeleton. It has blonde hair and lipstick and I'm cutting the head off."
>
> 11/15—He described his dough as a helicopter. He then took a man block-doll from the shelf, put the

man in the dough and began to pound the man very hard with a roller.

His kind of play with dough is rather atypical in the nursery Threes. It is evident that his affective preoccupation is not only structuring his use of materials, but limiting the pleasurable use of his skills and potential discoveries through experimentation.

Yet, Mike did change some in the course of the school year; the changes are described more fully later. Suffice it to illustrate here the kind of change that took place in his cognitive conceptions and causality reasoning, as the supportive, closely supervised relationship with his teachers brought him a measure of trust, at least in his school world, that things were controllable and predictable. Paralleling this affective change in his perception of others' feelings toward him, is some change in his own behavior towards them and presumably some change in his self-feelings. On his part, he had much fewer and less diffuse outbursts of helplessness and rage at people or things that one way or another got in his way. As in this benign way he began to experience himself as more controllable and expectable, he also began to evolve a more circumscribed conceptualization of violence expectable from outside sources. The direction of his cognitive change follows developmental lines, in that he is taking his first steps towards objective causality reasoning in differentiated percepts of the natural "impersonal" world, as his responses to rain show.

11-12/64—Mike told the teacher with evident anxiety that it was going to rain. She reassured him that it would be all right if it did since they had their raincoats and boots. Mike: "But rain could break you all to pieces!" This is especially interesting since in the first months of school his favorite activity on the roof

was to make "real rain." Standing on top of the slide roof he sprinkled water from a can on all who came by, exclaiming with gritted-teeth glee, "It's raining on you!" No one understood the significance at the time though all felt "attacked."
Spring/65—Shortly after the gym episode in record II. Mike, spontaneously to teacher: "There is a drill in the clouds that makes rain; it goes boom!" He was apparently referring to thunder.

It is evident that in the beginning he functioned on a primitive level of punitive magic causality reasoning that extended from his personal world to "animate" non-human features of his world. It is equally evident that in affect-charged situations as in B, he is still prey to the same type of "primitive paranoid" reasoning where the parental figures are concerned. Though he runs away from the situation where he is hurt, and does not seek comfort from the teacher, neither does he blame or exclude her when she follows to offer comfort. This, too, is a cognitive-affect change.

Identification with the Aggressor at Expense of Self

Jane's records suggest some answers to how and why self-representations in fantasy of identification with the aggressor can reflect a relatively enduring internalized system with ramifying personality effects. These effects are discernible in her behavior over a period of time, both in fantasy expressions and interpersonal relations with teacher and peers. It is valid to question whether the slight incidents cited merit such interpretations and to ask for the evidence that self-representations in fantasy are signposts of interrelated cognitive-affect developments. These are the facts:

In the Fours, Jane's self-representation in her mother-baby fantasy play is that of the Mommy always angry at the baby or babies because "they don't listen." Whatever records there are indicate that she was preoccupied with this theme and played it out with dolls by herself, in contrast to group doll-corner play. On one such occasion she confided to the teacher, "I dream about hitting my babies when they get big . . . [because] they don't listen. Hitting's the only way . . . !"

Record III

Jane

Fours Doll corner, 1963–64

The teacher's report[3] represented both her summary statements interspersed with verbatim quotations of Jane: Her most frequent spontaneous activity was in doll-corner play, where she often took the part of an angry, screaming Mommy having to deal with a bad child (doll). On one such occasion she stopped to explain to the teacher standing nearby—

A

(1) "I dream about hitting my babies when I get big."
(2) "I talk, talk, talk to my babies and *they don't listen.* Hitting's the only way! What should I do, leave them?"

T. replied there were ways of helping children to listen and also implied that she did not approve of hitting and screaming, much less of "leaving the children" to punish them.

B

Another time she was overhead talking to her doll-child:
(1) "Next time *you don't do what I say,* you'll get a licking, or I'll scream at you."

[3] I have broken up the teacher's descriptive continuity, assigning numbers to sequential responses for convenience of cross-reference in the text.

(2) Then suddenly catching sight of the teacher coming towards her, she screamed at her: "Don't come into my house!"

The teacher, at first taken aback, finally figured out what had led up to Jane's violent rejection of the help she was coming to offer her. It seems that shortly before, in the midst of her doll play, Jane had asked the teacher to help her with her shoes. (They were all getting ready for the music period.) Teacher had replied that she would, in a moment as soon as she finished helping Ben. It appears clear that Jane reacted very strongly to teacher's not coming *immediately*. She could not tolerate delay in being listened to any more than the Mommy she played at being.

C

(3) Jane continued with her angry, defiant refusal of teacher's help, despite teacher's efforts to get her to tell her why she was so angry. Jane was adamant: *"Don't* help me! I don't *want* you to!"

(4) "No! You can't help me! *You can't help anybody!"* (Thus at one blow, Jane disposes both of the teacher and of the cause of her rage at the teacher.)

The music period followed which the teacher made the following notes of:

(1) "I finally told her that I didn't like her to talk to me that way . . . screaming at me. And if she could tell me nicely what was bothering her, I really wanted to help her.

(2) "She seemed taken aback that I told her I didn't like that talk. She was quiet for about ten minutes, but stared at me intently.

(3) "Finally she came over to me in music and held my hand. She stayed close by me.

(4) "On the way back to the classroom, she said, 'I like you.' "

There is a confirmatory suggestion of inadequate internal separateness of bad mommy-bad baby representations in a reality interchange with the teacher during this period (record III in section B), when Jane like the mommy became furious with the teacher for "not listening" to *her*. Since the teacher did respond in a moment, it is evident that in a dependency relationship Jane strongly experiences a temporal delay in the adult's fulfillment as a humiliation, which militates against growth from an infant's sense of now-or-never urgency to frustration tolerance, at least in interpersonal areas. The sad circularity of the negative interaction which humiliation in these circumstances often sets in motion is illustrated in Jane's screaming outburst only *after* the teacher, in full friendly spirit, returns to give her what she asked. (The contrast with J.'s background experiences [Piaget], development of different identifications, and different concomitant means of coping with delay or refusal is clear.)

That Jane's reactions are a dynamic product of her relationship experiences, and that she retains the capacity to grow beyond these to more optimal cognitive-affect integrations in accord with different expressions of her self in an adult-child relationship, is indicated in the final outcome of the scene. What the teacher's *behavior* and words made clear, as though for the first time, were that screaming and hitting were neither the best nor "the only way" to get someone "to listen" to you, that delay could be a temporal contingency for objective or fair reasons involving another, not a measure of the worth or the regard of her wishes or her person. Jane was able to "listen" to this, and what she heard introduced another dimension of understanding that apparently she welcomed once she could believe it. (Since it is easier for an adult to intimidate or hit a child, than vice-versa, on sheerly practical, pre-moral grounds, a child can welcome an alternative to "might is right.") The moral of this incident is simply this: Jane could trust and like the adult better when she could find acceptable alternatives to categorical compliance or defiance, and in this process she could like her "self" more, too, even as a child—as her seeking to hold the teacher's hand without shame or uncertainty (and demandingness) of response implies. Naturally, such experiences would need to be replicated at home for an enduring intrapsychic effect.

In a fantasy recording a year later in the Fives (kindergarten, record IV), these related characteristics of Jane are observable: (1) she is neither a comforting mother nor a comfortable child; (2) as a mother she is largely bossy, though actually very dependent on one child (Rolly), who until this episode had always *chosen* to be her "baby"; (3) she is sadly ineffectual in getting the "babies" to listen to her, while her greatest satisfaction and highest praise still pivots on the early axis: "Baby's good. She listened"; (4) her effort towards the end, to get away altogether from the unsatisfactory mother-baby entanglements, is in a constructive direction, but reaching to be a "teenager" at Five is a brittle bridge for an "ideal" getaway. As indicated in (5) she feels being "one of the kids" as much of an insult as being a "baby." Overall, no matter how she tries, she cannot get an affirmative response from the other children. Only at the very end does she get them to "listen" to her, when she can leave the field of trying to control them and find instead a satisfying way of joining them, free of simple compliance and loss of face.

Record IV

Jane: Ineffectual Mommy

Fives Yard time, November 1964

Rolly (pretending to cry): I want my bottle.
Jane: Sit up, baby.
Rolly (lying down): I'm getting sick. Pretend I'm sick.

Jane: Let's take her to the doctor. He'll give her a shot. (!)

(Rolly lies on the blocks with her hands to her mouth holding a pretend bottle.)

Jane: There's a real fly on the baby. (She shows everyone a live horsefly which is on the ground. All leave the house. Jane gets a board and mashes the fly.)

Rolly: Keep the board here in case there are more flies. (She runs away again and they chase her. Again there is no talk.)

. . .

Jane: Baby, time for breakfast.

Rolly: O.K., just one minute. (She is busy drawing with chalk on ground.)

Jane: Make an apple and come. (Rolly does so.) All right, baby, time for breakfast. Judy! Judy! (Tries unsuccessfully to find Judy and then turns back to Rolly who is back drawing.) Time for breakfast, baby—you promised!

(Rolly keeps drawing for a while but finally goes in.)

Jane: *Baby's good. She listened.* (Turning to teacher): She's writing on the blocks with chalk. (To Rolly): Breakfast, eat it!

Judy: Oh, skip it, skip it! (Judy and Rolly draw.)

Jane: Now eat it!

Rolly (to teacher): We aren't going to eat breakfast in this house.

Jane (to Rolly): You always make up all the rules! (Some other girls approach to join them. Jane at first refuses to allow "visitors" then relents, but still trying to set conditions. They all sit quietly for a while until Rolly asks and receives permission from Jane to go outside and play. She invites the other girls to join her—which apparently is too much for Jane.)

Jane: Let's play another game! *No mother, no babies. Just teenagers.* (All go outside to draw, Jane trailing.) Rolly, we're all teenagers, Rolly. We're teenagers writing with chalk. (She is the only one *not* doing so at this point.)

Rolly: Pretend we go on a trip with our child, all right?

Jane: We're teenagers.

Rolly: I don't want to. Pretend we're playing school and we went on a trip, O.K.? (To the other children): Get a partner. I'm the teacher . . .

Jane (to Rolly): I'll be with you.

Rolly: Only one teacher. You be one of the kids.

Jane (very angry): No! I don't want to be one of the kids!

Rolly: O.K., we'll have two teachers. (Jane claps her hands.)

The "facts" in Jane's records establish that particular self-representations in fantasy expressions are valid, potential indicators of internalized identifications and related aspects of core self-image. The discussion extrapolated from this aims to demonstrate (1) the interrelated aspects of early identifications and core me-image; (2) that the character of these determines their potential viable connections with developing ego competencies, and (3) that general ego advances are relatively independent of these psychic features, but that for ego competencies to serve as sources of self-esteem or personal autonomy, and as sources of an expanding repertoire of adaptive defenses, the identification-self image relationship must have features which facilitate the growth of connections with ego functions.

Identification with aggressor, as one coping strategy of turning passive into active, is thereby a positive means of dealing with states of helplessness and pain in childhood. However, when identification with aggressor appears the ideal and sufficient means of wish fulfillment and avoidance of pain, it constitutes an interference in growth. Feelings of independence, born of humiliation and defensive reversal of position *and* of aims (e.g., "I *don't want* you to help me"), produce only thin stalks for genuine autonomy and self-regard to grow on. This is a reactive internal stance which tends to perpetuate experiences of humiliation, since a child in fact does need an adult's help in various situations, to fulfill needs not only wishes. Aspects of early mother-child struggle which lead to this type of reactive stance (as implied in Jane's records), will throw their shadow on all relationships, real and pretend. The cognitive capacity for comprehension of reciprocal relations may be achieved in "impersonal" areas beginning around age 4–5, but delayed in "personal" areas. Big *and* little, give *and* take are cognitive steps beyond the concept of relationships underlying the big *or* little view in a power struggle. Jane's coping and defense resources are "rigid," and limited by the struggle format in which she perceives social relations and the see-saw of reciprocal relations, for example. The position of control which Jane seeks, tends to become an end in itself, while the content of the issue (originally the end-goal) becomes the means to this end, instead of vice-versa. The overriding of substance by means in itself interferes with the expansion of new means—e.g., persuasion, detours, "reasoning," and with opportunities to discover new substance through compromise solutions.

Identification with the Aggressor: Some Implications for Theory

In the light of Jane's record and others to be cited later (e.g., Gerry, Scot, Dori), "identification with the aggressor" is not a singular entity in its essential characteristics or in its intrapsychic effects and influence on behavior. In some instances, the aggressor introject serves as a protective force for the child, who leans on it to make itself be good or safe in particular ways. In this case, "identification with the aggressor" represents a part-identification, which is associated with relatively delimited content of do's and don'ts. These then serve to facilitate a sense of safety, and differentiated social judgments of good and bad.

"Baby is bad because it doesn't listen" (Jane), is a global condemnation of the child who does not comply with the adult authority. Obedience in the relationship, not the specific substance of the conflict, is made the paramount issue. In such terms, the alternatives (compliance or defiance, good or bad) remain fixed to an either/or type of dilemma and solution. One may infer that the introject-ideal is endowed with general powers to fulfill or frustrate one's (or another's) wishes, while at the same time being able to command the other to do whatever it wishes. This is a concept of global and arbitrary personal power, having little specifiable connection with comprehensible or objective reasons for "listening" or "not listening" to a person. The "other" in this context is Jane's own needy but helpless, angry me-self image, which in the process of such an identification with the aggressor is also the attempted object of discard and a chronic target of her disappointments, however projected. Clearly, adult behavior on this level would fit in with a young child's natural mode of dichotomous thought and strengthen its belief in the reality potential of wish-fulfillment through power (or that disappointments are because one is not "great" enough).

The character of the child's cumulative struggle experiences with external sources can become internalized in such a way as to perpetuate repetitive experiences of the same type of struggle beyond the primary family. Since the child's devalued little-helpless sense of self continues to be at stake in power-format social conditions, the nature of the alternatives available (e.g., strong or weak) means that actual achievements or battles won can serve to enhance or reassure only for the moment, while defeat experiences serve as shaming, anxiety-arousing confirmations.

Though the nature of the control struggle imbedded in Jane's aggressor introject is global and primitive, the level of the punitive imagery components is not. Jane suggests "hitting" and screaming are the main punitive weapons, while loss of love and/or loss of face are the main threatening consequences in a conflict of wishes with the parent figure. Her imagery level of punitive consequences is more limited and internally "distant" from the primitive rage imagery with which some children endow their aggressor introject, and which also reflects the content of their own conflicted aggressive impulses. In other words, the behavioral and personality outcome of any hierarchically significant identification, as with the aggressor, depends on concomitant intrapsychic relationships, namely, the imagery level comprising the punitive or protective nature of the aggressor introject, the relationship with the child's core me-image entailed in the process of identification, and the kinds of viable connections with ego functions which these relationships make possible.

Background Features in the Development of Self-Representations and Individuation

Self-representations, as we have seen, are relatively complex psychic emergents that rest on a number of cognitive and individuation achievements, and are governed by various affective factors as well. To place self-representation phenomenology in the broader stream of development, I shall discuss some currents I believe contribute to forming self-representation surfaces.

Piaget ties the child's potential capacity for (cognitive) awareness of his separate self to the evolution of schemata underlying perceptual object constancy—i.e., as Wolff (1960) puts it, to the time the child is able to "attribute a substantiality to the environment which no longer depends on personal action." In this context Piaget (1937) writes:

> . . . if the radical egocentrism of the beginnings first leads the subject to attribute all external events to personal activity, the formation of a permanent universe subse-

> quently enables the self to be located among things and to understand the totality of the sequences which it sees or in which it is engaged as cause or effect (p. 315).

Wolff, aiming to find convergences between Piaget and psychoanalysis from "the point of view of behavior," equates Piaget's "awareness of self . . . among things" with "awareness of personal autonomy," and thus finds a parallel with Erickson's concept of a "sense of personal autonomy" (pp. 138–39). The difference between the two concepts, I believe, makes Wolff's point little more than a *tour de force*. "Awareness of self" as a causal agent separate from other things represents a cognitive capacity—potentially linked to a variety of affective experiences which may differentially influence the child's use or expansion of this basic capacity. The sense of personal autonomy represents a special utilization of this capacity, based on the child's affective experiences in conjunction with its cognitive and physical advances in competency. The former is a necessary but not sufficient basis for a child's sense of personal autonomy.

As Erikson elaborates in his epigenetic schedule, "basic trust" is an antecedent affective-cognitive orientation that shapes a child's sense of autonomy, though a child's actual experiences during the toddler phase continue to influence the character of its trust in others and in its own impulses. Basic trust, like its psychoanalytic conceptual relative, object constancy, is a psychic outcropping of the child's positive interpersonal experiences of permanence and stability. The studies of the toddler phase by Mahler and her associates (e.g., 1963) bring to light how such affective organizers influence a child's use and advances in cognitive capacities. For example, they have shown how the toddler who has reached the stage of being able to walk away actively himself (a requisite of personal autonomy) can be bound to orbit around his mother out of fear and a struggle against physical separation from her. He can become so involved in "repetitive, coercive, aggressive patterns of wooing mother" as to leave other cognitive and affective potentials undeveloped. One is moved to wonder what kind of self-representational materials might be characteristic of such children, if their preoccupying struggle for concrete direct contact with their mothers does not interfere altogether with their capacity for projective fantasy expressions.

Considered both perceptually and dynamically, a child's awareness of its self will be coordinated in various ways to the type and extent of its awareness of people and things. Supporting this view is a Harvard research team's discovery of a developmental characteristic they regard as a "revelation." In their investigation of the genesis and the criteria of "competency" and "incompetency" in 1–3 year old children, from low- and middle-socioeconomic families, they observed that their one-two year olds spent an average of twenty-two percent of their day in "*staring* at a person or thing with intensity, as if to study its features." Such staring was easily distinguished from just "sitting and doing nothing, without looking at anything in particular, or else moving about in apparently aimless fashion." (Reported by Pines, 1969). Moreover, the children rated high in competency spent more of their day in focused staring—as well as fifty percent more of their time in practicing skills and constructing things—compared to the children rated low in competency. Focused staring thus appears to be an important perceptual-cognitive means of advancing meaningful awareness in a child. Equally evident is that a child's capacity for sustained concentration of this type depends on both the meaningful variety in its objective surrounds and on the affective valence of the people around it. (It is of special interest also that the children rated high in competency spent about twenty percent of their day in fantasy role-playing activities—something low competency children virtually never engaged in.)

Looked at as on a developmental continuum, focused staring is suggestively an extension of the infant's capacity and experiences of "alert inactivity" and the antecedent to a momentous cognitive-affective resource observed (Greenacre, 1958) emerging around age two—a child's involvement in making "same" and "different" comparisons between himself and other objects. This cognitive advance is an extension and transformation of the child's store of information gained in its earlier staring activities. The relevance of a child's achievement for comparative assessments, for characterizations in its fantasy as for its advances in self and object representations, is evident. Also evident is that a child will react evaluatively, not simply impersonally, to its perceptions of qualities that it deems same or different from its own. Hence, the child's sense of self and core-self image will influence and be influenced by its particular selectivity and verity of its perceptual-affective assessments.

As an aside, it is interesting that in my prior efforts to glean developmental information through a study of J.'s longitudinal fantasy records, I characterized her earliest self-representation expressions as relatively "fleeting" identification strivings in contrast to more "enduring" strivings and identifications. That is, they appeared to reveal a child's lighthearted attempt to *grasp* (in active, concrete form) what it feels like or what it would be like, to be the other in the qualities it admires at a time when its own size and limitations were beginning to be cognized, but had not yet acquired a painful reality. Though this remains my impression of the quality in her early self-representations or role-playing, the value of a concept of fleeting identifications is dubious. Actually, many of the characters J. assumed in her early play, e.g., laundress, charwoman, grocery lady, farmer lady feeding her hens (after sister was born), reflect provider qualities associated with her enduring identification with her mother. (By age three, incidentally, her manifest strivings, in fantasy, "to be like Daddy" in selected respects, had become incorporated in her mother-child play where she, as mother, was at times also a gentle but persistent teacher.)

A concomitant psychic development, from another conceptual vantage point, that likely enters into a child's early imitative-type fantasy (and which its engagement in fantasy may facilitate) is its achievement of object constancy, in the psychoanalytic sense. Self-representations, with selected attributes of mother or father, appear at times in contexts that discernibly reflect its potential service as a defense against separation (which is one function of identifications). A brief example from Piaget's records. He overheard J. at age 1;10 in a monologue say to herself (in her first "what's that" question): "What's that, Jacqueline? What's that? There (knocking down a block). What's falling? A block. . . ." (Piaget cites this record only to illustrate advances in the child's use of language from simple communication of its wants to a demonstration of its ability to "talk" and tell what it thinks.) It is safe to assume that here J. is re-enacting a significant feature of her Daddy in his relations with her.

On one level of abstraction, I believe this record points to a means by which object constancy in the psychoanalytic sense is advanced and also suggests that a child's development of object constancy is intrinsically interrelated with delineation of a separate self, while also abetted by its progress in representational language that Piaget speaks about. In her manifest behavior, J. is displaying her cognitive capacity to encompass simultaneously two important concepts, that of herself "out there" and that of an absent other whom she brings close in this primitive distance-type of self-representation. Differences may be found to exist between children in the onset of this type of fantasy, and in the type of object and behavior chosen for representation—which will provide clues to distinguish factors which do and those which do not generate movement in children from such "as if" identifications to more self-imbedded identifications.

This example also illustrates how language development is rooted in and vitalized by the child's affective relationships—a point relevant for understanding the progressive problems in verbal skills often found in children from socio-culturally disadvantaged and crowded homes. The adult's affective responses to a child's early "what's that" questions are probably an important factor in determining whether it will enjoy "playing with ideas" (which is a *sine qua non* of pleasure in school learning, cf. Malone, 1966). This relationship factor is somewhat separate from the cultural differences that have been observed in language usage, e.g., for communication of affects versus for information and ideas.

A final point about early developmental features that may be inferred from the character of representations in young children's fantasy is also suggested in the analysis of J.'s records. One of the distinctive consistencies in her behavior in reality situations that stimulates and is a hallmark of her fantasy play from age 1;6 on is the persistence and ingenuity of her efforts to realize her wishes—by overcoming or circumventing reality obstacles that were imposed by her own limitations or by parental injunctions. For example, a number of J.'s records illustrate her assertive carrying out in fantasy an act that she carefully avoids doing in reality, either in response to her own or to external restraints. I have already mentioned her creation of Marécage, at about age four, as a girl who often *can* do with éclat what J. wished herself able to do. To cite one earlier illustration from obs. 84 (Piaget):

> At 2;7 J. "wanted to carry Nonette (i.e., L. who had been born shortly before). Her mother told her she could try later on. J. folded her arms and said, 'Nonette's in there. There are two Nonettes.' She then talked to the imaginary Nonette, rocked her, etc."

J.'s initial energic endowments and relationship experiences (adjudged from Piaget's reality references and reflections in her fantasy content) led her to expect an attentiveness to her wishes, and fulfillment more often than frustration or pain.[4] Her ability to "grizzle" loud and clear and to get "panana" therefrom, as in the following apt illustration of J.'s "generalizing"[5] behavior, is surely the kind of antecedent experience necessary for a "sense of competency" (White, 1963) and the more general "sense of personal autonomy." At about age 1;6,

[4] A child whose wishes are met inconsistently, or permissively with little connection to objective realities or its developmental needs, or met only when its tantrums lead the parent to yield, will not acquire a sense of entitlement.

[5] J.'s experiences are also reflected in her initial generalizing of "No." At about age two, "J. said 'No, no-o' to her blocks in tones varying between vexation and entreaty, as if to people opposing her wishes." (obs. 119)

> J. was becoming more and more skillful in using adults to obtain what she wanted [that she could not get herself], and always grizzled when they refused or pretended not to hear. One of her grandfathers was the person she found most accommodating, with the result that she began . . . to use the term "panana" not only to call her grandfather but also to indicate that she wanted something, even when he was not present. She would indicate what she wanted by saying its name, give a definite grizzle and add "panana". . . (Piaget, obs. 101).

I have conceptualized one of the ramifying personality outcomes of such experiences as a "sense of entitlement." Entitlement is the implicit message adults give a child when they readily, consistently meet its demands; "undeserving" or "bad" is the message when the adult refuses, ignores, or chastises a child for its demands. In relatively optimal circumstances such as J.'s, a sense of entitlement will be maintained as a vital "affect organizer" of thought and intentionality, with little or no interference with the child's development of ego resources for judgment and reasoning in reality. A comparison with other nursery records that will be discussed offers some evidence that a child's genuine (not defensively assertive) sense of entitlement is a positive substratum in core-self delineation, as well as in advancing reality testing and awareness of self—basic in the development of a "sense of personal autonomy" and a "sense of competency" (White, 1963). Among other things, denial of reality limitations and spirited defiance in childhood fantasy often serves to vitiate the moment of humiliation and help free the child to attend to objective realities, including alternative paths to fulfillment (hence, decrease reality frequency of impasse conflicts and certain defeat by adult), as in J.'s creation of Marécage, her own Nonette, and her own secrets.

In summary, the capacity of a young child temporarily in fantasy "to become the other instead . . ." of what it had only been before evolves from and in turn enriches its growth in complexity of affects and ideas in these ways:

(1) In regard to identification, self-representations in fantasy free the child in some measure from dependency on the actual presence of the parental figure for maintaining contact and a sense of well-being, representing a symbolic form of "refueling" which sustains the child's development of object constancy. Hence, such early expressions of self-representation may also be said to signify a child's capacity for enduring secondary identifications, in the psychoanalytic sense.

(2) The ability to engage in self-imitative fantasy play is evidence of the child's developing capacity of self-observation, hence of increased complexity in its awareness of self. Often the context of such play also reveals awareness of its own behavior related to awareness of the other's reactions to its behavior.

(3) The other side of self-imitative fantasy representations is the child's intentional impersonation of others. Projective self-representations as well usually reflect a simultaneous apperception of selected characteristics as same or different from (ideal) self, and value judgment of good or bad experienced in phase-specific dichotomies (big-little, strong-helpless). Together, the two forms of imitative behavior in fantasy convey the child's two-pronged strivings inherent in its reaching out for meaningful relationships where "life is with people," i.e., for the other to be like himself, and for himself to be more like the other. This is, of course, an oversimplification, since it leaves out the selectivity processes and defensive needs which may render these efforts optimally unequal in direction, or inappropriate.

(4) That a capacity for increased acuteness of self-observation tends to develop in conjunction with the emergence of evaluative comparisons with others may be surmised by the coincidental activities (around age two) of marked interest in making same and different comparisons, in reality behaviors, and projective or experimental identifications in fantasy play. Both the character and implicit selectivity in the young child's expressed observations of same and different (usually with respect to people), and in the attributes of its fantasy representation, often reflect the child's prominent affective strivings and experiences at the time.

(5) Correspondingly, one may assume that differentiation and individuation of self-image takes place in conjunction with differentiation of internal object representations. Where affective experiences and phase-level strivings combine to create unclarities and relative unsafety in the processes of separation-individuation (Mahler), oscillation, or fusion of negative self-object representations may be rather persistent psychic resultants, as we have seen them reflected in Jane's records.

3

Affective Factors in Regressive and Variable Cognitive Functioning

A valid appraisal of the influence of affects on thought can be made only within the context of knowledge of the optimal limit of expectable cognitive characteristics at different ages. Piaget's theory and the research findings he has stimulated provide the ground in which the individual figure may best be appraised.

While a detailed description of Piaget's contributions is not relevant here,[1] a brief review of some general points will serve to facilitate the subsequent presentation of fantasy analysis material. (1) In the earliest period of mental development (sensorimotor), there is little discernible differentiation between characteristics of thought in personal and impersonal situations. All things and events are cognized or imbued with meaning in relation to the immediate moment and persona, equally in wishful, playful ("ludic"), and reality-directed behavior. (2) The child's skills and knowledge of the real world advance in accord with its own transactions with things and experiences of people. The advances within the sensorimotor phase are reflected in a number of ways in the early stages of the next major phase of mental development—preconceptual, representational (symbolic) thought (from 18 months to age four or later). The child in this second major phase evidences, among other ad-

[1] There are a number of excellent accounts of Piaget's work, notably by Hunt (1961), P. Wolff (1960), and Décarie (1962).

vances, less frequent apperceptions of causality in terms of magical thinking, animism, together with a growing comprehension of reciprocal relations in classes of objects. (3) Normally, the gains children continue to make in their ability to deal objectively with spatial, temporal, and means-end features of their world, appear concurrently in all mental life, to some extent even in dreams in the early years.

Where affective realities are present, however (e.g., impulses, conflict, anxiety), and enter into means-end features, the gradations and distinctions achieved in causality comprehension emerge more slowly and are less stable than in impersonal, objectively structured situations. Affective realities selectively imbue the different objective components with meaning and significance that are not as universal as in more impersonal areas, and therefore can lend themselves more easily to pre-causal thinking. As Wolff (1960) points out, many of Piaget's observations "show that the transition from magical phenomenalism to objective causality is slow and painful. Long after the child has acquired an objective conception of spatial, temporal, and causal relationships, he tends to revert to magic phenomenalism whenever he is confronted by insoluble tasks which he intends to solve" (p. 139). An arousal of earlier modes of reasoning in affective circumstances is illustrated in J.'s response when she was six-and-a-half.

> (At age 6;6) "J. screamed with fright when the door of the hen-house, blown by the wind, hit her in the back. Then, crying, she said: "The wind's horrid, it frightens us."—But not on purpose?—"Yes, on purpose. It's horrid, it said we were naughty." But does the wind know what it does?—"It knows it blows" (obs. 119).

At any level of development, therefore, early forms of thought (magical thinking, etc.) may reappear in individual stress circumstances. By this token, past the age of three or so, the appearance of earlier forms of reasoning and judgment in particular situations (e.g., "fluctuating certainty"), is an indicator of stress and affective interference with optimal cognitive achievements. Such interferences may be passing or more characteristic of the individual's personality functioning.

Looking at psychic evolution from another vantage point, early functional and affective schemas (structures) may be described as less clearly differentiated within and between each other than they will become. Similarly, newly achieved levels of thought and skills will be more vulnerable to disruption (dedifferentiation of schemas, or regression), than well established attainments which have more numerous and various intrapsychic runners. Expectably, children will be more open and vulnerable to alterations in their "ego state" than adults. "The Witches" fantasy record (V), in a group of Fours, provides material for understanding variability and regression in thought and behavior. It illustrates dynamic conditions which lead to the re-emergence of an earlier level of ego functioning and of associated dependency feelings towards a significant adult (teacher, in this case). Several of the child witches will be seen to change from a relatively high level of resourceful, independent behavior to a lower one in terms of thought, activity, and goals.

My overall interpretive position may be summarized in this way: The transitory regressive reactions of the children represent a defensive position instigated by their driving need for "reunion" with an adult whose disapproval (interference) of their self-initiated aggressive activity aroused in them an anxiety experience of loss of love. The essence of this experience, as one child indicates, is a rather intolerable one of feeling "lonely." The children so affected not only abruptly cease the disapproved activity but become completely inactive for a while, rousing only to contact the teacher with, "Look at me!"—though all they are doing is rocking or sitting quietly. On a corresponding level, as the record illustrates, these children not only seek the teacher's approval in a regressive form but also feel dependent on her for direction and control of their behavior. The positive quality of their behavioral aim to recover the teacher's love reflects the relatively undiluted prominence in their development, of the wish to please. It contrasts sharply with the provocatively negative regressive responses to criticism (rejection), seen in children whose early experiences in attempts to please and be pleased have been fraught with humiliation and failure. "The Witches" also illustrates the different patterns of expression of "attachment," "loss," and dependency feelings in children. The latter concept is clearly neither superseded nor necessarily submerged in that of attachment.

Record V

The Witches

A

Fours Yard time, morning, January 1964

1. Laura and Aries (taking board as broom and starting to hop around): We're pretending we're witches and it's Halloween night.
2. Seth: Can I play?
3. Aries: You can be an assistant witch.
4. David: If I can't be the grandfather witch, I won't be your friend.
5. Aries: No you can't!
6. David (crying): I'm not your friend. I hate you!
7. Aries (softly): I was just *asking* Laura [the out].
8. Laura: You can be a ghost, or a goblin or a witch.
9. David (very serious, up close to Laura): Well, what do witches do again? I'm not sure.
10. Laura and Aries (making faces of amused superiority): They take children and turn them into gingerbread.
11. David (nodding): Oh yeah. They put a "spell" on them.
12. Laura (serious): What's a spell?
13. David: They cut them up and put them in jail.
14. (Seth, listening, suddenly hits David and Laura and races away.)
15. Laura (loudly): I'm not going to your house tomorrow if you hit me. (Seth turns back to her.)

16. David (under shed): Well, I tell you, we have lots of supper tonight. I put people in the oven.
17. (David, Aries, Laura, and Seth sit down.)
18. David (handing out): One for you, one for you, one for you. (All pretend to eat. Suddenly David lets out): *Oh! Oh!* We have only three people!
19. Seth, Laura and Aries (all starting to count each other): One, two, three, four. Four. Four!
20. David: No, I mean only three people in the oven to eat.
21. Aries: I'm eating Celeste.
22. David, Seth, Laura: I'm eating Celeste's head, I'm eating Rondi's, George's arm. (Eating motions.)
23. (They jump up, jump on their "brooms" and go for George, Celeste and Ronnie.)
24. (Teacher steps in and stops it. This breaks it up—few attempts to salvage group by Aries don't work.)

B

Rondi (from nearby ladder house): I'm your neighbor witch.

Aries: No.

Rondi: I have an idea. Let's be gorilla families and neighbors. (Aries won't, but David and Seth do.)

Laura (coming to teacher): It smells like the country—down where I swim and it's muddy. (She smells the frying codfish cakes from the kitchen exhaust fumes.)

C

David: It's nighttime in the witch house. (Lies down. No one joins him. All become two's or individuals. David and George on steps and sandbox. Aries and Laura follow ladder tracks to rocking boat. Laura rocks and sings.)

Aries (talking to self on rocking boat, sitting side-saddle): Mrs. F., look at the way I'm sitting.

Seth: Mrs. F., watch me. (Sits and daydreams.)

Laura and Aries: Mrs. F., we're lonely, there's room for two more here. One here and one here.

(T. asks Rondi.)

Rondi: No! (Could she be mad about the witches?)

(T. asks David.)

David (going to jungle gym—no one on it—asks): Girls, do you need me? (T. directs him to boat and he goes.)

Reality, Realism, and Fantasy

The children begin their play by clearly defining themselves as only "pretend witches." As they discuss what "real" witches do, and *do to* children, they become caught up in an increased need for *active* aggression on their own parts (A, 9–14). "Just pretend" then begins to spill over into increasingly realistic actions—really hitting or really going after real people, using a realistic prop (board for broomstick). However, they make only pretend moves to eat those they tried to catch for their "supper."

It appears that the initial pretend character of their talk about how they could be eaten up, cut up, generally punished ("locked in jail"), could not be sustained within the relative safety of the make-believe framework, and aroused real fears of such happenings to them. They did not take flight into reality, but became more deeply involved in the aroused fantasy—with defensive precautions of turning passive into active and reversing their position from victim to aggressor. The direction of their response may be understood on this level: Their discussion of what witches *do* aroused their own aggressive-impulse imagery; assuming the active role of witches afforded an expression both of their own wishes and of their defense against fears of being "destroyed" in these ways in reality.

Fantasy as a "Distance" Defense

The striking change in the behavior of the "witch" children (especially Laura, Seth, Aries) when they were stopped in their play by the teacher strengthens the inference that their own conflicted aggressive wishes and fears were underlying their fantasy activity. The distinction that fantasy expression can often provide for the child—that between his being "really" bad and being only "pretend" bad—was blurred when the teacher interrupted their crescendo of affect and threatening activity. Her intervention appears to have broken through their first line of defense provided by fantasy itself (relatively separate from other types of distance-defenses within it).[2] It broke through the distance of self from feelings of guilt-incrimination associated with their own aggressive impulses. The children may be described as experiencing an alteration at the time in the affective coloring of their core-self image, from good to bad, which simultaneously altered their level of ego functioning (section C). Their reactive behaviors resemble initially those stemming from a depressive position, but are followed by concentrated efforts to alleviate their feelings of loneliness through a regressive dependency route. (Feeling sad and lonely, as when the parents literally go away, is one of the ways guilt feeling may be experienced.)

This is certainly not the only possible inner experience and response-sequence of a child. But it does illustrate a basic model in situations where the person is unable to fend off internal acceptance of and self-image connection with blame (guilt feelings), and seeks to regain the real (or internalized) parental figure through efforts to be good, as defined by that figure. One alternative sequence is determined by the extent to which the child feels humiliated by the event. His longing for reunion thus blunted by a basic need to save face, he may be led to overt defiance of external directives and control, or covert revenge. A child not protected against repeated experiences of humiliation in a dependency relationship or when engaged in self-initiated activities may thus end up entrenched in a state of pseudo-independency and being a "bad child" in reality, not only in his core-self image.

[2] Teacher intervention is at times necessary, at times unwarranted. This observation is not to be construed as a value judgment on teacher intervention in general.

Individual Differences in Defense

Aries: Her reaction to David's tears and retaliatory threats of rejection goes beyond sympathy—into remorse for a crime she did not commit[3] (A,6). Nor was it out of fear of his rejection, since he was not one of her regular companions. Her response rather appears to illustrate both her special concerns about being good and not-bad, and an inability in affective circumstances to distinguish between her act and the evaluative reactions of the other to it. As will be shown later, a child's self-evaluation, though highly dependent for some time on the reactions of the other, begins to be a distinctive individual variable by age three or so.[4] Accepting the responsibility and blame for making David cry, she retreats not only from the offending content of her suggestion, but simultaneously from all initiative connected with it. Turning active into passive appears to be her primary defense against blame and wrongdoing—as in her later reaction to the teacher's intervention.

Rondi: In this episode Rondi displays a high level of ability to draw on her ego resources to integrate aggressive impulses and fears, with her wish to maintain social ties. She has developed the ability to resolve the either-or type of conflict apperceptions

[3] David's intense reaction to being assigned the role of "assistant witch" is akin to the young child's reaction to being called "baby." He happens to be the youngest in his family, but his vulnerability to this implication may be uniquely increased by his still unverbalized anxiety about a (congenital) sensory deficit. In his fantasy play, he was the most dedicated "Astro-boy" character in the group, and continued to initiate the same type of fantasy in the Fives.

[4] It is of interest that the following year, when Aries was routinely tested by the school psychologist, special mention is made of Aries' strong concern about being right or wrong. (She tested in the 99th percentile.) This observation suggests an inherent potential tie-in between a child's imperative controls related to good and bad, and achievements in terms of right and wrong. Thus, where a child's "performance" in anything continues to be connected to early anxieties about approval for being good, and early ideals or strivings for omniscience and omnipotence, one will find generalization and displacement in objectively unrelated spheres of good and bad (right and wrong).

(either victim *or* aggressor, for instance) by finding a differentiated position between extremes. Her suggestions to be "neighbor witches" or "gorilla friends and neighbors" are offers to share qualities of size and strength in the interests of mutual protection, without yielding one bit of her power to defend herself if need be. These are imagery concepts that draw on her most advanced cognitive capacities for differentiation, and also reflect her capacity for integration of knowledge and affects.

It is important to add that though this mode of response is characteristic of Rondi's coping-defense style, the fact that she was not herself involved in being an attacker "witch" (did not have to defend herself against aroused feelings of guilt or shame) left her freer than the other children to utilize her most advanced resources for adaptive defense solutions.

Regression in Level of Ego Function and Increased Dependency

When the teacher asked the children to stop their chasing, Seth, Laura, and Aries not only immediately dropped their broomsticks and "cannibalistic" gestures, but became inactive altogether. For a while they just sat—unresponsive to all suggestions to continue their theme in another way. It was clear that they were not simply tired. When they roused themselves, they did so only to ask their teacher to "look at me," though all they were showing her was their rocking or sitting sideways in the "boat." They had returned to a developmentally earlier phase of non-self-evaluative need for contact: "Watch *me*," "Look at *me*."

That the children had an experience of loss of love, that they were making reparative efforts to regain their lost object, is evident in their feeling "lonely." What is striking is that in these circumstances their reparative efforts take the form of increased *dependence* on the adult for approval, and *regression* in the use of their ego-skills and autonomous resources. They neither seek, nor accept offers to play with other children. They ask the teacher to arrange it for them. They yield not only their autonomy for impulse-controls temporarily to the adult but all spontaneous intiative to achieve or try anything on their own. In this, too, there is a developmental retreat to an earlier form of response to disappointment or frustration in their own efforts: "I can't, you do it for me."

One way of explaining their reaction is to infer that they had not yet achieved developmentally internalized defense structures to secure them against their oral-sadistic or conflicted aggressive impulses, which are intimately connected with primary family figures. When the protective cover of fantasy expression was lost through their own actions, their internalized basis for accepting blame triggered distrust of or "fluctuating certainty" with respect to their own impulse control. They regressed to complete reliance on external controls. In seeking to gain the teacher's approval and admiration, they also yielded their initiative and cognitive resourcefulness, in favor of her direction. The intimacy of connection, even at this age, between a child's view of his whole this-is-me self-image when his impulse expressions are involved with parental approval or disapproval is clear. What was a transient reaction in the "witch children" might serve as a paradigm of what can become consolidated in personality development when children are recurrently faced with expectations of "disaster" or blame. In keeping with these inferences of the dynamics underlying the children's behavior, not one of the "witches" protested "But we're only pretending!" when the teacher interrupted them. They had apparently not yet achieved the firm internal "distance" and acceptability of "bad" wishes, which it is possible to gain when the distinction between only "thinking" an impulse-wish and a deed is experienced as clear and valid.

Some Theoretical Conclusions

With growth in veridical comprehension and logic, there is naturally greater potential for intra-individual variations in level of thinking. Affective factors, including those induced by temporary physical circumstances such as fatigue and illness, give rise to variations in coherence and complexity of ideas and wishes, and in appropriate means-end sequences. Generally speaking, in fantasy or reality expressions, such variations in optimal level of comprehension and expression represent transient regressions to earlier forms of solution. Or they may instead represent a more established divergence in the child's processes of thought, in impersonal and affect-charged situations.

On the other hand, the extent to which wishes or fears can direct the nature of conclusions of reasoning, perception, or judgment, depends not only on the internal experience of the event, but also on the ambiguities inherent in the external situation for the individual. Various experimental and clinical situations demonstrate that affective circumstances evoke higher or lower levels of differentiated thought in adults as well as children. However, it is also clear in such experimental or test situations that the extent of influence of the affect arousal on the cognitive expressions depends also on features of the objective situation, i.e., whether these are extrinsically structured or call largely on the person's internal experience of the event to provide meaning to the materials. Which aspects of a situation are ambiguous and incite an affective structuring (as in fluctuating certainty), is also in part a developmental cognitive problem. The operation of wishful thinking cannot be attributed simply to the power of the affects.

Surprisingly, Piaget does not appear to take this clearly into account. For instance, he explains the similarities in the young child's ludic and reality-oriented reasoning in these terms: "Because [representational thought] enables him to go beyond the perceptual field he can *distort* [my italics] the reality to suit his wishes" (p. 233), and cites the following episode as an example of such distortion:

> At 2;0 . . . J. wanted a dress for her doll, which was upstairs. She said "Dress" and when her mother refused it, "Daddy get dress." As I also refused, she wanted to go herself to "mummy's room." After several repetitions of this she was told it was too cold there. There was a long

> silence. Then, "Not too cold!"—Where?—"In the room." —Why isn't it too cold?—"Get dress."
>
> . . . Thus the judgment "not too cold," made to meet the need of the situation, was subordinated to the practical end in view. . . . This is another example of . . . sensory motor reasoning (coordination of schemas for a definite end) . . . which transformed reality and served as a means of attaining the end (obs. 111).

Is J.'s "not too cold" simply a distortion of reality judgment to meet her need? Or does the incident mainly demonstrate J.'s strength of purpose to get her doll's dress? (There is ample evidence both in J.'s reality and fantasy records of such strength, related to her sense of entitlement.) One could speak of a distortion only if J. in reality had experienced the temperature of the room as icy and denied it. Here she is simply disputing her parents' opinion that the room was too cold to get the dress. Indeed, under the circumstances of wanting something very much in the room, neither J. nor her parents may have found the room "too cold" to go quickly into and out of. It seems to me that J. is moved to question their judgment not only because she didn't like anything to interfere with her wishes, but also because there was nothing in the room she was in to prove their contention. This cognitive sprightliness of hers is well established. From her beginnings, she had been encouraged to question what she heard, saw, and thought. Actually, though the parents were understandably reluctant to go into their temporarily unheated bedroom, to J. the objective situation in the room—to get dress—was ambiguous. So is the meaning of Piaget's question. An adult, let alone a two-year-old, might be hard put to answer his question, "Why isn't it too cold?" in terms other than "I don't think it is," or just "not too cold."

One may conceive the coexistence of different possible levels of cognitive functioning at every stage of development. The psychoanalytic concept of regression comes to mind at this point, as does Kris's (1952) delineation of "regression in the service of the ego." The latter refers to the temporary utilization of communication channels with more primary, generally preconscious modes of thought and feeling, for the sake of a creative outcome. The former describes a mode of defense invoked by the ego, which leads to a more or less permanent entrenchment of some portion or level of ego functioning tied to a previous stage of imagery, impulse, defense, and mode of thought. Anna Freud's (1963) more recent formulation of "regression in mental development" comes close to a proposal of "coexistence." She speaks of everyday instigators to temporary regression, such as fatigue, illness, disappointment, naturally more marked in children than in adults. One may investigate the concept of coexistence by studying individual characteristics of variability in levels of functioning for qualities that may be adaptive or maladaptive.

Differences between individuals (and clinical categories) may be found in the circumstances and speed with which particular levels are evoked and invoked in a forward or backward direction, and in the circumstances and speed of recovery to the highest level within the individual's developmental range. These angles are generally relevant, of course, in all investigations where individual variability, developmental age, and situation are interdependent factors. Some of the fantasy records will show "regression in the service of the ego" by means of the particular defense strategies conveyed in them, while others will reveal strategies that fail to yield adaptive outcomes.

4

Pattern Relationships of Defense and Individuation in Fantasy

Two defense categories, I found, particularly distinguish certain individual and developmental features of affective-cognitive response patterns: One is oscillation and fluctuating certainty, the other direct and distance modes of self representation and defense. Some introductory comments on defense reactions are in order before the two categories can be properly discussed with the help of the study records.

Defense reactions may be explained and understood at various levels of description. Broadly speaking, defenses may be defined as affective-cognitive control devices, aroused to direct or ameliorate the outcome of one's intentional efforts and interpersonal events. In this sense, defense modes have the potential of being reparative (internally and/or in reality), or merely repetitive, as in self-fulfilling prophecy behaviors.

At a dynamic descriptive level, defense reactions represent a person's behavior patterns that are primed by anxiety and have the foremost aim of protecting him against unendurable experiences of loss of impulse control, of physical integrity, of basic self-esteem. The effectiveness and variety of ego resources a person may mobilize for defense when so threatened differs with individuals, at different ages, and with the press of circumstances, internal and external. The identification of defense mechanisms represents one means of sorting out the processes and understanding the pertinence of particular defense devices in development and personality functioning. As generally understood, defense mechanisms (e.g., displacement, projection, reaction-formation) are psychoanalytic constructs denoting the types of primary or secondary processes that a person is able to draw on to ward off or to mitigate arousal of pain and internal sources of conflict-anxiety.

Anna Freud's classic study, *The Ego and the Mechanisms of Defence* (1936), was the first to establish developmental and diagnostic distinctions in the individual use of the different defense mechanisms. Hartmann's *Ego Psychology and the Problem of Adaptation* (1939) established a framework for the appraisal of given adaptational capacities and specific cognitive processes, which may be utilized in the function of defense. In the years to follow, a number of others (e.g., the works by Hartmann, Kris, and Loewenstein; Rapaport; Erikson) have contributed to the coordination of clinical insights with general psychology and generated interest in conceptualizing the "normal" as well as the ego, in psychoanalytic thought. A recent brief expression of this broader orientation is a brief article in which Sandler and Joffe (1967) introduce the idea of "positive" defenses. They define these as any defense that is mustered by a person to sustain his state of well-being or security, not simply to defend himself against anxiety or other negative affect. ". . . we can regard the defense mechanisms as being directed towards the maintenance of well-being, rather than specifically directed against the emergence of anxiety" (p. 513).[1]

Lois Murphy and her collaborators emphasized a positive and enlarged view of defense reactions in their concept of "coping strategies" in *The Widening World of Childhood* (1962). Coping devices denote the overall efforts and total range of resources children from age two to five may employ "towards a solution of

[1] It is known that individuals vary in their speed of recovery from negative affect experiences (shame, guilt, rage), as well as in the relative stability of their positive state of well-being. How these differences relate to or rest upon differences in characteristic defense patterns is an important question.

a threat, fear, or challenge of mastery." Coping devices draw on a child's general capacities for thought, speech, locomotion, and the like, whenever he "encounters something not yet mastered: . . . an obstacle or a conflict" (p. 6). The coping responses may range considerably in complexity from methods of "simply surveying the situation" to the use of cognitive skills involved in planning and action. "Adaptation" is conceived as the broader organismic foundation of coping based on ". . . habitual and routine, unchanged, automatic and reflex responses."

Coping or Defense?

The term "coping devices" enfolds defense mechanisms within a broadly conceived range of physical and cognitive resources, and quite different affective instigators. As a concept it does not distinguish between a coping solution attempted by a child when it is having a negative affective experience (threat, fear), or a positive experience (challenge of mastery). Are these differences in feeling-state associated with significant differences in the kind of cognitive resources available to a child at the time? On the face of it, it seems likely that the particular resources a child may muster when it feels threatened by internal or external sources of conflict-anxiety will differ from those that operate when he feels only challenged to master some obstacle to fulfillment. (This seems true even if the latter experience follows the former.) Individual differences in personality, related to characteristic range and deployment of resources for coping, certainly emerge in accordance with the child's proneness to one of these feeling-states, rather than to the other.

I believe there is heuristic value at this point of knowledge, in distinguishing defense reactions more specifically from coping devices in general, though both reflect a child's attempt to solve a dilemma it feels faced with. The instigating feeling-state of defense is anxiety, rooted in a fear of being overwhelmed, losing control, being humiliated. In contrast, feeling challenged to mastery is rooted in a person's sense of being able (through his own efforts)[2] to control, to overcome. In defense, the aim is essentially protective and restitutive; in the other, the aim is more expansive towards mastery and achievement. The outcome in either case may be positive or negative with respect to the child's attainment of its aims. But the means the child employs in the two affective contexts may well be associated with different psychic returns with respect to advancing growth and flexible use of resources.

In any case, whatever differences in feeling-states might generate differences in coping resources, whether a particular response of a child may be considered positive or negative requires judgment of the coping effects on the child's functioning and of the feedback outcome in the reality situation. In the comparative analyses of children's modes of dealing with anxieties that trigger or are aroused by aggressive fantasy content, I have been able to point out some criteria that distinguish between defense and coping in terms of the resource characteristics, apparent nature of anxiety aroused (or allayed), likely psychic returns, and the feedback outcome. A comparison of individual children in these respects is made possible by identifying some of the consistent features in the midst of their variations in specific defense ploys or mechanisms.

The nursery fantasy records of children across-time in a school year reveal consistency in these dimensions: (1) the child's characteristic use either of *direct* or of *distance* types of self-representation in the service of defense; (2) the direction of the defense (e.g., turning passive into active, reversal); (3) vulnerability to *fluctuating certainty;* and (4) the quality of "rigidity" or "flexibility" (Murphy *et al.,* 1962), which in essence determines the likelihood of a child's evolving a limited or expandable repertoire of defense devices.

[2] The child's relative prominence or lack of "sense of entitlement" is a differential mediating factor.

Fantasy as Coping or Defense?

What has been said about defense and coping reactions generally, is applicable to the analysis of fantasy itself. Apart from its aims, fantasying may serve a positive or negative function, depending on frequency, circumstances, and outcome (internally and externally).

It is very clear in J.'s records from age 1;8 on (Piaget) that her recourse to fantasy expressions represented an important positive factor in her growth of resources for mastery in her everyday living. Among other reasons for this is that a child's ability to verbalize affective stresses and dilemmas symbolically (however defensively) in fantasy scenes, tends to effect some psychological distance from terror or rage that might otherwise be expressed directly in behavioral symptoms. Suggestively, in the acting-out children in the nursery sample, fantasy play is rare; but more or less coincident with behavioral evidence of growth in internal controls and related decrease in overwhelming aggressive-anxiety affects is the initiation or elaboration of fantasy play. Hence, fantasy is not only a medium wherein the child may express conflicted impulses and the like, but his very ability to project these in some fantasy form often signifies psychic growth and furtherance of resolution.

Anna Freud (1936) succinctly stated that involvement with fantasy is a pathological defensive activity only "when it ceases to be a game and becomes an automatism or an obsession—a compensation for more than residues of 'pain' and uneasiness, but an attempt to master the whole of his acute . . . anxiety" (p. 92). In clinical experience "too much" and "too little" recourse to fantasy is a differentiating diagnostic symptom of cognitive-affect disturbance, while the character of spontaneous fantasy in the course of therapy may be used as a measure of progressive changes.[3]

[3] In a preliminary appraisal of spontaneous fantasy of "latency" children in psychotherapy, conducted by students under my supervision, I

Oscillation Between Fantasy and Reality Within a Fantasy

The study data mainly illustrate types of oscillation between fantasy and reality within a fantasy episode; records of concurrent reality-oriented behaviors by the teachers are incidental, too few to appraise differences in children's patterns of alternative involvement with reality and fantasy.

Three kinds of oscillation within a fantasy may be identified, two of which represent the same kind of defense reactions which child psychoanalysts have noted, with respect to children's shifts *between* fantasy and reality: (1) *flight into fantasy* or into deeper fantasy, and (2) *flight into reality*. Within the ostensible confines of a make-believe situation, young children can feel threatened when violence is projected or internally experienced, and they need to affirm their safety. They may do so either by retreat or flight into reality, or into manifestly deeper fantasy. (The concept of fluctuating certainty to be discussed shortly refers to a child's vulnerability to feeling threatened within a fantasy.)

The third type of oscillation, mentioned earlier in my description of group trends, and noted by others (e.g., Moore, 1964), is essentially a reflection of developmental trends and is nondefensive. For example, in the fantasy expressions of the Threes (more often than in the Fours and Fives) one finds shifts into reality which reflect the child's capacity at this age to swing freely between fantasy and reality, and to engage zestfully in both these

---

noted the following differences in "progress indicators": Progress (a) in obsessive-compulsive children was indicated and facilitated by their freshly acquired ability to engage in fantasy play, (b) in borderline children by a change in the cognitive affect characteristics of their initial refulgent fantasying, e.g., in a decrease in primitive aggressive and sexual content, and in magical causality thinking, accompanied by an increase in genuine rather than confounded distance-defense devices, (c) in schizophrenic children by their achievement of a capacity for direct "I" self-representation in fantasy depicting "dreams of glory" ambitions, in contrast to total absorption of "self" in an "as if" character, as well as by changes similar to (b).

worlds. Let me illustrate the three types of oscillation briefly now, from the study records:

(1) *Flight into reality*

David (to himself with distress): Oh oh, everything's broken. (Turns to teacher.) You know, my mommy shined my shoes last night. . . . (Returns to involvement in ongoing fantasy play; record X.)

George (to Rondi after she announced, "I'm a dolphin and I can make you bleed"): Stop the nonsense! (Record X.)

(2) *Flight into deeper fantasy*

George (rising quickly when David and Seth make motions of eating him, and proclaiming): I'm the STORM!

(3) *Oscillation swing, non-defensive*

Olivia (to teacher): What means "stripped of their beauty?" (Record I.)

Fluctuating Certainty: Indicator of Aggression-Anxiety

I have come to view the responses manifesting a child's uncertainty or confusion about pretend versus real implications in a fantasy context, as reflecting an underlying ego state of fluctuating certainty at the time. Individual children in my study differ in their proneness to such a state, as indicated in their misapprehension or flight reactions in either direction within a fantasy. A child may be thrown into a state of fluctuating certainty, either in response to content expressed by another, or even in the course of its own fantasy expression. What appears to happen is that some aspect of the ongoing context triggers a prevailing source of anxiety in the child, of a sufficient intensity level to blur distinguishing features of fantasy and reality. According to the study analysis, beyond the age of 3;6–4, the circumstances which evoke fluctuating certainty in a child are more individual than developmental attributes. Beyond this age, the child who characteristically uses direct "I" self-representation when expressing violence themes in fantasy is also the child most likely to manifest fluctuating certainty about the real danger to him in another's threat.

Different kinds of manifest indicators are seen as reflecting a child's state of fluctuating certainty. The defensive flight responses of George I have just quoted, exemplify types judged to be manifest indicators. In contrast, I consider David's flight into reality only a reflection of his affectively diffused moments of duress, when he briefly experienced everything around him as falling apart, and out of his ability to control. One could describe his flight response as an expression on a symbolic level beyond the toddler stage of a child's need to "refuel" in times of stress. (I am extrapolating Furer's felicitous term describing a toddler's recurrent returns for mother-contact, in the early course of its locomotion forays [quoted in Mahler, 1963].)

There are also other indicators of fluctuating certainty besides those in defensive flight responses. I shall cite two examples of these—Marya in the Threes, and Clara when she was in the Fives.

> Amy (taking her favorite position of director, was assigning roles to several girls. To Marya): . . . and you'll be the bad child (Amy's projection).
>
> Marya (heatedly): I am NOT bad.

It is relevant that Marya, who often engaged in fantasy play both with others and by herself, was at the time struggling in reality against being a "bad" child at home (cf. record XXI).

Clara, whose aggression-ridden fantasy monologues in the Fours will be quoted in detail, was by chance observed by me in a brief interchange with her friend Laura, when she was in the Fives. When I first noticed them in their classroom they were conversing, close together. What held my eye was seeing Laura move quickly back a foot or so, openly don some mask-like covering over her face (which she had been holding in her hand), then advance back towards Clara in a caricature of a menacing monster. Clara drew back, eyes wide in fright, saying in a half whisper, "Take it off, take it off." Laura did so promptly, with apparent surprise at Clara's intense reaction. She hesitated for a moment; then as though unable to resist the temptation, repeated her performance with the same success. Clara again reacted with obvious distress, and again half whispered the same plea, which this time Laura heeded.

Certainly Clara knew that the "monster" was Laura, and vice versa. Yet thoughts about real witches or monsters, or of people potentially turning into them, must have been vivid enough to her, for internal reasons, to evoke real anxiety and a state of fluctuating certainty in this objectively mock scare.

Developmental and Dynamic Features of Fluctuating Certainty

In Piaget's material, a child is able to make the distinction between pretend and real well before the age of two—when it is limited to activity it initiates itself as make-believe. Comprehension of the distinction between pretend and real meanings in the words and actions of other people is a later achievement, related to the child's advances in recognizing metaphoric phrases, along with its increased knowledge of objective probabililties. Within developmental lines, then, fluctuating certainty may be considered a transitional step in a child's grasp of distinctions between reality and make-believe, with respect to other people's intended meaning, from its initial phase of unknowingness or confusion.

Accordingly, it appears reasonable to assume that a normally intelligent child beyond the age of 2–2;6 would not usually experience fluctuating certainty in the course of his own initiated fantasy (scare himself) and that if he did so it would be an indicator of some affective interference in utilizing his ego resources for reality testing. Adam, in the Threes, manifests fluctuating certainty within his own fantasy construction, for the reason that similarly afflicts older children who exhibit fluctuating certainty with respect to other children's aggressive intent in a fantasy context. The effects of the persistence in Adam of the underlying affective factors, on his thought and behavior in the Fours, will be seen in the across-time recordings to be cited in the section on acting-out children. I shall quote an excerpt from these which shows Adam interrupting his make-believe activity of serving tea with real hot water from the sink (but not burning hot), to get a real potholder from the doll-corner. His decision appears governed not by his wish to enhance the concrete realism of his grown up activity, but by his need to be rid of the mounting anxiety within him about his ability to avoid (control) being burned.

> Lenny and Adam each had a small pitcher. Adam got up to get water from the sink. When he turned on the hot water, he exclaimed, "Boy, it's boiling hot!" (objectively it was not) and filled up his pitcher carefully. "I'm not gonna burn myself," he announced, "I'm careful." Then followed a repetitive game in which Adam made hot tea and Lenny cold tea, and served it to me [teacher] a number of times. At one point Adam suddenly jumped up, saying, "I forgot something," and left the room. He returned shortly with a potholder from the doll corner. As he applied it to the pitcher handle he remarked, "Now I'm *really* not gonna burn myself." ("Do you ever hold Mommy's pots at home?") "Oh no! I never did! I might get burned that way!"

My study materials suggest that beyond the age of four, children who are precipitated into a state of fluctuating certainty within a fantasy are thereby pointing to content that is powerfully charged for them for internal reasons. The source of the affective charge which interferes with the child's reality testing capacity (or development) appears to be preoccupying aggressive impulse imagery and anxiety. Other manifestations or consequences of such preoccupation, associated with fluctuating certainty vulnerability in a child, are: (1) a heightened selectivity of aggressive apperceptions of causality; (2) a related persistence of magical thinking; (3) a relative inability to develop distance modes of defense against aggression-anxiety, including a low level of creative deployment of fantasy expression. In such children, aggressive impulse derivatives and anxiety, in the balance of other intrapsychic features (libidinal counterparts), create islands of schemas separated from the mainland level of ego function advances.

Robby's record in the Fours (record VI) illustrates how phase-level aggressive impulse imagery and urgency, intensified by current life experiences,[4] may color a child's apperceptions of potential injury and serve to maintain magical causality thinking in associated content areas. His behavioral responses demonstrate that anxiety about aggressive impulses may lead to a total (temporary) loss of judgment in distinguishing between pretend and real dangers, resulting in a diminished range of resources for coping. His remarks in section B strongly suggest that when he was lost in thought, he was preoccupied with aggressive imagery on several developmental levels connected by his anxiety that physical damage might befall him.

Record VI

"No Kidding"—Robby

A

In the yard Robby was playing with Bob and Steve. Suddenly he hit Bob, who promptly hit him back. Robby

[4] In the teacher's report I subsequently read, the following notes she made are relevant for understanding experiential contributions and associated concurrent behaviors in reality: Robby had complained to her that he had no one to play with weekends, since his grandmother no longer walked to the playground with him because of trouble with her feet. When, during a parent conference, the teacher mentioned this, his mother reacted with total surprise, claiming he always had a marvelous time at his grandmother's. Several days later, however, she reported confirming these complaints by questioning Robby, but did not indicate to the teacher any changes in Robby's weekends, therefrom. During this period, Robby's "workaday" behaviors reflect his feeling uncared about, worthless. It was difficult for him to become involved in any activity; when he did he showed neither attachment to nor protective care of the nice things he made—buildings, paintings—so that they often ended up spoiled or destroyed. Though somewhat ambiguous, the implication is that he treated his products so carelessly that he or someone else inadvertently might despoil them. It is clear how Robby's ongoing relationship experiences could incite aggressive impulses and concerns within him, and create an overload in phase-level feelings of vulnerability to attack or damage.

broke into a torrent of loud, hard sobs, saying to the teacher who came to comfort him, "Don't let Bob come to this school ever again!" Steven then explained how it happened: "We were going to [pretend] burn some wood and he would be tied to it. *He didn't know we were kidding,* and he hit Bob, so Bob hit him back."

B

Robby (on coming out of being lost in thought, to student teacher): My foot hurts. It hurts all the time.[5]
Teacher: Show me where.
Robby (hand on groin): You know, where my penis is.
Teacher: Is it really your foot that hurts?
Robby: No-o. (And laughs.)

C

Limited distance aggression in reality, but with no signal remorse or empathy (cf. mother's apparent lack of empathy for him, preceding footnote): Robby persisted in flipping sand from a spoon on a child nearby despite the child's protests and several requests by the teacher to stop it. He continued doing so until removed from the group. Teacher then asked him if he knew how it feels to have sand thrown at you. He said he did and it wasn't "good." He showed no remorse, however, at having done it to the other child. Allowed to return to the group, he promptly began to threaten to flip the sand, though he did not carry it through.

It will scarcely be lost on the reader that Robby was well aware of the distinction between his foot and his penis. His remark may be considered a protective social convention, or beyond that, an illustration of displacement *in statu nascendi.* The particular choice of his displacement is explicable neither in terms of the symbolic potential of foot alone, nor in the social safety

[5] Note the associative connection with his grandmother's foot "hurting all the time."

attached to references to foot. It shows how experiential factors, however fortuitous, may serve as catalyst in particular psychic circumstances. That is, at his psychosexual phase-level, internal processes of anxiety and aggression (fed also by non-sexual sources) established causal-imagery connections between his grandmother's (damaged) hurting feet and his (endangered) hurting penis.

Psychoanalysis offers a basis for dynamic understanding of the affective conditions which occasionally or characteristically may propel a child into fluctuating certainty or total misconceptions. Accordingly, reactions of fluctuating certainty may be ascribed to the child's anticipation of retaliation for its own destructive impulses, and/or to the projection onto other objects of its revenge impulses, together with its uncertainty of its own impulse controls. A child's sense of helplessness to protect itself against its externalized, primitive revenge fantasies (often not in clear consciousness), will tend to increase its defensive need to *believe* in the power of wishes. In this way magic thinking and fluctuating certainty about the boundaries between real and pretend dangers are interrelated for motivational or affective reasons, and in selected areas will persist, even though magic thinking is no longer operative in general.

Further along on the cognitive developmental line, the more complex distinctions between possible and probable in judgments of a present event, or in expectations of future events in reality, may be blurred for similar reasons. Generally speaking, high levels of anxiety in adults rest on premises reflecting the either/or quality of early thought processes genetically associated with the anxiety content, which occludes distinction between possible and probable. The resultant anticipations derive their character from the person's underlying belief in, or chronic fluctuating certainty about the probability that his fantasy dreads (not necessarily conscious) will materialize. There is an interesting implication in a recent study of adults, that the vulnerability to a state of fluctuating certainty as noted in some nursery study children, may persist well beyond childhood. In a study of "hypnagogic and related phenomena," one of the findings is that "field-dependent subjects (in contrast to field-independent) seem more uneasy or even frightened by the experimental situation. They are more often caught up in imagery which, however bizarre, seems real to them" (Bertini, Lewis, and Witkin, 1964).

In summary, beyond age 3;6 or 4, fluctuating certainty indicators in behavior reflect a child's internal press and ego state at the time. Fluctuating certainty as a conceptual tool in analysis of data heightens recognition and understanding of a more or less transient affective source of interference with a child's cognitive capacities. More generally, the concept of fluctuating certainty may be considered an explicit if small addition to the perceptive tools of child analysts, not unlike Erikson's attentiveness to the types and meaning of irruptions in the flow of children's play in therapy sessions (1940).

Direct and Distance Modes of Defense and Self-Representation

The consistency I found in the across-fantasy records of individual children is a striking feature of self-representations. Some are involved in their fantasy constructions directly as "I," while others characteristically distance their self in the guise of another. Moreover, within each of these two types of self-representations, one finds children differing in the extent or character of their employment of other means of obtaining psychological distance from potential affective arousal. For example, a child engaged in a violence fantasy as "I" may in the same breath employ such distance-defenses as "isolation of affect" and physical constriction with respect to symbolic actions accompanying the violence.

Arly, in one group of Fours, often verbalized threats of primitive annhilation. But she made these threats in a completely unaccented voice, with a poker face, and total absence of active symbolic gesturing. If one did not hear the words, and just saw her angelic face, one would never guess the content. At times, she also projected the "arm" of violence, by ordering a companion to carry out the fearsome act—"Ben, chop him to pieces!" In Arly, the distance-defense devices appear in contexts where her own real self is directly implicated, where her target is a person who is directly present nearby (usually a child, sometimes the teacher), and where the verbalized aim is openly to hurt or annhilate.

There are types of distancing devices other than those utilized by Arly to be found in either of the two self-representation groups: generalizing the "enemy" that is present (as in getting after "the girls"); creating a far-out indeterminate character, or attacking one that is allegedly right "over there," but is in fact totally unseen; at the most extreme, expressing aggressive intents or commissions either towards or as a non-human, sometimes even inanimate figure (as George's "I killed the lighthouse," or "I'm the STORM"). In brief, among the distance forms of defense, one finds the self-representation characters varying in identifiable familiarity or irreality, the targets in generality or irreality, and the activities engaged in as more or less symbolic.

Developmental and Dynamic Features

It will be recalled that Mike's direct "I" representations reflected power attributes rather than identifications with persons, in part or whole. I described Mike as a child with a delayed or distorted delineation of self schemas, such that he was unable to project his self as a whole person, or even an animal. Some preliminary observations of a research group at the Hampstead Clinic support the significance assigned to Mike's responses. As reported by Sandler (personal communication, 1964), the research group was beginning to note differences between the fantasy characterizations of neurotic and borderline children. In the neurotic child's fantasy, the several characters appeared to be projections of different aspects of his self images or of conflicted parts of his self. In contrast, the borderline child seemed unable to project his self, and always remained as "I." These observations were made of children in therapy during their middle childhood, which suggests that beyond a given age, a child's direct form of self-representation in fantasy may reflect an obdurate interference in self and defense development.

The motivation to achieve or maintain a sense of safety from blame and punishment for aggressive impulses in fantasy expressions (conscious or not) usually arises more from the child's underlying premises than from reality dangers in the present (as in the "Witches"). All manifest distance-defense devices enable a child to achieve some psychological distance from direct responsibility as the possessor of the feelings, wishes, or actions he is expressing. But all distance devices are not equally effective in protecting the child against anxiety surges connected with the conflicted impulses and fears underlying his fantasy.

As illustrated in the nursery records to follow, the distance form of self-representation is the sign of the most effective intrapsychic organization for handling anxiety otherwise arousable by expression of aggressive impulses by one's self or in another.

Analysis of the records of Clara, Gerry, George, and Rondi suggested the hypothesis that distance forms in fantasy characterizations signify not only different but also later intrapsychic achievements than do direct forms. With this in mind, I first turned to Piaget (1945) and reordered his quoted materials in longitudinal sequences. When the evidence in J.'s records (the most complete in his book) confirmed a developmental trend, I sought an additional check in the fantasy activities of a severely disadvantaged Head Start group of Threes. Here, too, I found a developmental trend in that when fantasy first appears, the children's characterizations begin with direct "I" forms, and in a few proceeded to distance forms within the several months they were observed.

Dr. Carol Eagle was at the time the Director of Psychology and Consultant of this Head Start project. She recorded the children's fantasying for me, as time permitted, in the spring of 1967. During the first half of the school year there were virtually no fantasy activities. Only a very few of those children who did begin to engage in fantasy around the middle of the year achieved distance characterizations by the end of the school year. The total number of records is too small to warrant detailed analysis, but these observations appear valid and of interest, in comparison to the nursery children: Sometimes the distance form was a defense, like "I'm Batman," when the child felt threatened by the aggression of another; sometimes it was an expression of identificatory strivings out of admiration, like being teacher or a soldier. Expectedly, the thematic elaboration in fantasy was relatively minimal. Differences in real experiences, as compared to the study group's, were reflected in their mother-child play. As the Mommy, the Head Start child was likely to be involved in details of cooking and preparing a meal, whereas the study children were more involved in feeding their babies and/or putting them to bed. Finally, where oscillation between fantasy and reality occurred, the Head Start children were more likely to take leave of the fantasy level to engage in direct, real aggression, or real arguments, suggesting a more easily aroused state of fluctuating certainty, traceable perhaps more to their developmentally limited experiences with make-believe activity than to the greater prevalence in them of affective interferences.

I shall cite a few records of Piaget's J., before I discuss the nursery school children, to illustrate the developmental trends. It is of interest that the developmental changes from direct to distance forms in her representations are especially clear in fantasy expressions reflecting feelings of defiance and conflict.

I have placed episodes 1–2, and 3–4, in paired sequences to show just how J.'s use of various distance devices coincides with an overall increase in the complexity of her affects and ideas. Generally speaking, about age 2;8 is the time J. begins to shift from representing herself as "I" carrying out a forbidden or unachievable act, to portraying another as doing so. A similar trend marks the character of the other. In earlier fantasying the other is someone real, though never someone in the immediate surrounds or known well. Later the other becomes even more remote; they are figures freshly woven out of strands of her real experiences and internal world.

Episodes (3) and (4) show too, how a child's use of distance forms may also signify its developing capacity for internalized conflict (in comparison to prior experiences of conflict between self and external sources), as well as its means of dealing thereby with conflicted aggressive impulses. In passing, I may note that the bear-biting-mommy fantasy reflects J.'s early manifestation of her consistent, often ingenious efforts to eliminate aggressive feelings and conflict with her mother (as in #2, and also in the notable episode at age 2;1 shortly after her sister was born when she created baby Nonette for herself). During the turmoiled years between two and five, she expresses aggressive feelings towards her father (albeit through distance characters like Caroline and Marécage), but not once is her mother or sister a specifically designated target, and with one notable exception not a distance target in fantasy either. An aligned manifestation of the same developmental forces is her early and consistent self-representation expressions of identification with the provider.

Record VII

J.

1) At 2;4 J. not being allowed to play with the water being used for washing, took an empty cup, went and stood by the forbidden tub and went through the actions, saying: "I'm pouring out the water!"
2) At 3;11 she was told not to go into the kitchen because of the pails of hot water prepared for a bath: "Then I'll go into a pretend kitchen! I once saw a little boy who went into a kitchen, and when Odette [real maid] went past with the hot water he got out of the way." The story continued on this theme, by way of compensation. Then it ended with a symbol acceptance: "After, he didn't go to the kitchen any more" (both obs. 84).
3) At 1;7 (25) instead of biting her mother's cheek . . . [as she had], she pressed her bear's face to the same spot and said: "Oh! Oh!" (from obs. 75a).
4) At 2;8 J. was angry with her father, tried to hit him, etc., and since this seemed likely to have unfortunate consequences she suddenly cried: "It was much nicer when Caroline (a friend of her godfather) was cross with God-

father." She then related, drawing entirely on her imagination, how Caroline had struck Godfather, and she began to mime the scene in detail [n.b., words alone did not suffice, for the age, and for the occasion]. When later on her mother spoke to her about her original anger, J. would have none of it: "No, it was Caroline!" (from obs. 84). 5) . . . At 4;8 J. was jealous of her father and said: "Marécage has a horrid father. He calls her in when she's playing,"—and "her mother chose badly," etc. (ibid).[6]

Types of Defense and Variations in Level of Aggression-Anxiety

The across-fantasy recordings of four Fours will be cited to illustrate the preceding theoretical elaborations on types of defense responses.

Individual children will be seen to differ in their apparent preoccupation with aggressive impulse-imagery, and relatedly, in the level and effectiveness of their means of defense or coping with aggression-anxiety. Clara's records reveal the most primitive and interfering patterns of cognitive-affect reactions, Rondi's the most advanced and facilitating one. Rondi is the only one of the four children to consistently use distance forms of self-representation, and to manifest a flexible, varied defense repertoire. More than that of the others, her manifest fantasy content is characterized by creative elaborations and interweavings of reality knowledge in affective contexts. Gerry and George are between the two extremes. Each represents one of the two early defensive organizations of aggressive impulses—Gerry, identification with the aggressor; George, identification with the victim. Both express these in direct "I" form.

Clara

Clara often appears to be an unhappy, dissatisfied child; her fantasy content is suggestive of an underlying depres-

[6] In obs. 84, Piaget cites examples of one of his subtypes (of Type III), which he calls "compensatory combinations."

sive position. She is clearly an able child during the infrequent periods when she is not preoccupied with her admixed yearnings for closeness with her family (or teacher, as transference object).[7] In her fantasy monologues she deals almost exclusively with aspects of her reality world at home, selectively transformed and fragmented by the successive interplay between her transparent aggressive impulses, and the defenses against them.

Her use of direct "I" self-representations is relatively the most primitive, in the sense that her destructive declarations are contained by few protective distance devices, these being quite ineffectual in warding off anxiety and regressive thought processes. More specifically, primitive weldings of sexual and aggressive impulse derivatives comprise her fantasy talk; the aggressive depictions are openly directed against or otherwise involve her primary family (mother, father, little brother), else she threatens present transference objects, her teacher or certain children. She achieves protective distance mainly through gestural constriction and verbalization of highly improbable acts of violence centering on "cutting off" or biting imagery.

Internally she has not yet settled into a preferred defense position—either of identification with the victim or with the aggressor. She tends to fluctuate between the two. Outstanding is her concerned expectation and explicit support of a talion concept of punishment and justice. The talion sequence is repeated several times in her record; she "commits" some fearsome act, then attempts to "undo" it. But her "undoing" is on the simple level of reversal of position, so that she becomes the victim of the very aggression she (descriptively) initiated. The law of talion is swiftly applied (sections A, B, E, record VIII). The

[7] Clara, like other children with marked separation-anxiety based in ambivalence, suffers constriction in her ability to utilize the activities and social opportunities school offers, to develop thereby the equivalent of "transitory objects," which would reduce the intensity of her primary attachments, and help her to ford the separation void.

ideas of "reversal" and talion are both rooted in magical or primitive concepts, and when they persist for affective reasons beyond developmental limitations, they are likely to be associated with fluctuating certainty arousal—as Clara was to exhibit later in the Fives.

Record VIII

A

Fives October 1963

While eating toast she suddenly announces to teacher: "I'll break your head off, and eat it up so you wouldn't be Mrs. F. any more." Then grabs teacher's skirt tightly, saying over and over, "Stay right here! Stay right here!"

B

Shortly after, takes note of a puppy passing by the fence in the yard, where they were at the time. "Hey, look at the little puppy. He can't come into the yard because we have gates—and he can't bite everyone." (Her feeling of being able to control oral-sadistic impulses, however projected, does not last long.) Suddenly she screams out, "Get away! There's a bug on here! I hate bugs!"

C

(Back in the classroom the same day, she held on to the teacher with a monologue; excerpts from the teacher's account are cited below.) (1) "I *vomited* in my crib; after my sheets were changed I went back to sleep." (2) "When I was asleep a mosquito came into my room and bit me." (3) "I am two and a half (which is between her own and her brother's age). I am going to fall apart, and my mommy will glue me together." (4) "When I was a little boy-girl I vomited in bed. . . . I spit and my mommy came in and stepped on my dirty pillow case." (5) "I am a teacher—and you are a teacher." (6) "When my daddy comes home at night I get his coat and he takes me to his office . . ." (7) "I want my mommy . . ." (ends by crying, achieving temporary comfort only when held by teacher; cf. similarity of this reality ending to A and B above).

D

December 1963

(In the classroom.) She began with a verbal attack on the teacher, then on the school, and then on some children. "You stupid lady!" To Etta: "I hate you." To both teacher and Etta: "It's a stupid school. Some day I'm going to get a big bat and knock it all down and I'm going to break everything in the yard. And I'll knock down people's heads. I'm going to make people's heads bleed and cut Celene's head off with a very, very sharp knife. I'll bite them and make them bleed!" (The latter illustrates a typical breakdown even of distance defenses with respect to weapon of aggression.) "I'll cut your leg off!" George, who was listening to this, seems to have become concerned and had to test reality limits: "Cut—knife—cut—will you cut off my head?" Clara, promptly: "Yes." Teacher: "Teachers and mommies don't let children hurt themselves or other children." George: "No mommies let you have a sharp knife." Clara: "I'll sneak it while my mommy is asleep and—*cut my own face* and hands off—and feet" (my italics).

E

February 1964

Dictating a story to an assistant teacher several months later Clara reveals the same preoccupations with her intensely ambivalent feelings, primarily towards mother and younger brother but, as can be seen, readily extended or transferred to teacher and peers. The distractible, flitting and affect-shifting quality of her thought content accompanies the regression in her level of cognitive expression which is brought on by a surfacing of her conflicted, highly charged hostile and sexual fantasies. ". . . And my mother will let me hold him [brother] . . . if you hold him he can take little steps like this . . . Do you have a sister? You told me 'yes' already. Does she walk? *And then my mommy will cut my brother's head open—and then put a different one back* . . . Now he has a new head back *and my head is cut off. It doesn't hurt.* . . . and then my mommy had to cut my sister's head open." (She has no sister.) "And then my mommy will take a rest and she will get up a quarter after one. My daddy will get up a quarter after you . . . and my mother will get up at a quarter after *foot.*"

"My mommy painted on my brother." (Noticing some children painting.) "This is a stupid school . . . It has stupid Etta in it." (Etta is a particularly angelic looking and behaving child.) "My mommy will let me call Etta 'Monkey' and my mommy and daddy will let me call Laura 'Sweetie.' No! Call Laura 'Stupid.' " (Now examines teacher's notes and comments.) "That's not the way you write 'stupid!' I know how to write 'stupid.' And then my mommy would say 'sweetie' to my brother and I would hug him." (Note again desperate efforts to reunite with mommy—from mommy's approval of her condemnation of sibling-type rivals to joining mommy through loving her real rival. Not much nutrient for *her* in either solution at this level. The ways in which Clara's ambitious strivings become sucked into her intense affect conflicts are evident, and are intimately connected with her relatively unsuccessful efforts at a positive identification with her mother.)

It is clear, especially in sections A and B, that her anxiety about real punishment (separation or physical attack) for her aggressive feelings is easily aroused. A year later, as already mentioned, Clara exhibited fear and fluctuating certainty about the real (possible) threat posed by a friend who openly put on a mask-like covering and moved towards her in obvious caricature of a monster.

Evidence of correlative interferences in intrapsychic advances, which her elemental defense devices both reflect and contribute to, is found in various forms: in the primitive oral-aggressive imagery of her fantasy content, and in the way she uses speech to hold and clutch at the teacher;[8] in the blurred, unstable identity delineations (fluctuation and fusion, C 3–5, especially); and in the level of her cognitive formulations, which prominently include oscillating fantasy-reality content, offering little protective cover or comfort in either direction, and display regression in continuity of level and coherence in response to anxiety irruptions. The content reflects the operation of primary processes more than the other children's, has a more run-on quality, more primitive means-end sequences, and is generally more prone to regression (cf. C and E).

Analysis of the concomitant characteristics of Clara's fantasy content suggests the underlying interconnections between the level of defense, intensity of aggressive impulses, and the developmental level of aggressive imagery arousing the anxiety-defense cycle. The direct form not only points to the existence of relatively ineffectual defense resources, but also implies a relatively vulnerable, poorly delineated sense of self. Separation-individuation difficulties are interlocked with the problems she experiences in dealing with primitive ambivalence, separation anxiety, and aggression.

Not all children who manifest direct self-representation, however, need be on the same level of development in all these re-

[8] The teacher's report of Clara for school records, covering the first half of the year, came to my attention some time later. It includes comments such as these: "She found it hard to share me and would try to hit, cling, sit on my lap. *Often said, 'You stupid lady,' when I left her* . . . teases other children with 'mine's better, yours is no good,' etc. This lessened at those times when she was able to be really involved with what she was making. Lots of talk about what brother Jo *cannot* do . . . Her mother told me Clara would pull her away from the baby—not let her talk on the telephone, etc." The teacher's notes also indicated that the mother had difficulty separating definitively from Clara at the beginning of the school year.

spects. George and Gerry, described below, also express themselves in direct "I" terms in their fantasies, which too are almost exclusively concerned with violence and aggressive themes. Compared to Clara's, their fantasy expressions exhibit a higher level of organization, coherence, social relationships, and are not as prone to regression in form or content. Two other differences are pertinent: the boys never make direct references to primary family members (as targets or objects of longing) and each has a definitive mode of defense identification. These are signs of a more effectual system of defense resources than Clara's, or their greater freedom from anxiety (depressive) interferences to deploying their cognitive resources.

The likely key to the differences between them and Clara is that the boys' major focus of rage-anxiety and level of aggressive imagery is developmentally advanced beyond that incited by separation-ambivalence dilemmas. Ability to move past this phase-crisis permits development of relatively greater individuation (self-delineation), more circumscribed sources of anxiety, and a correspondingly different level of aggressive imagery.

The direct form of self-representation, in comparison to distance forms, is nonetheless a sign of an internal organization of schemas or systems more open to threats of anxiety irruption from aggressive impulse sources, i.e., of less effective or stable distance-defense resources. This is indicated in the greater proneness of such children to experiences of fluctuating certainty. At the same time, as George and Gerry's records illustrate (IX, X), when the content of the direct form reflects a clear defensive stance (identification with victim or with aggressor), this may be taken as a sign of developmental advance in internal distance beyond that available in the phase of predominant oral aggressive imagery, and related modes of anxiety and defense.

Gerry

In his fantasy expressions Gerry is solely preoccupied with aggressive action content. Some records illustrate how his preoccupation and associated tensions may limit his opportunities to become interested or involved with quiet learning activities.

In one section of the record (A), while the teacher is reading to the group, Gerry wanders restlessly around the room for a while, returns to tell the teacher that he is "making a knife to cut those girls over there," and goes off to make it. Shortly he comes back, makes a cutting motion with his "knife" across the back of the neck of a randomly chosen girl, which only the teacher notices. He makes no protest when the teacher quietly takes his "knife" away.[9]

The episode with Mark (B) reveals several significantly interrelated features. His direct "I" self-representations are insistently in the identification-with-the-aggressor mode. He cannot tolerate or even trust a distinction between pretend sick and really sick (damaged, passive). This indicator of arousal of fluctuating certainty in him is essentially similar to the state of uncertainty and ambivalence he evinces in giving George the chestnut "poison." It is quite clear that at no time and under no circumstances will he allow the position of victim to overtake him, and his vigilance in this respect can render the boundaries between real and pretend harm permeable.

Record IX

A

Classroom, November–December 1963

(Children listening to story)

Gerry (restless): Mrs. C., I'm making a knife to cut those girls over there. (Goes to dump truck and fills it with block people.) Look, Mark! My truck is full of garbage. I am rich! I want to be rich! (Goes back to making

[9] In accordance with my primary emphasis on vicissitudes of aggressive impulse derivatives, I am bypassing indicators in the study records of psychosexual phase-level concomitants, such as Gerry's, "Look . . . My truck is full of garbage. I am rich! I want to be rich!" (A)

knife. Finishes; returns to group and makes a cutting motion quietly on back of a girl's neck. Teacher moves Gerry away and takes his "knife." He goes on to something else.)

B

Yard

Gerry: Let's get a sharp knife and cut the (rope) ladders and the people. Just cut off everything!

Mark (fearfully): Not the people. People don't like to be cut up.[10]

Gerry: O.K.

Mark: I need a sick person. Will you be sick, Gerry?

Gerry: Not me.

Mark: Just pretend—doctor play.

Gerry: I got the gun and *it can lock the door too. O.K., now I can shoot* and just go out and kill people!

Mark: We can cut it (!) in slices and cook and eat it all up!

George: But don't eat me!

Mark: O.K.

George: It's a shark . . . (Teacher is called away at this point, though the boys continue.)

C

Gerry: I hate your shoes, George. (They are brown and white fur cowboy boots.)

George: Why?

Gerry: Because I hate brown. I like you, George, but I hate brown. I hate your shoes.

[10] Both Mark and George as well as Gerry experience fluctuating certainty in this record. There are too few recordings in which Mark appears to follow up the implications of his oral-sadistic concerns reflected in this record, and his more regressed imagery connected with cutting compared to Gerry's. I might add, however, that in the two dreams he spontaneously reported to the teacher the manifest themes were similar. In both there was a big character (witch, giant) involved with a little one (girl, mouse), and at the end the little one was scared, cooked, or eaten.

George: Indians kill animals. They ride horses . . .
Gerry (to teacher, writing): Say "kill people, kill animals, kill horses" and send it to somebody! I got a gun. No. (To George): I'll give you the poison stuff (Picks up chestnut. George steps on it and breaks it.)
George: It's poison.
Gerry: Then I can shoot you (not clear whether after the poisoning or instead of).
George (getting up quickly): I'm not dead! . . .
Gerry: No—it will hurt. It's very terrible poison stuff. (Teacher says it is not poison, just needs to be cooked. Gerry is uncertain, indecisive, and moves his hand toward and away from George. Finally decides to give it.) Here, eat this!

Though Gerry, Mark, and George all certainly know what pretend means and often engage in fantasy play, when aggressive content prevails they can be certain only of their own make-believe actions, as is the case in chronologically younger children. In brief, Gerry attempts to attain a safe and invulnerable position mainly through an identification-with-aggressor stance. His precautionary move to "lock the door" (literally present between the yard and the school proper, i.e., the authorities within) is a reflection of his relatively unintegrated internalized controls.

The formal character of Gerry's fantasy expressions supports the hypothesis that a child's freedom for creative elaboration of its aggressive thoughts and energies is limited when it needs to contend with internal sources of aggression-anxiety and defend against anticipated consequences in external reality. As seen, his fantasy expressions are largely confined to repetitive, declaratory statements of intent to cut, shoot, kill. Though his themes are mainly variations of "Kill, kill!" in comparison with Clara's diffusely permeating oral components his content level of aggressive imagery and implicit phase-level anxiety concerns appear more advanced, and his relationship with his teacher more age-appropriate.

George and Rondi

George and Rondi appear in a number of records together, and with others. Their behavior in records X and XI demonstrates individual consistency of defense style, and also illustrates differences in functioning related to their respective use of direct versus distance forms of self-representation. George uses the direct form, always in accord with identification with the victim. Rondi uses different forms of self-representation (provider and aggressor), but never one with the victim. It will be seen that though George's fantasy expressions are as confined to the victim theme as Gerry's to the aggressor, his fantasy happenings are more varied than Gerry's aggressive assertions. Whether this reflects simply an individual difference in creative resources, or a more advanced case of internalization of conflict and level of defense strategy (victim versus aggressor) is an open question.

George

Several characteristics of George's direct self-representation as victim are remarkable, particularly his ever wary efforts to control outcome and his vulnerability to fluctuating certainty. Whatever the disaster he depicts, however vociferous his cries for help, he maintains constant control over attempted rescue operations (record X). Indeed his fantasy expressions are centered primarily on calling attention to his desperate straits; he is little interested in, if not actively discouraging of, efforts to save him initiated by another child. Only when his descriptive or prescriptive control of events is threatened does George shift from his preferred mode of direct self-representation as victim. One such time he uses a distance form (A 22–23), but only to achieve defensive distance from the position of aggressor. And the way he does this confirms dramatically the strength of his internal reasons for an identification with the victim, and correspondingly for denial of his actively aggressive impulses or power to damage.[11] In "I'm the storm" (A 23) George takes flight into deeper fantasy and achieves distance as well as great power to destroy in a non-human representation. The consistency of his defensive need, not only defense style as victim, is evident in two other fantasy-play occasions. In both he was tempted into a type of aggressor representation by the strutting-aggressive boasts of other boys, but immediately reverted to being the victim. "I'm Astro-boy [too]!" is followed by "And I have the measles." "I killed the lighthouse" (record X-C), though achieving distance through a non-human, inanimate target, is nonetheless followed by "I got dead. Somebody killed me."

Several of George's records suggest that a defensive identification with the victim is not a reliable bulwark against the underlying conflict and anxiety. George is dramatically subject to fluctuating certainty when other children verbalize their assaultive intents. In record A (20–21) he sharply tells Rondi, "Stop the nonsense!" when she claimed, "I'm a dolphin and I can make you bleed." (She is, by the way, the tiniest girl in the class.) In record VIII (p. 91) he becomes visibly concerned about the "real" potential of Clara's threats to cut off head or leg, though they were not clearly directed at him. And in play with

[11] I was surprised and impressed some months after this write-up of George, based solely on his fantasy records, to discover in his end-year report that early in the Fours he had depicted himself as victim to his teacher. So convincing was his account of his very rough summer at camp, that the teacher was not only roused to sympathy at the time, but she felt moved to commiserate with the mother at the parent conference, held several months after his initial confidences. His mother emphatically disclaimed *all* of it: George never did "fall in the poison ivy and get it all over, in his eyes, mouth, nose . . . nor fall in a hole and only another doctor [his father is one] could get him out and give him a shot," etc.

Gerry he has to affirm, "I'm not dead" (p. 98) and urge Mark, "But don't eat me" (p. 97). In brief, George's direct mode of self-representation and the ready arousal in him of fluctuating certainty are both indicators of cognitive vulnerability in particular affective situations. They indicate relatively inadequate defenses against aggressive or sexual-aggressive impulses and fears, and point to his general defensive strategy of turning active into passive.

Record X

A

Fours — Gym, April 1964

1. George: I'm on the track of the choo choo train and the train's on top of me. Help!
2. David: Oh, my leg! It's broken. (Falls down.)
3. George: My neck came off. Help! The train is on me!
4. David: Ring the emergency and the train will come off you.
5. Seth (to teacher): What should we do with this captain? He keeps falling on the track.
6. (George gets up and screeches.)
7. Seth: Quick! There's a war!
8. George: Help! I'm shot in the war.
9. David: Oh, everything's broken. (To teacher): You know my mommy shined my shoes last night.
10. Seth: Quick! A storm—get under water!
11. George: We'll die and when we die the police will come along and take care of us.[12]
12. Seth: C'mon, you're sinking.
13. George: I'm the lifeguard. (But he falls into the water!)

[12] His comment is typical of the ready reversibility or uncertainty about the finality of death common at this age. The theme about a storm and the police coming to rescue is drawing on a current news item some of the children had talked about in class.

14. Rondi: I'm a fish.
15. Seth: Swim then.
16. George: Help! The shark is on top of me!
17. David: I'm trying to help you (and pulls him to side).
18. (Now Rondi, Seth, and David pick up George and drag him.)
19. Seth (growls with fingers up, David following, but breaks it off suddenly with): We're friendly to each other, right?
20. Rondi (to George): I'm a dolphin and I can make you bleed!
21. George: Stop the nonsense!
22. (Now Seth, with David in tow, walks over to George who is lying on the floor and pretends to eat him!)
23. George (gets up now and announces): I'm the storm!

B

May 1964

George: Get the poison from the rooster and throw it at me.

Seth: I'm shooting honey at you.

George: Seth shot a bullet at me so I'm dead.

Seth: No, it's poison. (Maybe "honey" was Seth's euphemism for poison to begin with. Seth also has difficulty in acknowledging or sustaining aggressive actions on his own.)

George: Seth shot poison at me so I'm dead! (Yelling): Give me some medicine!

C

George: Crash into the lighthouse.

Mark: Crash, crash, crash bang bash.

David: I shot the lighthouse. The lighthouse is dead.

George: I killed the lighthouse. Bang! I got dead. Somebody killed me.

David: Bang! I killed you. (This said in great high spirits, not upsetting anyone, including David.)

Rondi

In contrast to George, when Rondi was faced with the threat of drowning in a storm, she assumed the safest position possible: "I am a fish" (X, 14). In all three recordings where she appears (V, X, XI), there is similar evidence of flexible, effective resources: use of distance defenses when she makes menacing threats (e.g., dolphin, bee) and ability for identification with provider or with teacher; ingenious use of reality information within the fantasy constructions; capacity for compromise solutions in aggressive-conflict situations, beyond those confined to aggressor *or* victim alternatives. She is not provoked into fluctuating certainty. When threatened or in fact mildly hurt (XI, 5), she is able to move away from it in a way that not only diminishes the threat but creates a positive substitution (XI, 7, 10, 13). In "The Witches" record as in the bee record, she finds an enviable means of integrating two major sources of conflict, the wish for power and wish for closeness. As a bee, witch, or gorilla, she maintains her potential for attack if necessary, allows others the same potential but binds the aggressive powers within a caretaking friendly context.

Flexibility and a range in identifications are particularly noticeable in record XI. She maintains her self-representation throughout as a bee among bees. Her changes in character appropriately reflect a bee's actual potential. When she is "caught" by another she quickly becomes a bee that can sting (identification with aggressor, XI, 5), shifts briefly to identification with teacher when pushed down in the turmoil (XI, 7), then into the most stable and elaborated of these positions still within the bee context—identification with the provider. That is, she offers the children pretend honey, then finds some real sugar in her pocket to give to them. In these transactions Rondi is eminently fair as provider, and as hostess singularly gracious. She even gave her guests permission to leave *after* they had unceremoniously scattered (XI, 17, 18).

The defense style she is establishing, with its prominence of identification with the provider, represents a positive means of resolving conflicts and fears around aggression, arising from internal or external sources. Her compromise solutions help create opportunities for good relationships and feedback responses in reality, and thus strengthen internal schemas basic in the development of a relatively benign superego and a viable good self-image. Another way of putting it is that Rondi's defense devices are in the service of the ego, not simply directed against anxiety. They can thus be incorporated into, or may already constitute coping resources, whereas George's defenses are essentially confined to service against anxiety, or are in the service of the superego. Whatever the etiology, such differences in type and outcome of a defense organization lead to different opportunities for progressive synchronous learning and positive affect experiences in the real world. In this sense, one may consider a given type of defense and coping style to be a creative influence, as well as a reflection of growth in the range and flexibility of cognitive-affect resources.

Record XI

Spring 1964

1. Kata: I see the bees up there (imaginary).
2. Rondi (becomes a bee): Bzz, bzz. (Chases Aries.)
3. Seth: I'll save you. Bang! Bang! (Shoots the bees.)
4. Kata (grabs Rondi): I got a bee!
5. Rondi: My finger is the sting! (Mark pulls her; she falls and scrapes her knee slightly.) I'm going into the bees—
6. Aries: Look out! They'll sting you!
7. Rondi: No, I taught them a lesson. Where are those bees?

8. Kata: They must be under that board.
9. Rondi: No, they're in this piece of paper. (Aries and Kata hastily bid her "goodbye!")
10. Rondi: You can have a whole jar of honey. That will last for your whole life.
11. Seth: Oh, goody!
12. Rondi: You have to look for it. (All start walking under the slide. Teacher asks where they are going.) To Sugarplum.
13. Rondi: Here's the sugar. (Gives real sugar to everyone from a little package she had in her pocket.)
14. Laura (to Aries): I think you *should* put it in the hand without the bandage!
15. Doug: What about little old me? Where shall I sit? No room, Rondi! (Small scuffle then ensues between George and Doug.)
    Laura (again very self-righteous): Don't give George some.
16. Rondi (makes peace): Yes, I will, if he puts his hand out. (She gives sugar to George and Doug, shakes rest out in everyone's hands.) If you want any more you have to lick it off Aries. [No concern with Aries' bandage.]
17. (All leave when through with sugar.)
18. Rondi: Everyone may leave.

Beyond Identification of Specific Defenses: Concluding Thoughts About Developmental Features and Evaluative Criteria

Some defenses derive from more primitive modes of thought, such as magical thinking and global dichotomies, as in reversal of attributes, or fate. Others, such as isolation of affect, or intellectualization, represent more advanced "splitting" expressions. Still other defenses, such as projection, become more complex in the course of development, not in their formal characteristics, but in their intellectual elaboration and motivational context, reflecting the course of affective cognitive advances.

The analysis of the fantasy records demonstrates the feasibility and relevance of certain considerations for evaluating the character and influence of a person's defense reactions: the type or level of thought processes employed in the defense; the developmental phase symbolism; the relative prominence of the defense or strategy in the child's defense repertoire for dealing with negative affective (pain) experiences; the feedback consequences in terms of speeding "affect recovery," resolution of conflict, or facilitating interpersonal relations.

Either primary or secondary processes of thought may serve to promote or hinder a child's cognitive and affective expansion, depending on the developmental and psychological context in which they are deployed. For example, displacement is a characteristic of primary process thought; viewed as a cognitive capacity in early development it would be considered a mediating factor in the progressive development of thought organization from concrete, isolated meanings to more abstract concepts of equivalences and similarities.[13] In later development, the availability of primary processes "in the service of the ego" is a characteristic of witty and creative personalities (Kris, 1952). When the processes effecting displacement are encapsulated for defense purposes with the aim of avoiding conflict and unpleasure, they operate restrictively. In defense responses variously identified as "externalization," "denial," or "projection," displacement serves to blur or negate significant reality distinctions, and simultaneously awareness of own feelings. Rationalization, on the other hand, utilizes secondary process thought, but since the aim is to excuse, to defend against shame or blame, any actual validity in the explanation of the causal

[13] In certain personality disorders the capacity for displacement, in the sense of discovering valid equivalences in affective circumstances, is arrested at an early stage; no substitute or compromise solution is acceptable. In such instances, not even flight into fantasy may become an available resource.

factors is lost to the person as a potential cognitive gain, or basis for sustaining self-esteem and freedom from guilt.

The impact of such restrictive, defensive employment of thought processes, however, may be adaptive or pathognomic, depending on the place and consequences of the defense responses in the person's total functioning. It is clear that identification of a defense is only one step in evaluating its meaning for the individual and its significance in mental growth. Other dimensions of analysis that embody evaluative criteria are required, as others have also recognized. For example, Anna Freud's discussion of the "infantile ego" (1936) emphasized that a child's use of denial does not necessarily disturb his abilities for reality-testing, nor necessarily conflict with his eagerness to recognize and test the reality of objects. It depends on how and when he employs it. This emerges especially clearly in J.'s use of denial in some of her fantasy expressions. It is characteristic of her personality and stage of development that the denial of weakness in her fantasy or reality-defiance expressions was not *really* believed by her. Nonetheless the denial served at the time to relieve or protect her from anxiety and humiliation, which in turn helped her to face and deal directly with the offending realities. In this manner a defense mechanism constitutes a means or an aid in positive coping development. In the same way, a defensive flight into fantasy may be more generally a facilitating prelude enabling the child to mobilize resources to cope with the original source of pain.

Regression or Progression in Mode of Defense

Any defense may be described as regressive or progressive, in terms of its character at the time it is employed. A defense may be defined as regressive, for example, when a child characteristically retreats from an active, initiating position and turns active into passive to mitigate blame or avoid possible humiliation (e.g., Aries' defense against David's blame in "The Witches"). Regressive defensive behaviors may also be transient backward steps, as evidenced in J.'s records, which in effect create opportunities for affective experiences that strengthen the possibilities for enduring, progressive conflict solutions. For example, "At 2;6 J. was her little sister and mimed the action of sucking the breast, a game which often recurred" (obs. 79). Even in the midst of an acute stress experience in reality, the regressive behavioral defense J. mobilizes (crying like her baby sister) intrinsically includes a self-baby distinction that accords with her progressive modes of defense. At 2;8 "J. was screaming with temper, and as she was not given her own way she then said she was Nonette (L.), and went on crying, but imitating the crying of L. which *consoled* her" (obs. 84, my italics).

In the balance of J.'s defense repertoire, progressive modes of dealing with negative affects (envy, hurt, loneliness) or other feelings that bring her into conflict with her world, clearly predominate. An interesting example of a progressive defense is her successful effort, for some period following the birth of her sister, to keep her fantasy play with *her* baby "more and more secret." (It will be recalled that she created another Nonette for herself when her mother would not allow her to hold the real one.) In the positive affectional circumstances J. enjoyed, a secret marks a signal step along the path of separation-individuation that strengthens a child's sense of autonomy, much as its first use of "no" earlier initiated it. The feelings of humiliation and loss, which were the immediate instigators of J.'s largely progressive modes of defense, are a prototype of those inescapable negative experiences in early childhood that constitute spurs toward individuation and ultimate independence.

A discussion of two frequent types of manifest defense reactions found frequently in the fantasy records, projection and reversal, will serve to illustrate the nature of developmental and evaluative considerations.

Projection

As a term projection tends to be used loosely, to designate a type of mental process or a manifest resultant. When referring to the end-product, one is speaking of a form of displacement, or externalization of one's own thoughts or motives, which may be mobilized in the service of defense, or of identifying one's self with the other. The capacity for projection appears to be a mental given, which in early growth is operative more or less in conjunction with the inferred processes of introjection. It is clear that both capacities are basic in the growth of affective and cognitive resources, yet may also be activated in such wise as to interfere with reality testing, individuation, and interpersonal felicity.

In an analytic appraisal of J.'s records, mere identification of her prevalent recourse to projection as a defense mechanism would fail to identify the relevant meanings of its deployment in her personality functioning. As noted earlier, a young child's deliberate assignment of some behavior of its own to another object in fantasy play calls on its capacity for projection, and as a means of defense it may be observed before the age of two. At age 1;8, for example, J. projected her biting impulses onto her bear. One also may describe this early, simple expression of projection as marking the emergence of a mode of distance-defense. Beginning around age two, J. began to utilize projection as a means of dealing with physical or psychical pain. Integral in her use of projection, illustrated in such instances, are several individually distinctive features: her persistently stout defense against feeling helpless and a passive victim, and her characteristic self-representation as the provider-comforter. Moreover, she employs projection at such times always accompanied by additional forms of distance-defense devices (against potential aggressive impulse connections with "self").

With advances in mental growth beyond age three, projection is observable as part of more complex operations, as in Jane's "dream" of beating her babies when she grows up. In the Fours, projection appears prominently as a defense associated with an ongoing struggle and condemnation of own aggressive impulses. Excerpts from Evin's and Gerry's records offer a contrast between adaptive and maladaptive uses of projection. Evin's employment of projection may be described as a facilitating means in the progressive course of internalization of conflict, wherein the "good" core-self is distinguished from "bad" impulses. Gerry's use of projection, however, is more simply in the service of denial, hence blurs his self-awareness and subtly undermines in this context trust in self-initiated controls or good impulses.

> In the early months of the Fives, Evin did no block building himself, but would on occasions arise suddenly and swiftly kick down another's building. One day his teacher succeeded in persuading him to make a building himself. Proudly, he called her over when he had finished and instructed her to make the following sign: BAD BOYS—DON'T KNOCK DOWN THIS BUILDING!
>
> Towards the end of a school day, the assistant teacher observed Gerry playing with the newt, a class pet. Some time after, as the children were readying to leave, she became aware that Gerry had managed to "kill" the newt. Immediately on his arrival the next morning Gerry volunteered an account of the murder:
>
> "The newt bit me and I was getting madder and madder." (Newts don't bite.)
>
> "And Alex told me (questionable) to put a thumbtack in the head. He died."
>
> "He wiggled—he didn't like the cut."
>
> "He feeled it too. It went through his mouth." (Would need a magnifying glass to find.)
>
> "He's in heaven. I know where the newt is. He's in heaven. Poor newt. Shame on *Alex!*"

"Reversal" in Strivings and as Defense

The idea of reversal of position or reversibility of opposites (as in fairytales or Jekyll and Hyde themes, or Clara's anxiety when Laura "changed" into a monster figure) represents a form of thought congruent with magical interpretations of causality and the child's early experiences of feelings and wishes. Such ideas may be utilized to support positive ambitions—as in David and

Goliath themes, or a child's dreams of glory wherein he rescues the adult, or in conceptions of future relationships with the parent, such as "When I am big and you are little." This form of thinking lends itself as well to defensive aims.

Characteristic of children's early cognitions is the virtual absence of gradations or differentiations within affect dimensions or object categories. Their initial comprehension of differences is in terms of either/or, all-or-none, now-or-never alternatives. In the fantasy family play of the Threes, and to some extent of the Fours, the characters represent big *or* little, parent *or* baby, good *or* bad, and the like, whereas the Fives introduce more differentiated relationships. In the violence fantasies of Fours and Fives, "dead or alive" appears as a refreshingly reversible phenomenon: the same character may be "shot dead" and come alive many times. Or one may hear such announcements in a fantasy context: "We're dead! Get the Doctor" (to make them alive and well again).

These characterizations in fantasy reflect the same kind of dichotomous judgments the child is concurrently making in his reality-oriented comparisons of "same" and "different." This mode of cognitive ordering and evaluating is also matched in his relatively ungraded affective shifts between love or hate, admiring or totally rejecting. Moreover, having experienced his own affects as being so reversible, a young child will easily anticipate or fear that his place or position in the eyes and heart of the parent figure or peer is similarly transformable.

Reversal is frequently the conceptual means evident when a child is dealing with conflicted strivings to be big or little. This conflict is ubiquitous; the difficulties in evolving rewarding solutions (which may persist into adult years) stem from individual variations in deprivation and autonomy experiences. Indications of this dilemma are generally coincident with the child's cognizance, around age 2–2;6, of its little size and powers in comparison to the adults in its world. The special qualities of affective crisis posed by a newborn sibling may intersect with and influence the shape of this dilemma. The nursery school fantasy records point up individual differences in duration and intensity of the big-or-little conflict (e.g., Rolly and Jane, p. 42).

I quote an excerpt from J.'s records to show how reversal of position may epitomize early defensive aspects of identification characteristics, and also to illustrate how the processes which in effect engineer identifications and their emendations in development draw on those in concept formation generally. That is, while dynamic and affective factors instigate and determine the character of a child's identificatory strivings and internal schemata resultants, the processes effecting internalization are those operant in the progressive steps of mental growth.

> At 2;7 J. walked to and fro pretending to be holding a baby in her arms. She carefully put it down on an imaginary bed, made it go to sleep . . . then woke and picked it up. . . . The same day she pretended to be carrying her mother, "Mummy's very heavy," then imitated the farmer's wife feeding her hens, with her apron turned up but without anything in it. . . . The same day she was carrying in her arms a young lady she had recently seen . . . (obs. 81).

In this record J. attempts an identification with her mother through a reversal of position in concrete, physical terms. Perhaps her behavior exemplifies a universal transitional step in the progressive delineation of self and object representations. It is transitional in the sense that J. is here employing the earlier sensorimotor means of knowingness, in symbolic form, and in so doing her reality perceptions (of relative weight) are enhanced, and her internal representations of self and mother are sharpened. This record also suggests ways in which a child's widening awareness of its world provides a contributing motive and reality form for the affective generalizing phenomena characteristic of transference relations to other persons.

It is evident that (i) Reversal forms of thought (in children or adults) are basic modi operandi in revenge fantasies, fired by the arousal of shame-fury (envy, mortification). (ii) The idea of talion punishment, also a form of reversal of position, is shown in Clara's monologues (p. 91) to be a spontaneous emergence in the service of primitive morality, i.e., retributive justice. In such affective contexts, the idea of talion is directed against oneself rather than the other, for one's aggressive impulses against primary family figures or transference facsimiles. (iii) Past the age of three in J.'s records, examples of simple recourse to the seesaw notions implicit in reversal forms of thought become infrequent. When reversal does appear at a later age, it is primarily incited by experiences of mortification and is found in the company of other defense devices. It would appear that in adaptive development, the process or aim of reversal does not change with growth in mental development, as much as lose its value as a solution, with increased scope of defensive and objective alternatives.

Flexibility and Rigidity

In characterizing the qualities of their young subjects' coping devices, Murphy *et al.* (1962) found most useful the categorical distinctions between flexibility and rigidity. An analysis of these dimensional qualities provides another way of ordering behavior data to reveal interrelated contributions of genetic, dynamic, cognitive, and feedback consequences to defense patterns in a narrow sense, or coping patterns in a broad sense.

Flexibility refers to a child's "capacity to use one mechanism at one time and another later, as well as the capacity to use different ones together when they are needed" (p. 317). The personality assessment of their thirty-two subjects (age 2;6–5;7) clearly distinguished between children who displayed such flexibility, and those who characteristically displayed rigidity. Those who developed flexibility of defense patterns were descriptively summarized as "normal, happy children"; those prone to rigidity, in the sense of using relatively few types of defense repetitively, in no case could be described as happy.

They were children whose parents were described as "teasing, punitive, or in other ways aggressive." The children "responded by developing a protective pattern of *anticipating* blame, protest, accusation, or punishment from the adult and forestalling it by *projecting* threats to the adults, and by acting in a way which takes into account the possibility of threatening behavior" from others (pp. 317 ff., my italics). In other words, rigidity of defensive responses is symptomatic of a child's vulnerability and chronic concern with the possibilities of blame, humiliation, and/or punishment, and directly reflective of his pain experiences with caretakers. It is fitting in the present study that I spell out further the reciprocal cognitive-affect consequences of defense rigidity in children, particularly the ramifications of their heightened anticipation of negative consequences.

"Anticipation of consequences" in itself is a significant emergent of general intelligence, and more specifically a cognitive function basic to foresight. In Piaget's records (1945) the earliest explicit evidence of its development in any of his three children was at age 3;4. It is clear in Murphy's data, and inferrable in Malone's (1966) that experiential factors may enter in ways that will delay or distort or delimit the developmental emergence and use of this cognitive resource.

A group of three-to-four-year-olds from economically disadvantaged families were described by Malone (1966) as generally agile and well coordinated but "heedless" in their physical activities—which is to say that they failed to recognize in the physical surrounds or to anticipate possibly injurious consequences to how they jumped or ran, and the like. The experiential genesis of the delay or the delimiting of full use of foresight as a cognitive resource in Malone's children may well be related to two general features of their lives: a relative lack of protective, watch-out-for-yourself (anticipatory), parental reminders, together with a relative absence of predictable events. Poverty conditions tend to discourage routines as well as consistent protective caretaking, while encouraging family disruption and erratic outbursts of aggression and tragedy.

When the internal affective milieu in which this cognitive advance evolves is such that anticipation of consequences is hooked primarily to a need for defense, it not only leads to a narrowing of the defense spectrum but constitutes thereby an active interference with the child's reality testing, and with growth changes in the comprehension of causality in affective circumstances. In contrast, when anticipation is more a general tool of judgment and reasoning than an affective set of premises, it is a vital resource which leaves open opportunities for flexible adjustments of behavior to impulse. A child who is chronically concerned with fending off negative consequences that he anticipates is responding more to his preconceived cognitive premises than to his potential apperceptions of relevant cues of predictable differences between persons and situations. Depending on its rigidity, this limiting cognitive set will underlie fluctuating certainty, or will totally interfere with the child's ability to test or trust a distinction between pretend and real aggression, or to develop a basis for evaluating possible and probable consequences.

Finally, some comments about feedback consequences that tend to sustain existing rigidity. If the child's defensive response is of the aggressive nature described by Murphy, then his anticipation of consequences clearly leads to behavior which directly creates the conditions for self-fulfilling prophecies. If a child's internally rigidified anticipations (not necessarily in consciousness, of course) lead instead to retreating behavior, or even to attempts to woo a preconceived antagonist, his opportunities for positive interpersonal outcomes are certainly enhanced, compared to the aggressive child's, *but they may only* confirm his belief in the safety of his (automatic) strategy, rather than expand reality-testing. In other words, however important it is to understand the genetic and dynamic features generating rigidity of defense responses, it is of theoretical and practical import also to note that once established, it constitutes a continuing interference with the development of foresight and reality testing, and with the widening of both a range of affects and of the defense repertoire.

Distance Defenses: A Summary Overview

As indicated in J.'s records, a child's use of distance devices in fantasy expressions is an aspect of its general cognitive-affect growth, in spatial and temporal comprehension of persons and things beyond its earlier horizons. In the nursery records, one sees that distance-defense forms are not automatic emergents with general advances in cognitive capacities and characteristics. Children beyond the age of four who continue to use direct "I" self-representation are signaling some interference in growth. The indicators of cognitive interference in the nursery study records are the child's: fluctuating certainty with respect to the pretend or real danger of injury or loss from another, limited creative elaboration of aggressive themes in fantasy, rigidity in defense preferences and narrowed range, and at the extreme within the normal range (as in Clara), vulnerability to regression in imagery and diffusion of cognitive expression.

Clara's direct "I" self-representations are concurrent with relatively primitive expressions of oral-aggressive imagery (including "vomiting"), and direct references to primary family figures. Together, these may be considered indicators of interferences in the development of differentiated self-object systems, or of a child's vulnerability to dedifferentiation under the pressure of ambivalence and separation-anxiety. In any case, the source of cognitive interference, reflected in a child's persistent recourse to direct "I" self-representations, appears to be the child's type of concerns and conflict about its own aggressive impulses.

The general inference from these data is that the employment of distance defenses in fantasy constructions, especially in self-representations, indicates the child's achievement of a structural capacity for experiencing internal conflict about its aggressive impulses, and means of containing and coping with them without disruptive consequences. In effect, the manifest signs of distance defenses (including self-representations) reflect the extent to which the child has evolved distance resources internally, against anxiety irruptions.

In a clinical context, the concept of psychological distance usually refers to a sense of alienation from others as persons, as in psychopaths or schizoid personalities. In such persons neither care nor protection may be expected or sought from others. Among the cognitive symptoms of such developmental aberrations, one may well find fluctuating certainty characteristically blurring the distinction between internal fantasy and fact, or between the possible and the probable.

In current reality, reports of military operations are replete with distance-defense type phrases. Bombing and other such strategies are described in such abstract euphemisms as to create a psychological distance from the fact that weapons are being used to maim or murder human beings. It is an ironic commentary on civilized man's superego that to support such destructive acts he must regard his victims as thing-objects, not to be identified with as humans like himself. On the other hand, some people do not and can not attain such psychological distance from human targets. Clearly, the difference stems from both the politics of conscience, and from developmental features affecting the enduring structure of an individual conscience.

5

Morality and Superego Development Reflected in Fantasy and Reality Behavior

A compelling need to attain noble values and ideal behavior appears not to be inborn, any more than are proclivities for evil. But some notions of good and bad are inescapable and become as vital a developmental factor as the built-in urgency to survive physically. Powerful problems stemming from needing to be good or-else, and if good then-what, begin early in life. Associated as agent provocateurs or control-adjuncts of morality are guilt and shame anxieties—the two most penetrating affective assaults on an individual's state of comfort or pride in self. The arousal of shame or guilt, singly or in combination, gives rise to the most peremptory defensive responses which may, ironically, result in an amoral burst of behavior.

As a topic "morality and superego" represents volumes of thought and a variety of perspectives (philosophical as well as psychological) on the genesis and existential state of good and evil in human impulses and socialization. My references to psychological theory will be minimal, restricted to background comments or coordinated with the analysis of study materials and the extrapolated developmental outline of young children's concerns and struggle to be good, or not-bad.[1]

[1] Among key psychoanalytic contributions beyond Freud are: Beres (1958), Schafer (1960), Hartmann and Loewenstein (1962), Sandler, Holder, and Meers (1963), and Jacobson (1964). Nass (1966) provides an incisive overview of controversial areas of thought and research, including some inspired by Piaget.

What Is a Superego?

Freud's far-reaching, original formulations of the genesis and functional qualities of the "Super-Ego" (1923) in essence remain unchanged in later contributions by other psychoanalysts. Though there are sharp theoretical differences about "when" it is generally agreed that the neonate is untroubled by a superego—for a while. At some point the child begins to transmute its experience of parental do's and don'ts in such a way as to alter its own behavior directives. The superego refers to the internalized transmutation or "introjects" of authority-control attributes. As an interrelated but quasi-independent part of the child's total mental equipment, the attributes of its superego represent the major (not the only) sources of drive deterrence or control on the one hand, and of its "ideal self" standards on the other. The internalized dicta associated with these parental introjects are assimilated as categorical imperatives, and in a fundamental sense remain so always. It is evident that the impellingness and harmonious or conflicted integration of such control directives and ideals, with other psychic components (ego and core-self nexus), vary in individuals and at different developmental phases. How and why these variations occur in early childhood are the questions to which the analysis of the study records is addressed; the results fill in some gaps in present knowledge of developmental interrelations.

Fenichel (1945) summarizes the psychoanalytic concept of the superego in the most broadly concise terms:

> The superego is the heir of the parents not only as a source of threats and punishments but also as a source of protection and as a provider of reassuring love. Being on good or bad terms with one's superego becomes as important as being on good or bad terms with one's parents previously was. The change from parents to superego in this respect is a prerequisite of the individual's independence. Self-esteem is no longer regulated by approval or rejection by

> external objects, but rather by the feeling of having done or not having done the right thing. Complying with the superego demands brings not only relief but also definite feelings of pleasure and security of the type that children experience from external supplies of love. Refusing this compliance brings feelings of guilt and remorse which are similar to the child's feelings of not being loved anymore (pp. 105–6).

Fenichel, like most psychoanalysts, subscribes to Freud's original position that the superego as a structure comes into being not simply as the "heir" of the parents, but as "the heir of the oedipal complex." Among others, Hartmann and Loewenstein (1962), generally recognizing the relevance of ongoing developmental changes in the child, nonetheless give a primary causal place to the resolution of this particular psychosexual phase. They propose that the term "superego" be reserved ". . . as Freud did, to that momentous step in structuralization which is linked with the resolution of the conflicts of the oedipal phase" (p. 43). What are earlier discernible indicators of a superego influence in a child's behavior must then be called "precursors." In contrast, Susan Isaacs (1933), following Melanie Klein's position, believes that feelings of guilt and the superego develop as early as "the biting phase . . . but soon become linked with anal and urethral phantasies" (p. 373). Such theoretical differences can persist unchanged, as long as there is unclarity and imprecise information about the place in the developmental scheme of things of a child's notions of good and bad, and the influence of these on his behavior.

Within the framework of a "general psychology" orientation, Anna Freud (1966) denotes the ego functions that have a circular or reciprocal or necessary-if-not-sufficient relationship to superego formation and functions—bypassing the question of "when":

> Although intrinsically ego functions such as memory, secondary process thinking, reality testing, control of motility, have neither a moral connotation nor the oppo-

> site, social behavior and law abidingness cannot come about without them, nor . . . without ego mechanisms such as imitation, identification, introjections. It is a fascinating developmental study in itself to see each ego attribute, as it appears . . . contribute . . . Memory is indispensable for the individual's acting on foresight and experience, reason and logic for understanding cause and effect in relation to behavior, ego control of motility for preventing action on impulse, identifications and introjection for internalizing the external social norms, etc. (p. 25).

As a non-delineated idea, the "maturation of the ego" is often referred to in the writings of Freudians as an essential basis of the child's acceptance and internalization of "the moral standards, the moral directives, and the moral criticism handed down by the parents" (Jacobson, 1964). How and in what ways advances in ego functions lead to a child's acceptance, or in what ways particular variations in the character of a child's introjects or identifications may in turn affect maturation of given ego functions, are important questions awaiting detailed investigation.

In my analysis of individual variations in aggressive impulse derivatives and identifications, there are data suggesting there may be an optimal developmental period (beginning about age two) for the formation of organized schemas of good and bad as an aspect of its personality. Also suggested is a circular or reciprocal relationship in early childhood between drive control attributes and associated introjects on the one hand, and cognitive characteristics and synchronous advances on the other. Insofar as changes in superego characteristics (content, relative integration of the enforcing and self-critical functions) take place in some accord with changes in the child's developmental capacities for modifications of drive expressions, and for affective appraisal of parental demands and ideals (implicitly or explicitly conveyed), it is clear that the nature of the child's conflictual and protective experiences in its immediate and widening world will determine the opportunities it has to alter its primitive internalizations. Finally, it is conceptually expectable that a child's affective sense of self (including "sense of autonomy" vs. "shame") is also involved in the process, as both a cause and effect factor.[2]

Both Piaget's and Freudian morality constructs embody a developmental view, but their different primary focus leads not only to different formulations but to different discoveries about genesis and characteristics. With respect to terminology, "conscience" and "moral judgements" are equivalents in Piaget's system; there is no consistent usage in psychoanalytic literature. Sometimes conscience is used as a functional synonym for the superego, sometimes only to refer to the "self-critical" function of the superego.

For Piaget (1932) changes in moral judgment are continuous with and contingent on social-cognitive growth generally. The particular moral belief or practice at any given point is the outcome not of a particular affective cognitive phase or interpersonal relationship, but a resultant of the child's reaction to its total social world. He distinguishes two broad developmental categories in *Moral Judgement of the Child* (1932)—the earlier "morality of constraint" (sanction), and the later "morality of cooperation" (from age seven on).[3] The child's earlier morality constraints devolve from its ideas of "crime and punishment." These ideas reflect or are derived from its modes of thought characteristic during this phase—i.e., causality sequences are

[2] Interesting in this connection is Sandler, Holder, and Meers's (1963) conceptual discussion of the interrelated evolution of a child's self representations, "ideal self," "ideal child," and composite "ideal object." Their delineation of these concepts advances understanding and raises questions open to research, well beyond that inherent in the original, more global concept of "ego ideal."

[3] It will be recalled that the "morality of cooperation" is seen budding in the nursery school Fives. Beyond the question of age experiences, however, influence of particular interpersonal experiences on the manifest sequence of morality behavior is dramatically illustrated in Freud and Dann's description (1951) of the *initially* protective, "mutuality morality" characterizing the peer relationships of a group of young concentration camp refugees.

formulated in egocentric, concrete, magical terms, while alternatives are dichotomous and absolute. The later development, "morality of cooperation," as its name suggests, derives from and is directed towards reciprocity in action with peers (though not usually notable within the family). This evolutionary change in values and aim is also a function and reflection of the growth in cognitive level (away from egocentrism, magical causality, etc.); the cognitive changes in circular fashion are mediated and reinforced by the child's expansion in social horizons and physical competencies.

Piaget takes affective features into account, but believes these are adequately covered by reference to the child's dependency and "submissiveness." Even in these references, however, Piaget submerges the influence of the child's feelings in his appraisal of parental rules or threats, i.e., the child simply does not test these because he is not developmentally ready to test his own fantasies and magical beliefs.

> Just as, if left to himself, the child believes every idea that enters his head [4] instead of regarding it as a hypothesis to be verified, so the child who is submissive to the word of his parents believes without question everything he is told instead of perceiving the element of uncertainty and search in adult thought (1932, p. 409). (How often is the uncertainty clear to the adult?)

Piaget concludes with a casual reference to a process which is a crucial developmental outcome preliminary to a child's ownership of internalized moral dicta and values, and one neither simple nor inevitable: "The self's good pleasure is simply replaced by the good pleasure of the supreme authority." Piaget's unconcern, on a systematic conceptual level, with the motivational substratum or cosponsorship of cognitive behavior limits breadth of understanding for several reasons. For one, he

[4] The preceding discussion on children's defenses (e.g., denial), as well as his own observational records of J., make this statement questionable.

makes no distinction between the child's overt behavioral and cognitive "submissiveness to the word." Too, he makes no distinction between internalized conflict sources and conflict with external sources. And finally, he fails to take into account the contribution of the child's particular level of impulse-imagery, projection, etc. to its "accommodation" as well as "assimilated" schemas.

The importance of precise delineation of a child's cognitive resources at different developmental phases, for understanding his mode of comprehension and internalizing of given sanctions and values, surely cannot be overemphasized. Psychoanalysts would certainly not disagree. But their pursuit has been less than vigorous, their attempted dynamic integration of such knowledge has tended to perpetuate explanatory statements, which as Hartmann and Loewenstein (1962) described, represent different levels of abstraction, different specificity of connections with superego formation, or unclarity of referents to inferred content or functions. Psychoanalytic insights based on reconstructions, relatively uncorrected or amplified by direct observational studies of children, have led to some persistent generalizations of dubious worth. Among these is the recurrent assumption in the literature that "archaic" superego is synonymous with harsh and critical. At the same time, of course, a cognitive (or behavioral) framework alone represents only one level of description or explanation of moral beliefs and practices. Alone it cannot account for discrepancies between knowledge or belief and practice, or between the child's notions of punitive or-else constraints and the actual threats implicit or explicit in its relationship to parental figures. Nor can it account for individual variations in the predominance and intensity of coercive enforcement imagery governing good behavior and aspirations, though only through delineation of a child's cognitive capacities in early childhood can one begin to understand the more unrelenting, dichotomous quality of affects and ideas in early expressions of morality, compared to later ones.

Before I launch into a description of the specific points

backed by the illustrative study data, I would like to quote a record of Ben and Joe in the Fives. It is an interesting, relatively simple example of morality ideas confined to an in-group ("people like me"), which is not without parallels in the moral practices of adults. Ben is concerned about the threat of real physical injury to boys, and frames this concern in a moral context which somehow excludes the girls. That he does so may be attributed to a flight of alienation from girls which some boys of his age expressively convey (cf. Chris, record I). In his reality behavior, Ben is one of the least overtly aggressive boys in his group. Joe, on the other hand, often gets into scraps with either sex—but more like a colt than a lion. Joe is troublesome and gregarious, never menacing.

Record XII

Kill the Boys

Young Fives

Joe (stands up, looks toward jungle-gym where some boys are constructing a girl-trap): Trying to kill the girls again. I know it. Girls never fall in, but they might this time. (Climbs out of cart he is "driving," gets heavy iron pole.) There! I got it! A trap for all the boys. (Claps his hands vigorously.) They're trying to kill the girls—this whole thing could be my trap. (And starts singing as he works out a marvellous "Rube Goldberg" contraption with boards, bars, tires, rope and the cart.) Ha! Ha! Ha! (Laughs with wicked intonation and talks aloud as he works.) Ahhhh—they won't kill the girls today. The end of the ride will be in the tire where they'll be weak, and they'll stay there for two weeks. Then they'll learn their lesson. (Notes a board inside a standing up tire slightly balancing itself, and becomes excited with its prospects.) Look! A diving board! They'll jump high (points to tall railing in yard), go over the top, and die. They'll get killed.

Ben (comes over to see what he was doing): How does this work?

Joe: You'll see when the boys come. They'll die. . . . they start on here, and then get caught here, and go round and round here, they go through this, get dizzy in the tire, then they'll fall on the diving board, go high up in the air and die.

Ben (gets a sad look on his face): Why are you doing it?

Joe: Because the boys are always trying to kill the girls. Don't you want to help me kill the boys?

Ben: I love the boys . . . Would you do it to Johnny?[5] (Perceptive choice; seemed sure Joe would say no.)

Joe: Nah, just Jimmy. That's what *he* needs.

Ben (still sad, but trying to help Joe understand it's wrong): But the police will get you.

Joe: Ahh, I don't know.

Ben: But why not make a girl trap? (Implicitly better and safer from the police.)

Joe: But the other boys always make girl traps. I've got to protect the girls from them. (However, as Judy approaches them he shifts his morality line.) Oh oh, we're going to kill you.

Judy: No you won't.

Joe: Ahhh yes . . . ha!

Judy (perhaps scared): Soooooooo, soooowhat!

Joe (turns to Ben): We'll trap her. (Ben laughs, no longer sad.)

Judy: I just won't get into mischief and step in the wrong place.

Joe (to Ben again): She'll be very weak—but she won't die. (Happy with his compromise he starts singing to the Beatles' song, "I Love You, Yeah"): We hate you, yeah yeah yeah, we hate you, yeah yeah yeah. (Is doing things to his trap. Judy has left.)

[5] Johnny was a new boy, short and slight of build, who had a singular air of defenselessness.

The data analysis of the children's fantasy and interpersonal transactions with their teachers and peers aims to extract developmental and individual features of superego formation and function. I shall use the term "superego" to refer both to early and developmentally later functional structures. One can leave theoretical disagreements aside, with respect to when morality schemas may be legitimately designed as a "superego proper," [6] and find agreement in a general developmental view, namely that the formative attributes of functional morality directives are individually variable in some respects, and these variations are likely to influence the nature and potential of progress towards a superego maturity. What are the relevant variations? What may be considered progressive changes? We can agree these are the important questions to be answered.

Overall, the study analysis may be said to support Freud's original insight that ideally a superego functions as a protective, not merely as a "harsh and critical" psychic agency. The uniquely adaptive psychoanalytic approach to clinical investigations of maladaptive superego features has been the major source of the latter emphasis.[7] The study children's records point up the positive contributions of "good-enough holding" experiences (Winnicott's term, 1960) to the initial formation of internalized drive-deterrent values on the one hand, and on the other, the positive contributions of such superego morality schemas to the child's developmental resources in a wider sense (i.e., to ego and core-self attributes). Both circular and reciprocal intrapsychic relations may be inferred from some of the af-

[6] An offshoot of this position is seen in the almost mechanical reiteration (Jacobson, 1964) that a "feminine superego" differs from a (more firmly moral) "male superego" primarily because of differences in anatomy and type of oedipal problem to dissolve. I believe a similar basis for questioning this premise underlies a recent panel topic, "Genital primacy, in the light of ego psychology," in the 1968 annual meeting of the American Psychoanalytic Association.

[7] Schafer's paper in 1960, for example, came as a refreshing, corrective reminder of the potential "loving and benevolent" aspects of a superego in Freud's structural theory.

fective cognitive patterns identified in the study children's behavior.

Aggression-Anxiety and Developmental Influences on Ego and Superego

In a recent article, Stein (1969) pointed to some problems and gaps in psychoanalytic knowledge and singled out the relative inadequacy of the present state of theory and facts pertaining to aggression. There is a "lack of an agreed-upon theory of aggression," though there has been no lack of attention to it in various psychoanalytic writings.

> . . . we still have nothing to match the organizing power of libido theory with its specific phases, fixation points, and regressive pathways. . . . Meanwhile our knowledge of the *development* of the ego, as opposed to knowledge of its functions, remains a matter for considerable dispute . . . [with respect to] its origins, identification of specific phases and paths of regression . . . in spite of extremely valuable contributions . . . I suspect that this problem will be solved only when we have established a theory of aggression which is comparable to that of the libido (pp. 693–94).

The present analysis of developmental characteristics and changes in a functional superego, while not directly concerned with a theory of aggression, highlights the relevance of considering the meaning of different manifest expressions of aggressive impulse imagery and anxiety-defenses, for understanding variations in phases of ego advances more or less related to superego character. Needless to say, individual differences appear in the pervasiveness of anxiety about aggressive thought or act, in the developmental level of aggressive imagery (threatened or feared), and in the children's manifest success or struggle to contain aggressive behavior. I shall illustrate these differences as they are interrelated in the children's records with differences in synchronous ego advances, affects and identifications, and specific superego indicators (e.g., internalization of conflict, type of self-condemnation). Extrapolating from these data, it is likely that early indicators of subtle "cumulative trauma" (Khan, 1963) in the first five years will be discernible in a child's mode of involvement and concerns with aggressive impulses.

It is to be understood that a child's notions of good and bad come not only from parental do's and don'ts, but also from reactions to its own aggressive feelings against its caretakers—feelings which become developmental hindrances if they are fed by actual experiences of adult aggression or punitive controls (cf. Melanie Klein's *Envy and Gratitude*). Some of the points freshly arising in the analysis of the study protocols represent confirmation or elaboration of familiar psychoanalytic insights, with respect to the sources of aggressive investment of the enforcement and self-critical functions of a superego system. Briefly, these sources have been described as (a) actual parental aggression in introducing or enforcing rules, which includes recurrent teasing, contempt, or the silence treatment for the child's actual infractions or verbal defiance; (b) the child's projection onto the parental imagos of its own feelings and forms of aggressive impulse imagery (which may be especially intimidating to a young child who is prone to reversal types of defense and revenge imagery); (c) the child's self-critical capacity, which may be intensified by a defensive "turning aggression inward," to ward off anxiety about feared retaliation, or guilt. Of these sources (a) and (c) are variously referred to in the text. Different types of self-condemnation and their implications receive particular emphasis.

Self-Condemnation and Related Affects

Guilt-anxiety is a unique experience of self-condemnation and reproach. Simply put, it arises when a child's own aggressive (or sexual-aggressive) impulses are experienced as bad, because they are directed against the adults to whom it is attached, and as such become internalized sources of conflict within itself. Hence, experiences of guilt (conscious or unconscious manifestations) are considered the most singular indicators of a functioning superego. Inferences of the presence or absence of guilt feelings are difficult to make in ordinary behavior studies, since guilt may arise in a person without awareness of the instigating source, may serve as a deterrent to action (or urges) or as a punitive aftermath, and may be experienced only indirectly in somatic or psychic displacements. In the present study data, inferences of guilt appear warranted only in some behavior sequences, including particularly those in which children convey limited forms of self-condemnation. The related affect, remorse, is more easily adjudged, since it tends to follow rather directly on the person's apperception of his relatively circumscribed act (or too-vivid internal fantasy) as hurtful to another. As illustrated in J.'s and the study records, a child's feelings of remorse may be a prognosticator of internalization of conflict, or indicator of superego schemas.

I have chosen to use "self-condemnation" in preference to "self-criticism." In ordinary parlance, the latter is a general descriptive term which, psychologically, covers significantly variable components (derivatives) of guilt-anxiety, shame-anxiety (experienced as self-hatred or self-contempt), and a judgment-type appraisal of a thought or action. The term self-condemnation is intended to convey more precisely the automatic assaultive quality associated with guilt, in distinction to the self-critical experiences or expressions which are more a product of the person's (ego) capacity for self-observation and judgment. I have distinguished in children's manifest behaviors two forms of self-condemnation, "global" and "limited." I have found this distinction to be a revealing indicator of individual differences, and associated with a differential prominence of identification with aggressor manifestations. It is also my impression that global types of self-condemnation are in considerable part governed by the arousal of shame-anxieties at the time, and characterized more by experiences of self-hatred than likely accompany the limited forms. In this light, one may not be surprised that the psychic outcomes, not only the instigating affective-identification sources, of the two forms of self-condemnation differ. Analysis of the data suggests that global types of self-condemnation, in contrast to limited forms, both signify and represent hindrances to the child's achievement of "superego-core constancy."

Internalization of Conflict

Internalization of conflict[8] may be conceived as an ongoing psychic process, the instigating characteristics and functional outcome of which are variables in the build-up of superego schemas in the individual. Instigating characteristics and functional outcome, as inferrable in the study analysis, are significantly related to the prominence of a provider-protector or aggressor type introject; the self-and-object superego core, from which particular superego-content schemas radiate and are variously integrated in the personality, is formed in accord with one or the other predominant type introject. Internalization of conflict is conceivably ongoing, in one sense, because conflict-content is differentially heightened in sequential developmental phases in the early years. Successive experiences of conflict, as internalized, will more or less harmoniously add to and modify the child's preceding internalized sense of what will make it a good or a bad child. In another sense it is an ongoing process, because what personal or content attributes are internalized can become stable behavioral directives in the child to the extent that connective links with other psychic components of its person are established. The establishment of a network of links with the cognitive capacities and core-self aspects of a person is a multiple function of developmental possibilities and recurrent experiences of conflict resolution. That is, at each critical period of internalization of conflict, the time necessary for rela-

[8] Anna Freud uses similar terminology but with somewhat different connotations: "Internalized conflict" refers to an internalization of drive-conflict experiences the child had originally with external sources, while "internal conflict" is a conceptualization of conflict in structural terms—i.e., between superego-ego, or superego-id.

tive stability of the wish-to-please-one's-self to replace a refueling need for an active relationship and approval from primary figures, depends both on the extent of overdetermination of a child's contrary impulses and its positive experiences with significant adults. Hence, one may speak of a "variable" or "inconstant" superego as a characteristic feature of early development, but the range of developmental-phase behaviors subject to variability when the child is pressed will differ among children, in accord with differences in caretaking-relationship experiences.[9] The concept of superego constancy will emerge in this context.

Delayed Internalization: Aggressive Acting-Out Children

Anna Freud (1965) along with other leading psychoanalysts, has pointed out that a deficient superego is the consequence not alone of a child's inordinate aggressive impulses or experiences, but of its insufficient libidinal experiences in *the balance* of the two. I shall bypass the metapsychological implications of the distribution and neutralization of psychic energies and transpose this view to the abstraction level of a child's balance of "experiences," in the analysis of the records of aggressive acting-out nursery children. The records of Mike, Scot, and Adam illustrate the grounds for proposing that the children's relative imbalance of aggressive experiences (stemming from their insufficiency of dependency attachment feelings to family members[10]) is a major cause-effect factor generating delay or distortion in superego controls, individuation, and synchronous ego advances.

[9] Implicit in the interactive concept of experience, or "patterns of experience" as the causal unit in explanations of individual differences in situational behaviors (Escalona, 1961, 1970), is a recognition of the import of self-fulfilling prophecy in a child's transactions. That is, the characteristic ways of responding to its surroundings that have evolved in a child by age one or two, which reflect its *anticipations and demands* of others, influences, often unconsciously, the extent of initiation and affect quality of contacts with him. In this way may reality experiences confirm and consolidate early perceptions and response patterns.

[10] What differences may ensue in the characteristics of superego introjects and evolution of a superego in children who grow up in a positive, *extended* family environment represents a new and fascinating research

Three- and four-year-olds who come to school and act out in aggressive-destructive ways are more easily recognized than dealt with. They are more likely to be boys than girls. Though specific behavioral expressions may vary, and represent an outcome of different specific genetic-experiental factors, certain similarities and anomie-type behaviors may be noted. They bite, knock down other children's buildings, grab their toys, sweep things off shelves, hit out or go into unpredictable tantrum paroxysms. Some, like Mike and Scot, display a "psychopathic" reaction of indifference or positive pleasure (like a gleeful smile) when they disrupt or cause obvious distress to another child. Yet they also evince marked fearfulness of injury or punishment to themselves, and may not attack a child who attacks them or fights back.

Glimpses into the inner world of such children reveal a prominence of anxiety as well as rage reactions, preoccupations with primitive aggressive imagery, and in some the prevalence of a paranoid-type causality reasoning when physical or emotional pain is experienced (akin to Melanie Klein's description of the infant's "paranoid-persecutory" position). It should be emphasized at the outset that many of these children are bright, as manifested in their appropriate levels of reasoning in their limited impersonal or conflict-free areas. The following points summarize the cognitive-affect characteristics found in children whose preoccupation with (derivative) aggressive impulses and fears is associated with a deficiency in self-condemnation and delayed internalization of conflict (superego).

1. *Fearfulness of injury and punishment,* but no apparent anticipation of expectable consequences, i.e., no appropriate temporal or causality connections between the "crime" and the "punishment" he experienced or meted out to another child. Also, the fear of punishment does not effectively operate as an internal deterrent to aggressive acting out. By itself the wish to

area. Moreover, what differences in superego formation and character there may be in children who grow up in surroundings where they *need* aggression devices to cope with their reality world is also an important untapped problem for investigation.

avoid punishment cannot serve as a basis for identificatory internalization of morality directives, though it may be a behavior deterrent in intimidating circumstances. This has vast implications.

2. *Prominence of magical causality thinking and other primary thought processes* whenever aggressive impulses (and fears) are aroused (and they are aroused easily).

(a) Projection of own primitive level of rage and revenge imagery is common. In these children, the use of projection appears as a (circular causality) aspect of their relatively inadequate self-delineation and reality-testing orientation or resources. For example, in the early weeks of school when such a child is approached by a teacher immediately after he has done something "bad," he may quickly dash away or curl up desperately in a ball and scream if picked up, at times even articulating that he expects to be badly beaten, if not killed.

(b) In a world where black-magic causality abounds, there is no accidental bad happening; hence there is the relative prominence of a paranoid-persecutory type of causality comprehension. It will be recalled that Robby (record VI) was unable to distinguish between pretend and real when the fantasy content fitted into his own internal aggressive anxiety preoccupations at the time. (A state of fluctuating certainty represents an affective cognitive advance beyond this.)

(c) Displacement, or ready substitution of one target of attack for another, is not uncommon. Accordingly, teachers or other children are more likely to represent transference objects, than serve development as transitory objects in the processes of separation-individuation.

3. *Absence of signs of remorse, concern, or empathy with "victim,"* concurrent with no apparent expectation of any such responses to them when they are hurt. They do not seek protection or comfort from another at such times. Too, they seem unaware of choices open to them (e.g., verbal protest, persuasion, compromise) other than to attack the apparent perpetrator of their pain or frustration.

4. *Little or no engagement in overt fantasy expression.* When such expressions emerge, the content is limited and appears not to have the psychic utility of the fantasy creations and devices that less aggression-bound children may enjoy.

Adam

From the start of school at age three, and continuing basically unchanged [11] through the Fours, Adam is a child whose frustration and anger is easily aroused and immediately expressed in motoric ways, even though he could be articulate. These points may be specially noted: (1) In record XIII, episode 2, his behavior reflects unusual anxiety about injury to himself (being "burned"), along with the need to rely entirely on himself to avoid it. (2) Episode 6 in the Fours is testimony to his yearning sense of needing a *protector* of his own, albeit a ferociously aggressive one. The level of aggressive imagery he expresses suggests what a young child may experience when survival and wish-fulfillment powers remain relatively undifferentiated needs, and interchangeable sources of anxiety. The similarity of his cognitive apperception of, and affective reliance on, aggression in the Threes and in the Fours, indicates that the sources of such developmental "faults" are not simply out-grown. (On the other hand, defensive strivings for aggressive power, to allay anxiety about helplessness and aloneness, may be altered in young children by recurrent experiences with primary adults which eventuate as Adam's did in episodes 6 and 7.) (3) Incidents 4, 5, and 7 illustrate Adam's reaction of blame and attack on another (usually his only friend), when something painful happens to him.

[11] Regular nursery school experiences may have failed to modify Adam's primitive sources of anxiety, aggression, and premature self-sufficiency efforts, for a combination of reasons. His father, who worked at home and was reportedly very close to him, died suddenly—shortly before Adam started school. His mother, according to teachers' recorded impressions, tended to be overpermissive ("weak"), hence offering Adam little bulwark (or "protective shield") for security and safety.

Record XIII

Threes 1967, 1968

1. Shortly after arriving at school Adam was in the sandbox digging. Lisa climbed in near him; he threw a pailful of sand full in her face. She quickly scooped up sand and threw it right back. Adam was nonchalant as I brushed him off and didn't look at her again. A few minutes later Adam climbed out. As he passed Jenny, who was coming from the other direction, he pushed *her* down.
2. Lenny and Adam each had a small pitcher. Adam got up to get water from the sink. When he turned on the hot water, he exclaimed, "Boy, it's boilin' hot." It was not that hot. He filled up his pitcher carefully. "I'm not gonna burn myself," he announced, "I'm careful." Then followed a repetitive game in which Adam made "hot tea" and Lenny "cold tea," and served it to me a number of times. At one point Adam jumped up, "I forgot something." He left the room and returned shortly with a potholder from the doll-corner. As he applied it to the pitcher handle he remarked, "Now I'm *really* not gonna burn myself." "Do you ever hold Mommy's pots at home?" I asked. "Oh no! I never did. I might get burned that way."

Fours

3. Adam (to Lenny): Throw this away. (Gives him a piece of puzzle.)
   (Lenny looks at it, looks around for teacher.)
   Adam: Chicken, chicken-shit.
4. (Adam is seated on the floor next to a large enclosure block building he had made the previous day. Lenny and Noah are near him constructing a building of their own. As Adam moves he knocks down a wall of his own building.)

Adam (to Lenny who was not near the wall at time it fell): Now look what you did!

Lenny: I did not. (Yelling.) I DID NOT!

Adam: You little rat . . . you stupid rat.

5. Adam rebuilds his wall. A little later the wall again falls when he moves against it. He groans and begins to rebuild it, then looks over to Lenny and begins a scornful four-letter description of the toilet activities of "my friend Jackie." Lenny joins in briefly but then stops responding and Adam turns back to his wall. Lenny suddenly notices a block missing from the building he and Noah are working on and storms over to Adam demanding its return. Adam throws it on the floor, spins around as he is squatting on the floor, and knocks down the wall—I believe unintentionally. He is whining and almost crying; knocks the roof off his building, then turns to look at Lenny and Noah. He pokes his finger at Noah's bottom and Noah just moves away to the other side. Lenny and Noah discuss their building with assistant. Adam quietly goes back to his rebuilding. Once looks up at them and a friend who joined them and says in a low tone, "I could beat you all up. I could cut your heads off."
6. (During rest period Adam is on his cot opposite Lenny's. Adam is sitting, Lenny lying on his stomach facing Adam.)

Adam (in a sing-song): Lenny, Benny, Fenny . . .

Lenny: My name is Lenny.

Adam: Your name is stupid and shit.

Lenny: My name is Lenny!

Adam: My Daddy could beat you up. (Pause.) If I had a Daddy. (Then in a torrent of words, very quickly): If I had a Daddy, he would get you and get a knife and cut off your head and suck out all your blood.

Lenny: Don't! I don't like that. I don't, Teacher! (He turns to me with his face contorted and upset.)

(I told Lenny no such thing would happen to him and then turned to Adam and told him I was sure his Daddy had been a very nice and fine man who wouldn't do such things. As I stressed what a nice man his Daddy must have been, Adam half-smiled and stretched out on his stomach.)

7. Adam and Lenny are playing under the table. As they got more and more active I told them to be careful when they came out so as not to bump their heads. Shortly, Adam came crawling out after Lenny, and banged his head hard against the edge of the table. He began to cry, looked at Lenny for a split second, then made a dive towards him with his hand up, fingers claw-like, yelling: "You shit, Lenny!" I came instantly to comfort Adam, full of sympathy, and in time to take—restrain—his arm. Adam turned on me, tore at my smock, hitting, crying, shouting and cursing me out. "I'll cut off your head! I'll kick your shitty head in!" I kept telling him I was sorry he had hurt his head, that Lenny had not done it, and I had not, and he couldn't hurt us. It took quite a while before he was able to calm down and join the others. A little later in the playground he suddenly pedalled over on the trike to me. "Mrs. B, would you tie my shoe?"

In the records of Mike and Scot appear the prototype of early steps in affective interiorization of cognitive information of good and bad. In Mike particularly, one observes how the positive tipping of the balance of his aggressive/libidinal experiences at school arouses and focuses his dormant wish-to-please. Both records point up that "libidinal" optimally refers to appreciative and protective experiences, as well as to the more commonly understood aspects of gratification that yield a sense of entitlement. Relevant to the establishment of superego schemas, these behavioral changes are noticeable in Mike and Scot: Wishes and angry feelings begin to be verbalized more often; they discover acceptable alternatives, and also that they *can* make choices. As the internal impetus to aggressive acting out appears to diminish somewhat (in contrast to a temporary inhibition created when fear of punitive consequences is the exclusive deterrent), their capacity for pleasurable involvement in doing things increases.

Mike

It will be recalled that Mike was described earlier as a child whose behavioral records suggested a lag in his development of whole-self delineation. The following narrative account outlines the formation in him of a directive wish to do "the right thing," paradigmatic of a child's wish to become the adult's "ideal child" (Sandler, *et al.,* 1963). It will be seen that such a wish is also an interrelated aspect of ego advances and fosters self-delineation.

Mike was fortunate in having two teachers who were able to respond more to his needs than to his disruptiveness. They consistently protected and upheld him in such ways as rescuing him from situations in which he was frightened, avoiding or mitigating experiences of "loss of face," making restraints and prohibitions predictable, punishments limited, frustrations objective issues, and broadening his horizons of do's in conjunction with obvious interest in his expansion of skills.

After some months of such positive treatment, evidence of some internal changes in Mike appeared. He began to check with the teacher *before* he did certain things: "Can I . . . ?" "Is this right?" It is clear that his ability to delay action long enough to ask a question about things he had done heedlessly or provocatively before, marks a leap in his cognitive controls and time out for thought. His wish *and* opportunity to please his teacher by being good as defined more or less concurrently opened the door to various kinds of affective cognitive growth. He began to verbalize his demands and complaints instead of just hitting or grabbing, and the times that he did "blow" were marked by less violence. That his efforts to be good reflected a change in his focus of others, beginning with his teachers, is indicated in the comment to a student teacher quoted earlier, "My teacher, Mrs. C., . . . is my friend." It was during this same period that he revealed a comparable change in his causality comprehension of rain (pp. 37–38). Where he had been largely a loner, displaying a kind of as-if autonomy, he began to be dependent on his teacher, and to demand "stay with me," or "come back," when she went off. He was in the restitutive phase of being able to concentrate on materials (puzzles, blocks, and such) as long as the teacher sat by, and for brief periods even alone with another child. Then school ended, and the family moved away.[12]

These changes in Mike's cognitive affective focus, emerging as fruits of the trust-dependency experiences with his "friend" teacher, I consider signifiers of a beginning conscience in him, and of the causal circumstances in which a morality orientation is seeded.[13]

It is evident that Mike, as well as the other aggressive acting-out children cited, are only relatively lacking in age-appropriate impulse controls, only relatively lacking in the perquisites of age-appropriate internalization of conflict and knowledge of standards of good and bad

[12] In the young child, it is likely that good school experiences alone can at best serve only to ameliorate or strengthen internal trends created in the process of primary family interactions. Without comparable changes therein, the beginnings in Mike of a conjoined positive perspective of his self (as potentially good and competent) and his world (as potentially "holding" and responsive) can be minimally sustained or carried over to new teachers, new situations.

[13] In itself this point is not new. A. Freud and Burlingham in their wartime nursery experiences (1943) discovered early that only when deliberate attempts were made to woo the children into an attachment to a particular caretaking adult were the aggressive and recalcitrant children ready to care to meet the rules and expectations of their adult. On this basis alone could they develop a stability of behavior controls that then became increasingly independent of the presence, and finally of the ongoing relationship with the primary adult.

with respect to aggressive impulse derivatives. The point of their records is that identification-with-aggressor does not a conscience make. Rather, it tends to stimulate and magnify own and anticipated punitive consequences, sealing off primitive aggressive imagery and related magical thinking from developmental reality-testing and impulse-derivative modifications. In other words, identification-with-aggressor, relatively unmitigated by prior firm identifications with provider and protector, creates in effect a relatively undifferentiated ego-superego introject type of identification.

Scot

In another group of Threes, Scot engaged in more explosive acting out than Mike, but he also was more actively involved with people, however negatively. He reacted to teachers and other children as though they were only sources of interference, deprivation, or punishment. He was always eyeing and usually tried to take what another child had, always ready to drop what he had, as long as no one else appeared to want it. Like Mike, all his conflict experiences at first were only between his needs and external sources. After some months with a consistently soft-spoken, supportively firm teacher ("auxiliary ego"), he too was able to develop some measure of trust and dependency attachment.[14]

Like Mike, he showed cognitive growth concomitant

[14] His teacher's final school report includes these comments: ". . . in the first months . . . day after day, as I disengaged or restrained him from, e.g., trying to hurt another child who had something he wanted, I kept repeating, 'It's all right, I want to help you . . . It's all right, I want to help you get what you want.' . . . eventually the intensity of his anger at my interference diminished. . . . I kept demands on him at a minimum. . . . Left to his own devices he maintains distance . . . almost never asks for help or comfort . . . refuses help, but when confronted with something he cannot do, he demands it immediately as though we had not offered help in the first place. In April, I noticed him beginning to accept help when offered and to enjoy it. . . ."

with diminished impulse-urgency, and in his case, increased dependency and achievement satisfactions were also accompanied by a decrease in his automatic envious focus on other children. His gains were real but clearly limited by recurrent sources of distrust and rage outside of school. Invariably he returned from a vacation in a far more combustible state than he had been just prior to it.

In the early spring, Scot was able to have a revealing exchange with one of his teachers on his expectations of being spanked (record XIVA). Some time after, when his behavioral advances at school were most evident, he was observed in the fantasy episode with Bea—possibly his first fantasy expression (C). It is clear he was having trouble at home with "aggressor" parents during this period (B). What emerges in his fantasy is a stark depiction of the traditional picture of a primitive superego, one infused with intense, merciless, and senseless aggressive intent. A comparison of his behavior towards the "bad baby" with Bea's, illuminates both the character and causal concomitants of his identification-with-aggressor.

Scot's attack on the bad baby is unprovoked and with a violence shimmering with murderous rage. Bea spanks her bad baby moderately and for a specified cause. Bea's baby had a chance to be taken care of, i.e., to feel good before it was punished and knew thereby that it was bad. That is, Scot not only metes out a painful punishment, but one that lacks specific cause-effect referents and an ameliorating caretaking context. In the differences between his and Bea's behavior is an expression of different internal experiences of caretaking, associated not only with different introjects (and ideal objects), but also with correspondingly different cognitive-affect resources for dealing with bad impulses. Scot's violent attack on the "bad baby" is a clear example of the investment of an aggressor-introject with the measure of the aggressive feelings mobilized in the child towards the "bad" parent.

Moreover, where rage responses are recurrently triggered, they not only tend to consolidate aggressive imagery on a primitive level (and associated magical defenses), but simultaneously to wipe out positive core-self images in the child along with its wish-to-please. Superego constancy does not appear a feasible achievement, in such circumstances. The import of a more provident relationship context in which a child experiences parental aggression, on the character of its superego-core and resultant internalizations, will be demonstrated in additional records to follow.

Record XIV

A. (Scot and I were alone in the music room after I had taken him out of the classroom for attacking two of the girls by pulling their hair. We were looking out the window.)

Scot (in a baby voice): Mama 'panks . . . Mama 'panks . . .

T: Your mama spanks you?

Scot: Yeah, she gets mad at me and spanks me.

T: Do you do something that makes her get mad?

Scot: She gets mad at me when I'm bad.

T [galloping to the rescue instead of further inquiries]: You're not bad. You just do bad things sometimes.

Scot [clearly responding more to the affective flavor and its practical implications than to the specific niceties in the content]: Teachers don't spank?

T: That's right, teachers don't spank. I want to help you stop doing things like pulling Sara's hair.

Scot: I wanna go back now.

B. During March Scot was much concerned with spanking, several times was heard asking other children if their mommy or daddy spanked, volunteering the information that his daddy spanks him and he doesn't like it.

C. Sometime at end of March or early April, Sara and Bea were washing their rubber babies. Scot wanted to wash a baby, too. As he put his baby in the water, Bea's baby dropped to the floor. She pounced on it, spanked it *for getting dirty,* complained, "Oh, I'll have to wash you again," and put it back in her tub. Scot watched for a moment, then quickly dropped his baby on the floor and pounded it with his fists as hard as he could, muttering, "Bad baby, bad baby." Then he grabbed it and slammed it down into his tub, submerging it. "Now I'm drowning you, I'm drowning you, you gotta get dead." He picked it up, dropped it on the floor, and began pounding it again, repeating this process three or four times.

In summary, the predominance of primitive aggressive imagery is unrelated to intelligence, but in a circular fashion it is associated with and maintains primitive prelogical causality reasoning with respect to actual or threatened pain and frustration events. This affective-cognitive state creates a "sense of unsafety" with respect to own impulses as well as those of others. Characteristically, the distinction between accidental and intentional is either irrelevant or incomprehensible, as much for pain inflicted as for pain received. The nursery records of acting-out children suggest that a child's not-good-enough experiences of nurturance, protection, and opportunities to experience pride in *being* as well as pleasing by its *intentional* doings not only maintain the "rages of the oral phase" and revenge fantasies, but lead the child to *need* aggressive powers to cope with its sense of unsafety, pseudo-autonomy, and consequent sense of aloneness. In such psychological circumstances, a child's development of capacity for sympathy and remorse is blocked off, along with possible internalization of moral injunctions and ideals related to aggressive-destructive intent and behavior.

I shall elaborate on the wish-to-please as an adaptive developmental variable and affective organizer in relation to moral ideas or behavior more fully subsequently (Ch. 6). Suffice it now to note that Mike's and Scot's readiness to care about being good in the eyes of the teacher, for them represented in effect the beginning of their morality. In turn, their wish-to-please orientation stemmed from their orderly experiences of protection and gratification, i.e., from the appropriate ways the adult conveyed its caring that they be good.

Early Internalization Exemplified in J.

It will be recalled that J.'s personal world provided her a generous portion of gratifying, protective, and autonomous experiences, along with prohibitions and limits. Earlier I presented evidence in her fantasy records of her consistent identification with provider or protector. The following incidents (age 1;8–2;7) are cited as indicators of early internalization of superego schemas (as defined), the core of which is presumed to be shaped by these identifications. Like Rondi, and in contrast to the aggressive acting-out children, J. seems to fit Jacobson's (1964) description of a child enabled to experience many of his parent's demands and prohibitions as "joining forces with his own ambitions . . ." [15] (p. 96).

Both the bear fantasy and the incident in the garden are concise illustrations of a child's relatively easy internalization of specific parental condemnations, in the spirit of *joining* the parents rather than of submission to them. In the bear fantasy, J. represents herself as the protesting mother who is hurt by the bear's bite, thus indicating her mode of distancing her self from her bear-self. The garden incident not only reflects J.'s sensitivity to parental disapproval, but also suggests that the affec-

[15] In Kohlberg's (1963) study of moral development, a "naïve" sixteen-year-old boy describes this feeling: "I try to do things for my parents, *they've always done things for you* (my italics). I try to do everything my mother says, I try to please her. Like she wants me to be a doctor and I want to, too, and she's helping me to get up there" (p. 26).

tive-cognitive context in which the disapproval occurs encouraged alignment with their evaluations of "naughty." On a behavioral level, such alignment will tend to limit the frequency and range of a child's bad behaviors. (Even J.'s expression of bad impulses in fantasy are rather limited.) Also suggested in this record (XV-C) is how a parent's affective designation of a child's act as good or bad may serve as a particular organizer of memories which "stand apart" from others and constitute particular superego schemas, or serve as a modus operandi in forming them.

In the reality incident at age 2;0 (which Piaget cites as an example of J.'s first verbal reasoning), J.'s behavior suggests she experienced both early guilt-anxiety and remorse. Her "piercing screams" coming as they do "after a long silence" bespeak a complexity of feelings, internal struggle, and thought in a two-year-old that is often unrecognized. Instead of the "crime" she did commit, she confesses to one she did not in reality commit, but could expect to be punished for if she had. Remembering J.'s persistent, ingenious efforts to overcome obstacles to the fulfillment of her wishes (sense of entitlement), it is not far-fetched to infer that during her period of silence she experienced an internal conflict between her impulses to be a good ("ideal") child, and angry impulses to defy her parents and in revenge do something forbidden. Remembering also the strength of her attachment to her parents, it is likely that she experienced guilt-anxiety about her aggressive impulse fantasy, which then promoted her screams. It is evident from her parents' reaction that her screams suggested terror more than a tantrum-like demandingness. J.'s feelings of remorse and "confession" follow her reality perception of herself as aggressively hurtful to her parents, since her dreadful screams not only made her parents come back, but obviously frightened and pained them. Such responses bear the marks of a conscience or superego.

The last episode quoted (D) is a surprisingly complex "undoing" and "redoing" type of fantasy for one so young. Overall this incident illustrates J.'s already characteristic means of dealing with anger and disappointment, particularly in relation to her mother. Beyond the expression of remorse Piaget sees as forming J.'s fantasy, one may note these aims and positive modes of recovery: She arranges to be alone with "the lady" and effects a reunion (overcoming the internal loss suffered through anger) through identification with the provider. Her good treatment of "the lady" can be seen embodying her ideal of a mother-child relationship. J.'s feelings of remorse, possibly guilt (since primary family dyad vs. triangle situation is symbolically represented) not only suggest internalization of conflict and a functional superego, but her modes of coping reflect the character of her superego core. J.'s behavioral manifestations contrast sharply with the study children depicted as possessed of a prominent identification-with-aggressor superego core.

Record XV

J.

(Implicit limited self-condemnation and means of "recovery")

A

At 1;8, instead of biting her mother's cheek herself as she usually did, she pressed her bear's face to the same spot and said: *"Oh! Oh!"* (obs. 75a).

B

At 2;0 J. had no inclination to go to sleep in the evening and called to her parents for a light and someone to talk to. We went to her room once to tell her to be quiet and warned her that we should not come again. She managed, however, to get us to go to her a second time, but understood that it was the last. *After a long silence piercing screams* were heard as though something *dreadful* had happened. We rushed in [obviously frightened] and J. confessed that she had taken a toy from the shelf above her bed (which she was *forbidden* to touch at bedtime). She even looked really *contrite,* but everything was in its place and it was obvious that she had not touched anything. She had thus preferred to pretend that she had done wrong and believe it, in order to get the light and the company she wanted, rather than to stay alone in the dark and have nothing on her *conscience* (obs. 111a, all italics mine).

C

At 2;2 J. was in the garden walking on the landlord's flower bed. Her mother stopped her from doing so and J. at once replied: "Me spoil Uncle Alfred's garden," i.e., she was identifying this situation with another very similar, but which she had experienced in another town (obs. 106a).

D

At 2;7 a friend of her mother went for a walk with them. J., who did not care for the presence of a third person, expressed frankly what she felt: *"She's naughty* . . . she can't talk . . . I don't like people to laugh," and especially, "I don't understand what they're saying." Then, as soon as the walk was over, J. accepted her, put her beside her in the bath, then in her bed, talked to her, and went for a walk again with her (all in imagination) (obs. 86).

Internalization of Conflict and Differences in Self-Alignment

In a descriptive sense, all superego schemas laid down in the course of individual development are not equally or sufficiently anchored in the psychic structure of the total personality. Young children's behavior reflecting internalized controls or drive-deterrents is subject to varying extents of instability, expectably because they are more responsive than they will become, either to external excitants or to temporary disruption of their affective bonds to their significant adults. The little girl in Mother Goose who "when she was good was very, very good, and when she was bad was horrid," describes the extreme manifestations of what I shall call a "variable superego," or "superego inconstancy." It takes developmental time and propitious circumstances for the establishment of superego constancy, as herein defined. The point my data analysis supports, however, is that the latter is an unlikely attainment unless an early positive core, in identification with the provider, initiates and sustains internalization of ideal drive-deterrent (moral) values. In the text superego constancy refers to the psychic outcome and growth potential in the functioning of a child whose differentiated superego schemas are formed on the basis of an initial (and experientially sustained), largely positive affective alliance with parental ideals and dicta.

Let me recapitulate the developmental view of the superego described earlier, which emerged in the course of my data analysis. (1) Internalization of conflict is considered a recurrent step at each critical peak of a psychosexual-aggressive phase, in the service, or as a function, of the child's (conscious and unconscious) strivings for alignment with its real "mothering" and "heroic" parental principals. Relative resolution of internalized conflict experiences marks and reaffirms the establishment of a superego constancy at developmentally successive conflict phases. The interrelated propitious circumstances for such resolutions are the child's cumulative stability vs. everyday shifts in its positive alignment-attachment feelings, and a sufficiency of experiences of *internal embattlement,* leading to enmeshed viable connections with the child's "this is me" core-self system and its cognitive values. All other things being equal, one would expect a child's most recent drive-deterrent schema accruals (or the most difficult for the particular child to achieve) to be the most vulnerable to sources of variability in the functional valence of superego schemas.

(2) Accordingly, the establishment of superego constancy (affective and functional) is likely evolutionary, akin to object constancy, and like the latter, dependent on the composite operation of positive affective features and a requisite level of intrapsychic differentiation. Depending on the degree and character of internal conflict engendered in the process of internalization, the child's actual balance of "pain" and "holding" experiences in relation to its real adults will influence its sense of alignment with, expectations of, and readiness to please the caretaker-authority figures in ways defined as good or ideal.[16] On this level of conceptualization, individual and developmental differences are expectable, in the digestible or intrinsically conflicted (regurgitable) facets of the cumulative superego core content, and in the ease or resistance to functional oscillation (in part or whole, momentarily or longer).

Some inferences congruent with this general developmental view and in some measure supported by the study data analysis:

(1) Proneness to a variable superego will be more or less in accord with the intrinsic ambivalence and aggression associated with (persistent) superego-core identifications. One may expect a child whose behavior indicates a prominence of identification-with-aggressor also to manifest signs of variability in decisive superego influence beyond developmental limitations. In different ways, Gerry's and Dori's records will illustrate this.

(2) Proneness to a variable superego may become a characteristic more or less in response to marked changes in the child's affective alignment with its caretaker figures. Ambivalence and associated variability may be fixated in a child's evolving psychic structure by the onset (between the ages of 2–3;6) of psychological changes (arousing anger, etc.) in the child's heretofore close, relatively unconflicted attachments to its adults (e.g., Evin). Or ambivalence may be intensified, emerging as a kind of regressive disconnecting affective influence, when neg-

[16] At the extreme, one would expect an autistic child, relatively devoid of attachment feelings to its human caretakers, among its other psychic deficiencies, to be unable to internalize conflict experiences and develop a superego.

ative changes in the child's relationship and well-being experiences occur between the ages of 5–8.

(3) The child's experiences of internal conflict, engendered by the schemas laid down in the process of internalization of conflict, expectably involve some measure of its own condemnation of interdicted impulses affectively linked by it to its "this is me" sense of self. A relatively limited experience of such self-condemnation may be expected to facilitate the development of a superego constancy, and a global type of condemnation to hinder it. (Marya and Jono will be cited to illustrate explicit expressions of limited self-condemnation, Dori the global type.) In keeping with the presented viewpoint, the data analysis points to linkages between characteristically limited self-condemnation and a relatively positive superego core, and between global self-condemnation (or its projection as in Gerry) and relative prominence of identification-with-aggressor (or chronic state of ambivalent attachment). Forms of self-condemnation, therefore, are treated as indicators of internalization of conflict, and within limits of predictability of future events are considered prognosticators of superego constancy or variability.

I shall now describe the individual differences in early affective superego constancy (relative superego constancy) discernible in the very young and how these may be seen as the fountainhead of ultimate stability or inconstancy of moral directives in conflict situations.

Lisa: Inconstant Superego

Lisa's records dramatically reveal the generating factors and features of her variable superego in her fantasy and reality-directed behaviors over a period of years. Lisa's disparate levels of cognitive, affective, and motoric functioning betoken problems clearly beyond the normal range. I am citing her because the nature of her difficulties in adaptive integration generally are reflected in the variable character of her superego-directed functioning, and they reveal macroscopically some problems in development which are more faintly limned in ordinary circumstances.

The records of Lisa in the Threes will help to understand the quoted observations of her in the Fives. The latter provided a unique record of the persistence of a type of variable superego related to impediments to intrapsychic integration, which in Lisa are physical and psychological in multiple ways. The fact that Lisa manifests her capacity for internal disengagement from superego schemas far more often on a reality or fantasy verbal level than in aggressive acting out, does not in my view diminish the significance I have attached to her records.

In the Threes and later, Lisa is in the main a child who is more eager than able to make close contact with other children, and who tries too successfully to make verbal contact with adults as though she were not a child. As reflected in her early records, Lisa's violent alienation from her sense of baby-self is in some causal way coexistent with her efforts to deal with primitive aggressive imagery urges and anxiety. Her defensive attempts to substitute wholesale identification with a "concerned-aggressor" maternal representation for her feared and hated "baby self," may be seen as seriously interfering with the potential inherent in internalization of *conflict* (involving core-*self* and introject) for equally advancing individuation and ultimate superego stability.

A description by her teacher in the Threes of Lisa's way of hugging her teachers when she arrives at school in the morning, reveals the sad incompatibility between her continued yearning for basic "baby" closeness, and her defensive identification strivings with its characteristic unchildlike verbal-level means of effectuating contact.

"In the morning, Lisa comes to school with a very excited, intense look in her eyes (as if she were about to eat a delicious cake). She smiles broadly, holding it fixed until it turns to a grimace sometimes. She rushes to hug Miss M. . . .or myself, squeezing us hard about the hips or waist, sometimes trying to reach for the neck, often pushing her head into the teacher's stomach. I believe she would stay there a long time if allowed. At the start of this hug there is usually a rapid jumping up and down, as if she cannot contain the excitement she initially feels." (I would gather from this that Lisa's internal excitement sharply abates during the time she spends in body-burrowing with her teacher, and returns more or less when this contact is severed.)

Lisa in the Threes

When first observed [17] in the Threes (at age 3;6), Lisa's behavior revealed considerable gaps in integration of body-ego, ego-impulse life, and also significantly weak connections between her "self" and her internalized drive-deterrent content. Her body movements were relatively unco-ordinated, her usual tonus flabby. "Though one of her greatest pleasures is dancing," the teacher wrote several months after school began, "she uses only peripheral movements, flapping her hands about like flippers, leaving out the middle of her body entirely. When she ran for the ball, it was as though she had never moved her body before." (In the Fives, Lisa loved most to enact herself as a ballet dancer, but her movements and dancing were graceful more in her imagination than in reality.) Though Lisa was clearly very bright and articulate, at the same time there was a definite unchildlike quality in her conversations with adults, and a quality of not being on the same wavelength when talking to children. "Cognitive egocentrism" describes her verbal exchanges with children,

[17] The observations were recorded at my request by Lisa's teachers, Miss B. in 1960 and Mrs. F. in 1962, several years before I began specifically to collect and study the children's fantasy expressions. It happened, however, that I became concerned about Lisa, and requested observational records, when I noticed her doll-play in the classroom: the general theme, carried out with much body excitement, was "burning." "The house was on fire," she readily informed me, and the babies were about to be or were already burned. The relationship of these fantasy themes to her real experiences is indicated in her mother's comments about Lisa's celiac condition, quoted below.

and mimicry of adult talk, her conversations with the teachers.

Most dramatically, when the order and controls Lisa tried to maintain failed, "a wild frenzy" often took over —arms and legs flailing wildly, accompanied by high-pitched screams. The following notes by the teacher of the first parent conference she had with Lisa's mother need no comment.

"Mrs. F. talked to me for an hour or so about herself and Lisa. . . . She had an offhand, jazzed-up, humorous-sarcastic way of talking. Though interested, conscientious, and thoughtful in relation to the child, she emphasized continually how 'hard' it was. 'You have no idea how *heavy* she was to pick up—I couldn't pick her up after she was two-and-a-half.' She complained she hadn't been out of the house for five years (Lisa was 3;6 at this time). She stated frankly that Lisa was sent to all-day nursery so she could have some time to herself finally. I asked about Lisa's illness. She was a celiac child, I was told, for three years. (No explanation offered for its remaining relatively uncontrolled for that length of time.) The mother described most dramatically that she would take the child to the park, and after changing her pants, in twenty minutes Lisa would start the most horrible screaming and crying. The B.M. would come very often, and if allowed to remain in the child's pants it would act 'like a meatgrinder and eat away the skin on the inside of Lisa's legs.' I saw the terrible frustration and the general horror of it in Mrs. F.'s gestures . . ." (cf. Lisa's dramatic play and reactions to stressful situations).

But only two months later, during a second parent conference which began with the teacher's sketchy description of Lisa's behavior at school (her brightness, dramatic play preoccupation with adults and adult roles, dread of being a baby, the medicines, etc.), including a casual reference to Lisa's celiac experiences, "Mrs. F. first expressed surprise. 'When Lisa was a celiac child she was not really sick,' she said. 'She rarely cried—I cannot *stand* crying!—and she did not have to stay in bed,' etc. When I mentioned the pain of the burning, then the mother remembered it and elaborated on it . . . Then she mentioned some comments other people had made about Lisa, such as, 'She is so grown up,' 'She gets on just great with adults.' . . . Then she read the questions she wanted to ask me, from a piece of paper: (1) Lisa has great interest in death and dead presidents. Wasn't this unusual? ('Lisa has a photographic memory, and knows almost all the past presidents and the dates they died, from a book we have at home, with the pictures of all the presidents.') (2) Also, Lisa keeps talking about election day.[18] (3) 'Family plans to go to Europe and leave Lisa with another family. The thought made her most uneasy. Should she do this?' "

The teacher's observations, some of which are quoted now in sequence, give a clear picture of a child whose behavior swung sharply between two poles: precocity of ego controls and deficiency of back-up impulse controls, in the face of considerable inner-generated "excitement." The few observations of Lisa as a mommy are telling in their omissions of simple caretaking-comfort experiences.

Record XVI

9/26 (first day of school)—Lisa made some bold attempts to organize children in the doll corner. "You can be the sister, you can be the husband." None played with her.

9/27—Today she showed less push towards children, but directed many questions towards me. "Where is the teacher's closet?" "Is there a toileting time?" ("You can go when you need to.") *"I never go!"* ("Oh, sometimes you

[18] Cf. the stories including references to election day, 11/30 and 12/1.

must have to go.") *"Is it all right to wet sometimes?"* [my italics]

9/30—Lisa looks quite unhappy, as if she might cry any moment. She wants to keep everything for herself. Does not know how to play with other children, nor how to enjoy herself.

10/5—Lisa comes to school with an excited, anticipatory look in her eyes . . . as if she cannot contain the excitement she feels. . . . This kind of excitement is in most of her dramatic play ideas. "I am the second grade school teacher, Miss B. . . ," she announced. "Will you be my assistant?" Or, "Miss B. . . , can you tell me where my child is? What is her schedule for the week? When will she be staying for rest? When am I to pick her up?" (All said with excited jumping up and down.)

10/7—Her favorite play is in the doll corner, where she gets dressed up in a white, fluffy ballerina gown, carrying a feather duster as an umbrella, and packing a doll carriage full of pocketbooks, animals, scarves, and one baby. Lisa: "I am going to the park. My child is sick, her temperature was down and now it went up. Where is the hospital?" Some days she wheels her baby carriage to the block corner and rather loudly asks the children in general a question that none usually replies to, e.g., "I am looking for an apartment house, do you know where one is?" (I think her mother was looking for a new apartment at the time.)

11/15—One afternoon Sara approached Lisa saying, "You promised I could be the mother today."

Lisa: I want to be the mother.

Sara: But you promised I could be the mother. *You* could be the big sister.

Lisa (at that very moment, perhaps before she heard "sister," heaving a powerful fist in Sara's face, screaming fiercely): I WON'T BE THE BABY. (Her face was full of terror and rage.)

Lisa has never been the baby or child. She has tried to get others to be it. Often she asks a student teacher or myself, "Will you be my child?"

11/20—In the yard I participated actively, calling up the "fire engines." The wild, screaming engines and rushing around of the children suited Lisa very well. She joined in freely. After several such calls from me, Lisa asked, "Miss B., will you keep calling the fire engines all morning?" It was one of her happiest days in school.

That Lisa's defensive flight reactions (including violent rejection of "baby" or "child" self-representations) are attempts to maintain distance from terror and rage experienced on a primitive imagery level of annihilation is suggested in the following story, dictated to the teacher. Lisa volunteered to dictate this story after other children had volunteered (or agreed to the teacher's suggestion), following the teacher's reading a story to them "about a school that talked."

11/30—"Santa Claus hit a bad child, because he didn't want to give him any presents. (!) And he got unhappy (the child). And then he went to California, and California said, 'They have no children in town.' Santa Claus went to Mississippi and all the houses in Mississippi were on fire. And then he had to go out of the United States and he went to Colorado and then he hit everybody in Colorado. Then he went to the North Pole and shot one of the reindeer. 'Hey yey, yippeeyay today is election day, and there is no more United States, and today is Christmas,' he said to himself. He went to Colorado. He found the children screaming out of the window, 'We want presents!' Then there is no more world and no more children in the world and then everybody died—and then people were born again and then the world was there again; the buildings got higher and higher and higher."

12/1—"The election day meters (going round the world on election day), went up to visit Santa Claus and Santa Claus locked them up in jail. And then there were no more schools. No more world. Everybody was locked up in jail and everybody died. The jail got on fire." (Story Lisa spontaneously wanted to dictate to teacher.)

12/1—Mara and Manda are babies, sitting in a packing box and screaming.

Lisa: I'll be the mother. (Does nothing beyond the announcement.)

T: What does the mommy do when the babies are screaming?

Lisa (gives me a quick look of shock, then): I'll get them some medicine. (She hands them some dirt in a bowl and they knock it on the ground. With hands on hips): I'm trying everything I can, but they're not listening!

Nat (the daddy): Leave them alone, for God's sake.

Lisa (calmly): I'm going to the store. (Returns shortly, and jumping up and down wildly): I'm the mother of you and I know better than you!! I worked very hard taking care of my babies. (Later referring to Mara): She is a bad good baby, a bad good baby. (Then off and on repeatedly): I am the mommy and I am going to the store for medicine. . . . I'm the mommy. Hello, husband.[19]

(After Nat went away, Sara became the father.)

Lisa (to Sara): What about the babies? Are they good good good?

[19] Lisa's attempts to set up differentiated relationships (sister, aunt) when she tried to get other children involved, and they wouldn't agree that she be the mother and they the baby, was unusual for this age group, as was her reference to husband.

12/10—Lisa is playing with tiny rubber babies and doll house furniture, using cheese boxes as floors, plastic blocks as steps. I overheard this part of her conversation between herself as mother and a baby:

Mommy: Are you mad?

Baby: Yes, I'm mad! Hey! Not that program!

Mommy: . . . It's 12 o'clock, she has to go to bed. Oh, the baby hit me. (Squeezes baby, scrunching up own face.) I'm going to put *him* in jail. [my italics]

12/15—After her usual enthusiastic greeting to me when she arrived:

Lisa: I missed a very important part of the *movie* . . . about Sally. She had a cold for a whole year.

T: My! But then she got over it, didn't she?

Lisa: No. She had the remains. (Later): You know why she got sick? She didn't listen to her mommy and daddy. You have to listen to your mommy and daddy.

When her mother came to call for her in the afternoon, she noticed that Lisa's nose was running. (She has had many colds this year and mother is concerned that either "the child is not healthy, or it is her way of not going to school.") The mother made some remark to me about Lisa's getting a new cold. Lisa then turned to me: "Did you know I have a little sister? She is two years old and she ran and ran and ran and ran and ran," etc., all the while spinning in place.[20]

A year later, the therapist to whom Lisa had been re-

[20] The marked defensive flight Lisa engages in at this time, to avoid the implications of getting a cold because of not listening to parents that she had spelled out earlier, is no doubt evident enough that it will be no surprise to learn that she is an only child. I have italicized words in her records that mark her defensive distance. Her displacement of annihilation fantasies from humans to impersonal, inanimate referents (states, election meters), like her seeing a *movie* about (bad) *Sally* who had colds, represents a type of extreme distancing from one's "self," not simply from particular implicating impulses, described earlier as distance-defenses.

ferred, recorded these comments of Lisa's mother: "Mrs. F. said, *'I'm terrified of violence.* [Now that she's with you in therapy], I can make a fuss about big things and let little things go.' " Apparently Mrs. F. had continued to treat Lisa's negativism or fury if she couldn't order or learn certain things her own way by attempts to divert her, as one might an eighteen-month-old.

Lisa in the Fives

Lisa was given a battery of psychological tests in the Fives. There was no evidence of neurological or organic damage. Confirmed was her ability to function well with structural, conceptual materials (Binet I.Q. of 138), contrasting sharply with her infantile emotional underpinnings, or vulnerability to regressive thought processes in nonstructured situations. The tester made these comments, among others: "Lisa impresses me as a confused youngster who seeks her orientation and clues from her mother, and seems not to know where she begins and her mother ends. . . . It was most dramatic to witness Lisa's body go limp like a rag doll when her mother began to . . . [help her in dressing]. When *I* handed her coat to Lisa she attempted to put it on herself . . ." Her mother is "literally obsessed and absorbed with Lisa's every production. Mrs. F. created the impression that she is Lisa's source of all knowledge, inspiration and appreciation."

After about two months in the Fives, Lisa began to take a prescribed dosage of benzedrine,[21] which clearly helped reduce her vulnerability to regressively unintegrated behaviors. Anticipating that some mornings the drugs might be forgotten about, and curious about manifest behavior differences at such times, I persuaded the teacher to record behavior observations for several months. I received a sufficient number to permit me to reorganize her notes,

[21] Later other amphetamines were substituted for benzedrine.

so as to obtain parallel column comparisons in a number of areas of Lisa's behavior when sedated and when not sedated (for paradoxically this is the effect of benzedrine on certain types of hyperactive children). I shall quote only those juxtaposed comments from the total notes that demonstrate the persistence of a developmentally earlier phase of variable superego. The persistence of relative variability in Lisa is likely a consequence of both the nature of her affective bonds and primary introjects, and of her constitutional difficulties in binding and integrating cognitive, affective, and early body-ego individuation aspects of development.

Record XVII

Lisa

Benzedrine	No Benzedrine
Tends to be amenable to teacher direction and suggestions.	Along with random body motions and a wider vocal range with greater predominance of high screeching notes, is fanciful, angry, provocative in talking, scapegoating; resistant to authority and routines; secretive plans to thwart teacher or a particular child; much toilet talk.
Is quite conspicuous about her conformity to the regimen of the room or the routines of triptaking. She often acclaimed her conformity in a loud voice to	All of this is delivered in a gleeful, giggling, mischievous manner: "Let's talk at story time today so no one can listen. I hate to listen to grownups, don't

Record XVII (cont.)

Lisa

Benzedrine	No Benzedrine
the class at large, or would ask the teacher in a loud voice, "Don't I listen the best of everyone in the class?"	you? Let's have a school with no grownups!" [22] "We're going to live with dinosaurs and make them eat up all the teachers and children in the world except for me and Bea and Steve. . . ."
After a good deal of resistance she was prevailed upon by T. to taste the foods she pushed away. She then wished acclaim for the compliance: "Am I the best eater in the class?"	"Let's not listen to Miss F. when she tells us to taste food at the lunch table."
She began by not liking to rest but then complied, again wishing acclaim: "Am I the best rester?"	At rest time she is not only in frequent motion, but will flaunt her refusal to rest verbally. Or: "Let's get Kenny to be a bad rester at rest time today!"
These are recurring themes in her conversation: being the best; being biggest; and being liked. In the midst of a conversation or discussion, will often	"Let's not play with Alex!" "Do you like Ada? I hate her. She's a doodybum. Let's no one play with her!"

[22] Lisa's greater clarity at this time of expressions of defiance of adults, as well as wishes for their acclaim, as her own (child-person) "I," likely reflects the developmental advances in separation-individuation fostered in her therapy.

Record XVII (cont.)

Lisa

Benzedrine	No Benzedrine
suddenly interject: "Are you my best friend?" "I'm your third best friend—right?" If responded to affirmatively, she will clasp her hands, squeal or be soundless, smile prolongedly.	"Let's put Andy on top of the Empire State Building and then drop him down and he'll tumble forever" (laughs gleefully, claps her hands, eyes shining with delight at the thought).
Helping Alis with her block-building, says softly: "Give some more blocks to Alis." To Bea nearby: "I like you. You are my third best friend."	Usually will wander around the room seeking others to join her in mischief, or at least contact. Will verbally provoke.
Relationship with T. casual, only at times teasing, testing, resistive. She likes to be cuddled and kissed. At such times, simultaneously with the kissing, she generally pours out words: a show of knowledge, recollection of a particular experience, declaration of some intentions.	If companionless at such times, she will attempt to annoy or provoke a child alone, seemingly for sheer contact. When she has the companionship in these verbal taunts, she seeks to maintain exclusiveness of contact with the particular child or group, actively excluding others wishing to join.
More involvement with materials than with fantasy. In blockbuilding (active, creative) she was the first child to make a build-	She will readily stop this taunting, rebellious talk when T. asks her to. But her ability or readiness to control lasts only 20 min-

Record XVII (cont.)

Lisa

Benzedrine	No Benzedrine
ing with room divisions, stories, steps, etc. She is involved in the conceptual challenges of construction.	utes. When kept in close contact with an adult, she is more quiet physically and less inciting to riot.
Gets completely absorbed in crayoning . . . work is usually representational, most usually a female. "Is it a girl, because I only draw girls?" They are most accurately detailed —eyes, ears, nose, mouth, cheeks, fingers, designed blouses and skirt. Only sometimes, though, she adds tree, ground, and grass—*and she has never yet made a house.*	Coloring, which she loves, and doll-corner play can also have quieting effect. Or she is able to snap herself out of incessant physical movement and irrelevant talk when in a small group situation she is asked some information question. The conceptual materials she then deals with are relevant and lucidly presented.
(Manually she is the most dexterous, able to write her name in small spaces, etc.)	

To conclude the record of comparison between sedated and non-sedated states in Lisa, the following excerpt by the teacher recounts how circumstantial exacerbation of her angry feelings at mother induced recourse to aggressive fantasy, etc., despite the drug.

"Lisa has played in the doll corner more frequently than other children, but her interest in this and in dressing up subsided after the first month. She returned to this play and to dressing up early December, when her parents were preoccupied with the Fair and were away, and the [new] apartment was all disrupted. During this time her dramatic themes were home and family (in contrast to the historical figures played out earlier: Betsy Ross, Eleanor Roosevelt, going to the funerals of FDR, George Washington, etc.). She *had* to be the mother. She tends to be imperial in her commands, orders the children about in a grande dame manner, but is frequently not listened to. She tends to be not only definite, but most rigid about having *her* plan followed. She began to express many hostile, aggressive fantasies, attempting to get some children involved in the talk or dramatic play. Most of the children (many of whom had sought her in the beginning of the year because of her vivacity and wealth of interesting ideas and information) dropped away during this time, so that now she is involved primarily with a loose group of two or three, all of whom are intelligent, and are coping with problems of hostility and low frustration tolerance."

I last heard of Lisa when she was nine years old, after she had spent her first summer away at a camp. (I had heard nothing in the interim, except that she had been in therapy since the Fives.) I was sent a copy of the camp director's report, of which the following excerpts are relevant: "Lisa is an outgoing child who wants very much to make friends . . . even though she keeps herself away from a group more than is good. She would gain friendship more easily if she would not rebuff others in her own special way. She has to clown in order to get attention and this is at times disturbing. *She is easily influenced by misbehavior of others, but seldom takes the role of instigator.* She seems to feel that, in order to be popular, she *has to copy the bad manners and ideas of others. Whenever she is reprimanded, she feels very badly, but her remorse is short-lived.* In the beginning she had difficulty accepting adult guidance and some of our rules . . . Her table manners leave a lot to be desired . . . She is obedient . . . Whenever the group put on a play, Lisa's suggestions and ideas gave the play a certain charm. . . . She is a very interesting child" (my italics).

Some Concluding Inferences About Lisa

Though Lisa is a deviant child in a number of developmental respects, there are aspects which on a conceptual level are more widely representative of psychic interferences stemming from premature suppression of experiences of overt conflict with significant caretaker adults, and relatedly, premature repression of primitive rage. The repression appears to be a defense against an early level of anxiety activated in part by her own aggressive impulses and her expectation of retaliatory abandonment (annihilation) by the real parent, because the context in which the child experiences hate or rage against the "bad" parent may be so structured (unconsciously) by the parent as to leave her always feeling unjustifiably bad and destructive. Generally speaking, such affective-cognitive structuring is abetted by parental figures who are genuinely concerned on a caretaking level, who abjure overt conflict (violence), but are completely intolerant about the child's not experiencing good feelings, especially that its caretaker is invariably good and the standards of right and wrong invariably admirable. (In Lisa's case, her celiac condition diminished, for her mother as well as herself, possible good experiences of being taken care of protectively and with comfort; in more ordinary circumstances, the effects of the constellation described would begin at a later point in the child's individuation progress, and with similar pain experienced only on a psychological level.) In other words, aggressive, bad impulse reactions in the child, whether phase-intrinsic or situational, appear as threatening the necessary coexistence of ideal child and ideal parent introject.

As suggested in Lisa's records, one consequence may be described as a psychic embrace of should's, such as more or less effectively cloaks gaps as they recur between what "I want to do" and what "I should want to do." Awareness and experiences of internal conflict thus being blocked, progressive modifications of superego schemas and interconnections with ego functions and core-self image are similarly blocked. Characterologically, the consequence of such a strangulating internal embrace of the introject's should's is that the person's sense of well-being and esteem remains on the level where it was purchased, i.e., almost entirely in the coin of the other's mien of approval.

The effects on behavior with respect to good and bad in conventional moral terms of such relative failure of functional integration of superego with other components (as with the effects of "cumulative trauma" generally) may not appear until adolescence, and if overt morality aggression conflicts arising at this time are not resolved differently than they were in childhood, they may appear in adult years. In adult years, persons with this type of developmental fault may suddenly and unpredictably, both to self and others, engage in behaviors totally at variance with their genuine conscious convictions about moral values and with their prior highly moral behaviors.

Evin: Developmental Fixation of Variability

Though the data are scanty, Evin's record exemplifies the thesis described earlier: Consistently provident experiences in the first eighteen months or so nurture a strong wish-to-please (internal orientation) and give impetus to early internalization of conflicts. An abrupt, sustained loss of the accustomed closeness and ability to please the parents occurring around twenty-four to thirty months will tend to fixate developmental conditions underlying variable superego functioning (e.g., reliance on parental figures for emotional refueling and as auxiliary ego), without necessarily interfering with the accrual of drive-deterrent content in subsequent development.

According to his mother's report,[23] Evin probably experienced a sharp change in the stimulating, attentive, close relationship with his parents, and in the evident pleasure he could give them, beginning when he was about 2;6. The three years he spent in nursery school, from age three through five, were characterized by considerable unevenness of his own behavior controls. He began each school year with relatively frequent bouts of bad behavior, which diminished once he had established a positive relationship with each new teacher, but then his behavior controls became variable (though to a lesser extent) when she was not sufficiently available to him for one-to-one times. In the Threes he was for many months a frightening bad boy in the eyes of the children because of his lightning-swift, unpredictable biting a nearby child on occasions. Subsequently, his outbursts of bad behavior consisted of suddenly knocking down another child's building, or stubbornly interfering with and disrupting other children in play, or being mischievous during lunch (e.g., throwing food around) or chanting "doody heady, peny head" defiantly at the teacher when she remonstrated with him. On the other hand, in each of the three years whenever he and his teacher were alone together, he was invariably a charming companion—as a conversationalist and a listener. Needless to say, though he was clearly a

[23] In a parent interview when Evin was in the Fours, his mother informed his teacher that she had become depressed subsequent to the birth of her second child when Evin was about two and a half. Parental interrelations and relationships with Evin deteriorated at this time. They were making efforts to improve their situation by therapy, with only mild (variable) success so far. Most significantly for Evin, she became disappointed in him when he was two and a half or three because the promise she thought he had of being a great intellect was dashed for her. (No specific reasons given.)

most able child, he engaged relatively little in any sustained interests in materials, or in carrying out his very good ideas himself. He was, for example, more likely to proffer helpful ideas to a child block-building, than to make his own.

His changes in behavioral controls and eruptive manifestations largely reflect age-appropriate accretions of internalized do's and don't's, while his withdrawal into isolated play which often followed his bad behavior testifies to internalized conflict and sadness about being bad. At the same time his behavior indicates an early level of variable connectives with self, along with his wish-to-please being subject to a related level of ambivalence and alternate arousal of oppositional impulses in revenge. His motivational alignment with superego schemas varied in accord with the satisfaction not simply of his dependency needs but also the early conditions of dyadic closeness which had initially made him feel like a good boy. Having lost this abruptly and incomprehensibly (though without violence or physical neglect), being a bad boy at times and in these limited ways may be seen as a declaration of independence and a relief from the periods of his completely contained, isolated fantasy play. But as long as "good me" and "good boy" remained linked to his early ideal mode of relationship, he could evolve no means of owning either himself.[24]

Davi: Return to Variability

I had only a chance encounter with Davi when he was six, some months after he had newly arrived at the school from another city. I noted it at the time because it struck me as a paradigm of a child's "bending" of its cognitive resources to

[24] It will be recalled that the incident of the sign cited earlier ("Bad boys! Don't knock down this building!") was an outcome and expression of his feeling good about self-and-teacher. But at the end of that very day, just as he was leaving to go home, he was seen to hesitate briefly near his building, and then to tear down his sign. On the other hand, he did not also destroy his building.

maintain a positive internal alignment with a parent, in the face of some conflict and doubt which threatened to disrupt it.[25]

I cite him now briefly, to illustrate that while the conditions encouraging or hindering superego evolution in the first five years in ordinary circumstances persist, and leave enduring psychic precipitates, actual experiences for some time thereafter, particularly with parental figures, determine whether the acquired superego shape and constancy will continue or sustain congruent growth trends. In the account that follows, it is clear that the interdependence of ego and superego functions continue into later childhood. It is also clear that the extent and character of the impact of later opposite influences are limited and shaped by the earlier formative features. In his middle childhood Davi became a depressed, oppositional child, not, for example, an acting-out delinquent.

Record XVIII

Davi

(A compromise solution in the service of attachment)

The class chameleon had been found dead by the children when they arrived at school that morning—mysteriously "squashed." When I joined a small group at their lunch table later, they immediately told me about it, since we happened to be sitting close by the dead pet still resting in its glass bowl. Davi, with several others, jumped up to look at it again, and as he turned back I heard him say aloud to himself, with a shake of his head, "It's still dead."

I: Did you think it might come alive?

[25] Clinical evidence has amply demonstrated that young children normally struggle to avoid disillusionment with and alienation from parental figures—akin to their struggle against "separation loss." Premature disillusionment creates the intrapsychic equivalent of and to some extent similar consequences to premature actual loss of the other.

Davi (promptly): Yes. (Although some of the other children are vigorously shaking their heads "no," he adds): I'm sure it's true but I don't believe it.

I: I don't get it. How can you be sure it's true and not believe it?

Girl (bright-eyed, excitedly): That can't be, can it? You can't *do* [think] that!

Davi (unwaveringly): I'm sure it's true but I don't believe it. (To repeated questions of "How can you . . ." he simply repeated his original statement until I thought to say that I *really* would like to know what he meant and that I was sure he had a *reason* for saying what he did. This somehow reached him and after searching my face for a moment, he explained): Well, my mother told me that after Jesus was hung on the cross and buried, several days later he came alive. I'm sure what she says is true but I don't believe . . . it.

Davi was charming, alert, and companionable for the better part of his first year. In the last two months the teacher noted that he had become rather subdued and seemed preoccupied. In the following three grades, as could be gleaned from his teachers' reports, Davi became increasingly truculent and defiant towards the teacher, but more detached than aggressively involved with his schoolmates. At the same time he became increasingly indifferent to school learning. Seeing him once in the third grade, joyless and sullenly slumped in his seat, one could not believe that this "behavior problem" child was the same vibrant, thoughtful, really nice boy I had met in the first grade.

The basic reason for these profound changes was a marked change in his experiencing of both parents, beginning some time during the first grade. At this time the relationship between the parents markedly deteriorated; Davi's father began to stay away from home frequently, ostensibly on business trips at first, then openly effecting a separation. One may assume that in the course of these events Davi suffered a relative loss of both his real parents in different ways. There were clear limits to his behavioral decline at school, likely set by the solidity of prior relationship nutrients which had founded an internalized positive self-alignment with parental standards and ideal child. At the same time, it is evident that some of these nutrients were leached out as a consequence of his premature disillusionment and functional loss of his prior attachment to his parents, with the result (among other concomitants) that the continued evolution or consolidation of superego constancy as well as ego ideals were impeded.

Gerry: Identification with Aggressor

I have cited Gerry's fantasy records earlier (#IX) as illustrations of a child's consistent identification with the aggressor, associated with some vulnerability to fluctuating certainty, and have also quoted his complex projective defense manoeuvres to ward off condemnation of himself. In the earlier discussion I pointed out his symbolic act of "locking the door" against school-authority figures to gain internal freedom and safety to "shoot, shoot!" people in his fantasy play.

The most dramatic expression of Gerry's superego shape and operational inconstancy is to be found in his "murder" of the newt, the class pet of the Fours. The assistant teacher had been nearby most of the time he had been playing absorbedly with it, and recorded her observations shortly after the newt's demise (record XIX -A).

Gerry's preoccupation with the newt's mouth, beginning with his unsuccessful searching for it and ending with his putting a tack through its "mouth" because "the newt bit me" reveals a marching concern with aggressive impulses on the oral "cannibalistic" level I commented on earlier as not unusual in the nursery Fours. However, Gerry's acting out is in contrast to the children in "The Witches."

The morning after, Gerry swiftly volunteered an exonerating explanation of the event to his head teacher (B) which is remarkable in recapitulating well-worn palliatives, for in essence he claimed "the newt bit me first" and "the other guy told me to." After thus freeing himself of blame and responsibility (and self-condemnation or punishment anticipated during the previous night), he proceeded forthwith to become the newt's chief mourner. His compassion for the death of his avowed enemy followed by his idealization of it ("He's in heaven. I know . . ."), brings to mind a parallel sequence as Freud described it in *Totem and Taboo* (Ch. 2) in the idealizing ceremonial rituals of certain primitive groups after they had beheaded and/or devoured the enemy.

Record XIX

Murder in the Classroom

A

March 1964

Gerry had been playing with the newt and I was sitting at a table writing. I was also speaking with Gerry about the newt. I asked him if he would like me to get a library book about newts. He said yes. I asked him the name of the newt and he said "Newty." He came over and showed me the newt and said it did not have a mouth. I then asked him how would the newt eat his food. He was holding the newt in his left palm, sometimes letting him crawl up his wrist. He quietly played with the newt near the aquarium for about twenty minutes. At one point, he put the newt in the clam shells and closed them. I told him that I didn't think the newt would like this and explained that he would not have air. He hesitated and took the newt out. Then he continued playing with the newt, while

I emphasized that he should be gentle and careful while holding it. Then he put the newt in its aquarium but was watching it. Doug came into the room and went over to Gerry at the aquarium. He was loud and boisterous, running as he joined Gerry. The two of them were playing with the newt and then other children came in, and it was time to get dressed to go home. Gerry and Doug were still with the newt. Then I heard, "Let's kill the newt." I am not sure if Gerry or Doug said this. Then other children came into the room. I remember hearing, "The newt is wiggling. He's not dead." Mrs. F. (the head teacher) came in and she talked to Gerry about the incident. (Content of this talk was not recorded.)

B

"The newt bit me and I was getting madder and madder."

"And Alex told me to put a thumbtack in the head. He died."

"He wiggled. He didn't like the cut."

"He feeled it too. It went through his mouth."

"He's in heaven. I know where the newt is. He's in heaven. Poor newt!"

"Shame on Alex!" [26]

The defenses Gerry mobilized to divest himself of blame, or to ward off some punishment he anticipated, suggest that he experienced some guilt-anxiety and that he had developed some type of superego organization. His guilt feelings, however, appear to have been most active *after* the act, rather than before it. One might say he locked the door on those feelings, or was able to when the pressure or support of external controls diminished with the physical distancing of the teacher. In

[26] It is unclear from the teacher's account how Alex came into it and why Gerry did not hold Doug responsible, even leaving him out of it altogether. A hypothesis is suggested but with awareness of missing facts.

this context, "out of sight, out of mind," acquires a special aptness.

A detailed inspection of Gerry's behavior may serve to highlight the nature of his internalization of conflict, and to support the inferences drawn regarding the constituent characteristics of his superego.

To begin with, Gerry did not commit his crime "in cold blood." He was apparently in a state of conflict and excitement before Doug or Alex joined him. I am assuming that Alex did come by "when the other children came in," and that the teacher did not notice him because he remained a silent, hence *uncritical,* observer. Alex was a child who got into acting-out trouble at times but always obviously, not silently. In this sense, Alex was a more handy scapegoat than Doug, but to attribute a Machiavellian talent to Gerry's unconscious would of course be sheer speculation.

In any case, it is clear from the teacher's report that Doug was present, and at least an accessory to the crime. If either Doug, or Alex if present, had condemned Gerry's jabbing at the newt, it is likely that he would have been constrained. I believe it was the absence of external deterrents, including that of the teacher's nearby presence, at the time of the pitch-point of his aggressive fantasy and anxiety that constituted the necessary and sufficient condition to free Gerry to kill the newt. In this sense, one can understand how, strongly pressed to avoid blame, he could experience someone or something outside of him having "made" him do it. One may assume, further, that Gerry's defense signals a desperation to avoid *internalized* anticipated consequences wherein his main teacher served as a transference object. For in the final twist, Alex alone is the bad one, and Gerry emerges as the good one, as though united with an internalized ideal.

On a more theoretical level, Gerry's compassionate denunciation of Alex and his idealization of the newt along with himself suggests a Janus-faced or indigestible introject.[27] Gerry's behavior as reflected to some extent (perhaps even foreshadowed) in his fantasy records suggests that his preeminent modes of dealing with internalized sources of conflict between drive-impulses and superego standards, are to avoid blame if "seen" in transgressions, and to avoid being "seen" if transgressing. Thus, a major attribute of the do's and don't's standards that he appears to have internalized is a punitive-restrictive one. His form of identification with the aggressor suggests that he experiences the disciplinary parent more as a policeman-aggressor than as a protector-aggressor. I use policeman in a traditional sense—one who is there because you are "expected" to do wrong, who has to see to it that you do not, who is ready to catch and to punish you when you do. In children's fantasy play, including cops and robbers, the policeman-representation is generally a threatening, punitive figure—someone to run from, not to, less admired than feared.[28]

Self-Condemnation: Indicator and Prognosticator of a Superego

I have proposed that indicators of self-condemnation in a child be considered guilt equivalents or a composite shame-guilt expression. It will be understood that mediating and un-

[27] In "Miss T," Walter de la Mare provides an impeccable description of the psychic process and outcome of an identification, in contrast to incorporation of an indigestible object:

It's a very odd thing—
As odd as can be—
That whatever Miss T eats
Turns into Miss T.
Porridge and apples,
Mince, muffins, and mutton
. . . ; the moment
They're out of her plate
Tiny and cheerful
And neat as can be
Whatever Miss T eats
Turns into Miss T.

[28] I later found in his teacher's report statements to the effect that a German-type of paternal discipline prevailed in the home, that the father appeared to be affectively distant and was also away from home periodically. His mother, on the other hand, appeared to be sweet, gentle, ineffectual. Gerry was an only child at the time. Neither parent was comfortable with the progressive school attitudes and disciplinary techniques; they were distinctly at variance with the father's.

derlying the development of guilt-anxiety is the child's capacity for empathy with the "victim," which is born out of its positive affective early human relationships, as well as an internalization of morality schema interdictions against aggressive-destructive impulses. Optimally, self-condemnation as a resource represents a child's alignment of its core-self with internalized morality dicta, along with its sense of intrinsic justice, developmentally in line with other adaptive turning-passive-into-active moves that help build a child's sense of autonomy.

The study record illustrations that follow will delineate different types of self-condemnation and their ramifications; these may be overt expressions or inferrable in the child's behavioral expressions as in Clara's and Tim's talion punishment sequences. Implicit or explicit, self-condemnation types differ in ways that suggest developmental and individual distinctions in the following respects: whether it is merely an aftermath expression or serves as a deterrent to the urgency of acting; whether it tends to be *global* in the attack on self and in the relative diffuseness of the reasons given for the condemnation; whether the self-attack tends to be *limited* in character and the act condemned more precisely, specifically delimited. Indicators of talion concerns in children may be described as diffuse though complex expressions combining some level of guilt-anxiety and magic thinking, where intrinsic justice is felt to be meet with retaliatory reversal. In consideration of these qualities, proneness to talion concerns may be considered the most undelineated (self-object) expression of self-condemnation and justice, the primitive counterpart, perhaps, of the defensive position of identification with the victim.

A word here of the nursery children's use of the epithet "Stupid!" which appears either directed against the self or as a taunting condemnation of another child. Usually it means "You're bad!" in the sense of a moral transgression, not a mental deficiency. It expresses a scornful condemnation of overt aggressive behavior such as hitting and biting, sometimes of teasing too. As used, it suggests a relatively undifferentiated shame-guilt affect.

Tim: Talion Concerns in an Oedipal Context

Tim is a very articulate, well coordinated just-Four, who for the first month of school liked nothing better than to cuddle up with or near the teacher and listen to a story. After about a month he became overtly aggressive when his wishes were somehow interfered with. At these times he might attack the teacher (biting, kicking, threatening never to come to school again); less frequently he would push or occasionally bite other children. His fantasy play during the first three months, which gave him his "greatest relaxation and serenity," consisted mainly in his being the baby to some maternal little girls, but only a sleeping baby. "He would lie stretched out on the floor perfectly still, or curled up covered with a doll's blanket. His only block buildings were simple enclosures for himself, the baby, to sleep in. (His sister, the only sibling, was three–four months old at this time.) Outdoors, however, he was actively involved in riding the tricycle, and on this he would pretend to be a speed-racer, a fireman, or a *mailman*" (my italics; cf. fantasy below).

Two–three months after school began, he made his first real friendship and gained an accomplice. Together, in an unholy alliance, "they tear around the room, shouting newly discovered four-letter words, teasing children and teachers with 'mushy diaper' and 'big baby.' He's fond of mocking the teacher with 'Okay, baby' whenever she speaks to him." About three months after school began, his teacher observed the following fantasy, which signals a change in the dynamics of his internal struggle coincident with the change in his reality-oriented behaviors: "Seeing him stretched out, perfectly still, on top of the sandbox with two little girls next to him, I asked if one was his mother and he the baby. To my surprise he said no, that he was the father, adding, 'The father's dead, he drank poison juice.' 'Where did the juice come from?'

I asked. He replied that it had come in the *mail,* and '*nobody knows* who sent it.' "

A week following this fantasy[29] the following incident was recorded by the teacher because it seemed "strange" to her: "His mother was having lunch with us. At one point she left the table momentarily. Tim turned suddenly and asked me, 'Mrs. C., am I going to die?' This was not apropos of anything being said, and was all the more strange since he is not a particularly questioning child.

Marya: Limited Form of Self-Condemnation

In behavior and affect range, Marya (record XX) and Jono (XXIII–XXIV) are more typical of middle-class Threes who enter nursery school than Mike or Scot or Dori. They have more stable internal controls, appear to have had more fulfilling, age-appropriate experiences of autonomy-assertion, and to have developed a more solid wish-to-please. Marya and Jono were in the same group of Threes in which the two teachers recorded extensively throughout their school year.

The early recordings of Marya suggest that a limited form of self-condemnation is causally related to and a manifestation of a relatively balanced provider-aggressor super-

[29] Until the advent of his sister, Tim's personal world enveloped him closely in an adult-triad cocoon, a world which included unusual closeness with his father whose studio was a part of the home. In his school behavior it is evident he has no fear of physical punishment by adults. At a regularly scheduled parent conference shortly before or after the "dead father" fantasy, his mother spontaneously reported that "recently in their afternoon time together he has asked her to engage in fantasy play with him of two kinds, in sequence. First, he is the baby and she the mother; then he becomes her husband, while she is to be his wife." There are no steps in between for Tim as yet. His records and inferrable psychic development and problems provide an interesting contrast to Scot's, and a suggestive similarity to Clara's separation experiences and anxiety. It will be evident that prominent involvement with talion mode of thought tends to blur and impede the development of distinctive clarity of core-self and object representations (individuation) and to be associated with, if not also foster, magical thinking in affectively associated areas.

ego-core introject. Marya seems able to condemn a specific aggressive act (or thought), rather than to reject her whole self, in order to be aligned with the parental imagos.[30] Scot's murderous attack on the "bad baby," for some reason connected with its being or getting wet, contrasts sharply with Marya's moderate slapping of her bad baby for talking back to Daddy (record XX-6). Marya's recorded behaviors are congruent with experiencing parental controls and standards as relatively predictable and comprehensible in the situation, and as more often protective than arbitrarily punitive or unclarifyingly permissive. Her father uses hitting at times to discipline. But as Marya makes charmingly explicit, the parents' powers and prowess as perceived may be admired more than feared and envied, when experienced as available *for* the child's protection and upholding, not simply *against* his person and pleasures. From different vantage points, both Marya and Jono have a basis in their actual experiences for developing positive means of wooing or pleasing the parental-type figures *and* themselves—in contrast to other children who more often than not find that they can please only the parental figure *or* their selves.

In Marya's record, item 5 illustrates an early manifestation of progress towards stable, internal alignment with ideal child standards. Her responsiveness has several positive attributes and feedback consequences, aside from its obvious social benefits. Her self-alignment with being good as defined is apposite to an experience of power struggle and submission, and facilitates development of coping resources that can aid ego growth as well as foster super-

[30] Present data permit only broad references to positive and negative relationship features. As may be hypothesized and yet to be investigated, the influences of maternal and paternal figures have different internal consequences for a child, depending on different relationship experiences with each at different developmental phases, and also on whether the superego qualities and moral behaviors of both provide an ingestible continuity or negating factors.

ego constancy. For example, she is able to withdraw spontaneously from her impulse to project blame and not to feel impelled either to deny or to justify her act. Both she and Jono are able to be honest about their transgressions.

Record XX

1964

1. First three days of school she is very concerned with everything being in proper place. She takes teapot from the stove and asks, "Can I play with it?" Goes to put it on the table and asks, "Can I put it here?" This continued with every item she used. In the yard she stood by the jungle gym and asked, "Can I go in? Can I climb on it?" [31]

2. 10/21—Volunteers to teacher: "Daddy says, 'My God! My God!' He gets angry and smacks me."

3. 11/9—(Daddy is to be admired as well as feared.) Marya watching through the fence with Tommy and Johnny as fire engines go up the street. Tommy and Johnny are excitedly following the fire engines' progress and talking about firemen with great admiration. Marya breaks in: "My daddy's a fireman, real fireman!" She stamps her foot in the face of the other children's disbelief. "He puts on the hat and goes out to the fire. HE IS!" (He is a volunteer fireman.)

4. 12/23—(Daddy is her protector, too.) Shouting at a child who was bothering her: "Stop that! I tell my daddy and he shoot you. My daddy's a cowboy. *A cowboy with a gun!*"

[31] Children differ in their reasons for as well as in type of cautious surveillance of a new situation. Questions may be directed to protect themselves from physical injury, criticism, or humiliation (for "not knowing better"). In any case, it is clear that Marya begins school with a concern about being good and not-bad in the teacher's eyes.

5. 12/18—(Playing London Bridge with E. and H.—early adaptive internalization of parent-teacher disapproval; cf. item 6, too.)

Marya (hits Eliz): Stupid! (But she says this looking directly at Helen.)

Helen (very offended): I am not stupid.

Teacher: Oh, Marya, Helen doesn't like you to say that to her. She wants to play the game with you.

Marya: I'm not saying "Stupid" to Helen.

Teacher: To whom?

Marya: I say "Stupid" to me.

Teacher: But why?

Marya: Because I hit Eliz.

6. 1/2

Marya: Baby's crying because I spanked her.

Teacher: Why did you spank her?

Marya: 'Cause she's naughty. She was angry on the daddy and the daddy smack the baby.[32]

Dori: Global Form of Self-Condemnation

At age 3;9 when she entered school, Dori was an unusually tall, attractively pudgy, articulate child whose periods of keen, focused activity alternated frequently with bursts of toddler-level emotions and behavior. When propelled by her need for the adult's sole attention, or a desired object held by another child, or for less apparent reasons driven to defy, provoke and disrupt, her thinking and even her motor coordination regressed. The biggest problem for Dori as well as for her teachers was created by the negative, intrusive aggressive means she used when roused to get the physical contact, attention,

[32] In a number of other fantasy scenes not cited here, Marya also represented herself as provider and comforter, indicating thereby the range in her superego or ideal identifications. Obviously it is the range of identifications rather than the presence or absence of a particular one that determines the character of a superego.

and approval "she was almost ravenous for." Her unappealing, determined efforts antagonized her teachers,[33] and led only to negative attentions, or active rejection by almost all the children she approached. This vicious circle continued for some time, until the teachers (with guidance) were able to work out sympathetic, supportive techniques, including very specific, consistent ground rules.

Early in the fall it became evident that water-play was a pleasurable, relaxing activity for Dori. The one fantasy overheard and recorded during this period (record XXI-1) took place during water-play (as did several others later in the year). In it she directly expresses death-wish imagery towards her father with no apparent anxiety concomitants. (This is very different in anxiety and distance defense manifestations from Tim's dead father fantasy—as well as in the probable genesis of such wishes.) Only later in the year, when in fantasied exploits she attacks her mother, does she feel impelled to give justifiable reasons for her aggression. Her evolved need for some sense of orderly justice to account for her aggressive behavior (impulses) against her mother appears concomitantly with expressions of (global) self-condemnation when she experiences having "lost" her loving teacher through her unjustified aggression against another child. To what extent these manifestations of internalized conflict were simply developmental emergents (in her home-world), or were fostered by the relatively consistent protectiveness, means-end teachings, and expectable social rewards (loving teacher, friends) in school, is open to speculation. There is no doubt, however, that the cognitive-affective progress she was able to make in the fall was directly

[33] From her teacher's report in November: "I am reading to a small group . . . Dori suddenly flings herself across my lap, indavertently bumping other children with her legs, and in a whiny rasping voice (obnoxious!) starts pointing out the pictures, or telling me some unrelated story, not even coherent at times—all the while blocking the others' view . . . will not stop when asked . . . has to be taken from the room . . . in the meantime the other children have been distracted and excited."

related to her teacher's ability "to anticipate and sympathize with her demands," while maintaining ground rules. She became "less distractible, more able to involve herself constructively with materials (beyond water-play and such), increasingly able to sustain play with other children without antagonizing them."

But after January, Dori's line of steady progress was broken. The gains were still evident some days, but for most of the rest of the year, she would often become frantic and angry for a time during the day, physically attack other children (hitting, biting, pushing) or taunt them ("Stupid!"), again having many negative experiences with her teacher, or alternatively, going off by herself. It was during this period that in fantasy talk or reality asides she referred to quarrels between her parents, or to herself being physically hurt and therefore hurting her mother in return, and it was during this same period that she also had the bursts of global, intense self-rejection (section B and C). In one episode (#9) she manifests alternating victim and aggressor identifications—with fantasied content (presented as facts) constituting a transmutation of actual experiences, rage impulses, and internalized conflict anxiety about these.

It is evident, or at least understandable, that a global type of self-condemnation which is so murderous of one's core-self is more likely than a limited type would be to oscillate with externalization against the primary parental figure or transference figures. Though externalization or projection, as in Dori, may be seen as an adaptive rescue effort of her self, it is still also essentially a form of defense with negative feedback consequences internally and in reality. In her records, global self-condemnation is clearly a despairing total denunciation: "I'm stupid, stupid, stupid . . . ," and one that appears associated with almost tangible attempts to divest herself of her self: "I'm not Dori."—without being able to find a sustaining alternative, for "Sattita" too ends up being stupid. The motivation underlying such fierce, global self-condemnation in a young child, and its resultant identity confusion is suggested in items 4 and 6—"I say I'm a monster. My mommy says I'm a monster"—while in 8 and 9, Dori virtually describes her mother as a monster. Similarly, one finds the same type of global condemnation and almost tangible efforts to divest herself of her parents (items 1 and 7) as she had expressed toward her self-identity.

Record XXI

A

1. Dori had for some minutes been absorbed in playing with thick soapsuds. She begins speaking, continuing to stare at the soapsuds, in a singsong voice devoid of feeling. "My father called my mommy 'stupid' and calls me 'stupid'—I wish the cops would come to our house and get him and lock him up in a jail in a zoo and give him something to make him go to sleep so he'll never be able to move"—11/13.
2. Dori had just arrived. Miss H. (once-a-week student teacher, gentle, friendly) arrived, smiled at Dori. "Good morning." Dori stared at her for a moment, suddenly frowned and retorted angrily, "You're *stupid.* You're a stupid teacher. Get outta here!" I quickly said, "What made you feel so angry this morning, Dori?" She answered, pouting, "My mommy was yelling at me this morning." (11/26)

B

3. The day after Christmas vacation, when I called her name she stood up, frowned, and said, "Don't call me Dori, call me *Sattita.*" "Sattita," I replied, "that's a pretty name, too. A special nickname, Dori?" She shook her head impatiently, "No, it's not a special name. Don't call me Dori. I'm not Dori any more. I'm Sattita," and she ran off to the table. (1/2) For several weeks on and

off Dori continued her assertions that she was Sattita. When I asked her where she had heard the name—story, TV, mommy, or daddy—she would blurt out, "Nowhere" or "Nobody," and dash off. When I asked her mother about it, she knew nothing; she was not even aware Dori was using it.

4. One day (1/17) Dori and several other children were at the bathroom sink in water play, supervised by the assistant teacher. She made a comment on Dori's play. Dori: "I'm not Dori. I'm Sattita." She turned on steaming hot water and put her face into the steam. Mrs. A. backed away, reporting later, "Dori laughs with a kind of evilness as if she got much pleasure from bugging me."

Mrs. A: Well, I know Dori. She's the friend I really like.

Dori: Sattita is in the wall, turning on the hot water. (Turns to Adam who is standing next to her.) Sattita is Adam. Sattita's stupid.

Mrs. A: We don't need her here. You're not stupid. You're smart, Dori.

Dori: No, Dori's dead. Sattita killed her.

C

5. Several times, right after I have prevented Dori from attacking another child, or have stepped in right afterwards, she has stamped her foot, shook her head angrily, saying loudly, "I'm stupid, I'm stupid, stupid, stupid!"

6. Before Christmas, Dori's aggressive encounters with other children were limited mostly to bumping into them, grabbing toys, calling them stupid, and barging into play situations where often she did not fit in. Since then incidents such as the following with Joshua have increased. (1/30)

Joshua had just arrived, had put his coat away, and was standing near his cubby. Dori, talking to another child a few feet away, broke off her conversation, ran over to him, grimaced and called out to him, "Stupid, stupid, you're stupid!" Joshua angrily lashed out at her with his fist. Dori screeched with rage and tried to scratch his face. I restrained her before she could hurt him. She pulled away, ran to her cubby, flung herself down and hid her face in her coat. When I came near her she screamed, "Get away from me." When I knelt down and said I was there to help her, she shrank back, then blurted out, "I'm stupid. I'm a monster." I asked who says she is. "*I* say I'm a monster. My mommy says I'm a monster." By then I was urgently needed elsewhere and had to leave her.

D

7. They were making pictures which they wanted to mail to their mommies, all but Dori who pouted "No," when I asked her. She made another picture which she said she wanted to mail to Eddie, a friend of her daddy's. When I said I would mail it to her house, since I didn't know where Eddie lived, she said, "No, don't. Anyway I don't live there any more. I live in Brooklyn." (This is not true. It may be related to my having told her some days ago, when she asked, that *I* live in Brooklyn.) (1/20)
8. Out in the yard, Dori has been embroiled in one conflict after another. I finally lead her across the yard away from the others, explaining, "I'm just not going to let you hurt any more children today." Dori looked up at me sideways, and frowning, said, "But my mommy hurts me." The conversation ended as another child came over. (1/22)
9. (Identification with victim as alternative defense.) Dori wanted to come indoors with me when I went in to get mittens for someone. While there she found a roll of adhesive tape; she said she wanted me to put some on her finger.

Teacher: Why, Dori?

Dori (holding out her finger for me to examine): See? Right there. (She points to a red mark above the nail which looks to me like a sore hangnail.)

Teacher (sympathizes): Oh, yes, I see. How did you get that sore?

Dori (clutching her finger tight with her other hand): My mommy did that to me. She hurt me.

Teacher: How did she do that?

Dori: First she put red hot oil on my finger and then (talking very fast) she poured Clorox on it and it hurt me and I got mad and I punched her in the nose.

Teacher: And what did she do then?

Dori (in a high singsong voice): She got upset and she poured all of the food out of the pots and then she cried. (Stops, stares at the floor.)

Teacher: That must have been a very hard time for you. Now I think your finger really needs a band-aid, don't you?

Dori (sudenly rousing herself): No, I want to go out now. (Turns away and runs to the door.) (1/23)

10. (As assistant teacher is buttoning her coat at the end of school day, which Dori always waits to have done for her)

Dori: Shut up.

Mrs. A.: O.K.

Dori (rapidly, without being asked): Because my daddy tells me to tell others to shut up. He tells mommy to shut up, and mommy tells me to shut up, and I hit her. Daddy tells mommy to shut up and mommy gets angry and she has a fit. (Punches into the air a few times to show what a fit is.) (1/31)

Dori depicts aggressive happenings to herself or to her parents, directly as herself. Though many are likely in fantasy, they are reality-anchored and told by her as if they were believable facts, at least for the moment (cf. #9). There is no evidence in her records of fluctuating certainty, so much as a vulnerability to a transient loss of distinctions between wish, fear, and real happenings when she is caught up in preoccupying aggressive, retaliatory imagery of struggle with her mother or father, or as a part of their struggle (cf. #10). Her fantasy expressions, unlike Clara's monologues for example, never include mention of pleasurable familial or caretaking experiences, nor the fact that she has a baby sister. It may be recalled that in reaction to her *verbal* aggression, Clara was immediately galvanized into undoing efforts to hold on to and regain the adult she feared to lose thereby. In contrast, Dori does not express apparent separation anxiety, but rather efforts to sever ties with the bad parental figure she has "lost" (through her anger or disillusionment) and to become attached instead to another good object (e.g., #7). She also appears to expect such severance when she is bad, to the point of bringing it on—as the time she simply ran away from her teacher and possible reunion in a spasm of despair and self-condemnation, after she hit Joshua (#6).

As mentioned earlier, after January Dori's direct "I" depictions of herself as aggressor were always related as a form of justice; that is, "retaliation is right" for a crime committed against one first. But as aggressor or as victim, the physical attacks described predominantly reflect primitive aggressive imagery of real violence (beyond symbolic phase-related transmutations), and an absence of comprehensible causality for either punishment or crime. Dori's identification with the aggressor is on occasion replaced by a sweepingly global self-condemnation. In either manifestation one has the impression of these associated features: unclarity of ideal images, internal oscillation or confusion in representations of self and her caretaker figures as good or bad: an ambivalence which is partly expressed in aggressive, physical efforts to make contact (which in turn foster negative feedback reactions to her in reality). Such features create and characterize a child's instability of self-alignment with good versus bad behaviors. The self-same factors which are likely to impede the evolution of object constancy in her may thus be seen to interfere also with her developing a superego constancy, and readiness for internalization of conflict.

Jono and J: Examples of Superego Constancy

Both Jono and J. give evidence in their fantasy and reality expressions of basic identifications with the provider, of internalization of conflict, of adaptive means of resolution, and of recovery in response to limited self-condemnation. Both have developed distance forms of defense, a capacity for creative fantasy beyond defensive deployment, and are relatively free to engage in widening-world interests. Jono has a more difficult time than J. in dealing with his aggressive impulses in reality and appears to get into more overt conflict situations. On the other hand, J. has a more difficult time in "owning" her aggressive impulses, i.e., acknowledging them as her own. Her aggressor representations in fantasy expressions are make-believe figures, in contrast to Jono who can say, e.g., "I'm a tiger." J.'s extraordinary penchant for utilizing fantasy when experiencing conflict with external sources, or with one that is as internalized, may have created a side-effect in that she seems to have retained a vulnerability to magic thinking connected with "naughty" thoughts.

I shall present Jono's records in detail during his third year, and J.'s records in as much detail as possible, during her fourth year.

J. (Jacqueline)

I have already described the indicators of J.'s formation of an early positive superego: her positive registrations of "prohibiting schemas," her consistent recourse to various distance devices when moved to express aggressive feelings against her parents,[34] and her responses of remorse and undoing—before she was three years old.

"Aseau" and "Marécage" are companion-type characters created by J. and reflecting in different ways her internal struggle with her particular moral introjects, and phase-related anxieties.[35] Aseau came into being when J. was 3;11 and lasted for several months (until 4;1); the Marécage cycle began shortly thereafter and lasted for about six months. In both, one finds support for the conception of conflict and oscillation as inherent in psychological growth. The most outstanding differences between Aseau and Marécage are: Aseau generally represents moral authority, Marécage the wishes and desires of J. that are in conflict with the internalized or external limitations; Aseau is essentially endowed with non-human figural qualities, Marécage is always a little girl.

The sequence of changes found in J.'s fantasies dealing with implicit or explicit parental prohibitions is suggestive of a norm model of steps in the process of internalization of reality and superego demands: (1) internalization of early prohibiting schemas in identification with provider-protector, with relatively mild conflict; (2) evidence of variability or externalization of drive-derivative expressions, in conjunction largely with reality compliance with authority's demands or ideal expectations; (3) indicators of internalized integration or resolution of conflicted as-

[34] It is a striking feature of J.'s aggressive reactions in fantasy or reality that they do not appear directed against her mother, only against her father.

[35] It is interesting to note that in their attempt to categorize the purpose of the companion-characters they found in their nursery school group of children, Ames and Learned (1946) mention what may be considered a series of steps or individual variations in children's internalized struggle with wish and moral dilemmas. E.g., "Companion very smart, can do anything and not get hurt (or punished)"; "Companion very weak and is bossed around or cared for by the child"; "Companion allowed to do things child may not"; "Companion blamed by child for things child does wrong" (p. 155).

pects of interdicted impulse derivatives and painful consequences.

The *Aseau* phase: Aseau's physical characteristics changed often; it was a dog, or a bird, or an insect, depending in part, according to Piaget, on her ongoing "discoveries about zoology." At times, it approached human identification—it was "huge" or had "long hair." J. once commented to her mother, "You've got long hair like Aseau" (not vice versa!). Sometimes J. was herself Aseau, growling when it was a dog, or flapping its wings when a bird, but mostly it was a creature separate from herself. That is, Aseau was not as much or as often a self-representation as Marécage.

Unfortunately for our purposes, Piaget summarizes more than he quotes fantasy content involving Aseau, but the moral authority aspect was prominent enough to invite his comment: "In a general way, this strange creature . . . was a help in all that she learned or desired, gave her moral encouragement in obeying orders, and consoled her when she was unhappy. . . . These mythical characters no doubt also acquire some of the moral authority of the parents, but only so far [?] as it thus becomes easier of acceptance in reality" (p. 131). For example: J. (3;11): "You mustn't do that" (speaking for Aseau in reference to her thought or act of tearing a piece of paper). "Aseau will scold you." Or, two days later, "J. tried to eat nicely so that Aseau should not scold her" (obs. 83). Piaget also notes that the character of Aseau "who goes so far as to scold, is particularly interesting, and recalls the examples given by Wulf, Ferenczi, and Freud of what they call 'infantile totemism' or invention of animals which dispense justice" (p. 131).

With respect to the justice Aseau dispenses, it is evident that its apparent voice and posture in laying down the law are very different from the angry, scolding moral representations found in some of the nursery school records described. Similarly, J.'s representations of the good child are in striking contrast to the "bad baby" representations of some of the nursery school children. Aseau sounds not too difficult to please, and appears more like a benevolent despot than a stern or wrathful Jehovah. Its emphasis is largely protective, pointing the way to pleasing it rather than threatening or-else consequences to non-compliance. I consider these qualities reflections of J.'s developing superego and the basis of her superego constancy, i.e., the benevolent-protective core (internal transmutation of her actual experiences). These qualities are congruent with her prominent recourse to identification with provider or comforter in her fantasy records from the time she was twenty months of age.

The consistency of J.'s defense style in dealing with her aggressive impulse derivatives during her fourth year, reflecting her superego constancy during this period, is evident in the following two records. The first devolved from a reality event at age 4;1, when "expecting to see a dwarf she had seen several times before in a village, J. learned that she was dead." Immediately she told a story, "about a little girl dwarf who met a boy dwarf: 'Then he died, but she looked after him so well that he got better and went back home' " (obs. 84). During the next few days, Piaget reports, the girl dwarf was associated with "everything in her life." The affective impact of this reality event, and the cognitive affective complexity in her response to it, are in part clarified by noting two new features of J.'s life around this time: her brother was born a few months earlier, and according to Piaget in another context, verbal expressions of penis envy were beginning to be evident about this age. (Too, particular anxieties and concerns about the meaning of death are often noted in children in the Fours and Fives.)

The second record illustrates J.'s characteristic way of dealing with her ambivalence and aggressive concerns in fantasy constructions centered on family relationships. At the same time it clearly reveals her general developmental advances in thought, and reality scope, as well as some loosening in her previously strict adherence to self-representations as the ideal provider, or comforter. "J. at 4;7 was carrying a long stone to represent the jug of milk Honorine brought every morning. J.: 'I'm Honorine's sister, because Honorine is ill. She's got whooping cough. She coughs and spits too sometimes. It would be a pity if the little girl [J. herself] caught it. (She said all this with a local accent . . . and it was all made up.) . . . 'There's Honorine coming.' (J. now changed her role and coughed as she became H.) 'I won't come near the little girl, so as not to give her whooping cough' (she makes the gesture of pouring out the milk). 'I don't think I can give the milk whooping cough.' (J. then becomes herself taking the milk) 'I want a lot, you know.' (This feeling is immediately modified and countered by including other children who would also want 'lots of milk') 'Marécage told me that she would bring back Julie, Claudine, Augustine, and Philomene from Arolla. All those children need a lot of milk for supper' . . ." (obs. 88). Arolla is where J.'s mother had gone that day and had not yet returned. Also notable is the fact that all the children she names are imaginary.

J.'s use of projective characters to inform her father of her anger at him,[36] reveals developmental changes in the midst of her consistency of internal controls and defense style. It is not easy to understand her detour solution, since

[36] On the subject of the absence of even such projective expressions of anger by J. at her mother, Piaget's comments are interesting: ". . . The father is the object of ambivalent feelings—he is loved, but he is often a nuisance and his removal is not too serious a matter, while rebellion against the mother is much more disturbing." Also, ". . . How frequently in play the attitude toward the father varies according as the parents are together or the father is alone" (p. 175–76). When concurrent dream reports of Piaget's children are examined, one finds a range of feelings manifested towards female figures as well as male ones. A "horrid lady" appears in several dreams, so called because she is not exercising impulse controls but doing something "nasty."

she leaves her father in no doubt about her anger, and seems without fear that he knows it. Manifestly, it is beyond her affective acceptance to express it directly as her own self.

At 2;8 "J. was angry with her father, tried to hit him, etc., and since this seemed likely to have unfortunate consequences she suddenly cried: 'It was much nicer when Caroline [a friend of her godfather] was cross with Godfather!' She then related, drawing entirely on her imagination, how Caroline had struck Godfather and she began to mime the scene in detail. *When later on her mother spoke to her about her original anger, J. would have none of it* (my italics): 'No, it was Caroline!' " (obs. 84).

At 4;8 "J. was jealous of her father and said: 'Marécage has a *horrid* father. He calls her in when she is playing,' and 'her mother chose badly,' etc." (obs. 84). (Piaget's recourse to "etc." is, of course, an unfailing frustration for present purposes.)

At 5;8, "being for the moment on bad terms with her father, X. charged one of her imaginary characters with the task of avenging her: 'Zoubab cut off her daddy's head. But she has some very strong glue and partly (!) stuck it on again. But it's not very firm now' " (obs. 96). [In context, it appears reasonable to infer that the anonymous "X." is J.]

The *Marécage* phase lasted about six months, beginning about age 4;2. Marécage is a little girl like J. in all respects, it would appear, except that she was Negro.[37] There are familar ways in which Marécage served to express J.'s feelings and modes of defense, such as to affirm her sense of entitlement to her wishful strivings, to rid herself of feelings of shame and humiliation endured in

[37] The reality basis for this was J.'s first sight of a Negro woman shortly before, while on a boat trip with her family. It is a matter of pure speculation whether the color as such has psychic implications for J. which lent impetus to her incorporating it as an attribute of her protagonist.

reality situations. But Marécage also reflected the drama of J.'s internal struggle with her introjected moral authority in a way and at a time that phase changes in internalized sources of anxiety may be inferred and related to superego evolution.

The intrapsychic changes reflected in the two Marécage records (XXII-1, 2) and particularly in the subsequent episode may be most readily appreciated by comparing J.'s reactions to body injury during this period with those she experienced from age two–three. At these ages, beyond the pain of the injury she seemed mostly "insulted" by the happening, and proceeded to project the injury onto a more or less imaginary character, whom she then usually comforted. She did not seem particularly fearful, nor ever appeared to connect the cut or fall with being naughty. But now, in the middle fourth year, she expresses concern about the possibility, if not probability, of relatively uncontrollable events ("rolling for four nights") or injuries, as *consequences* to acting on naughty, hence dangerous impulses. In #3 she apparently experiences a surge of anxiety about possibly injuring herself, in response to an unspoken fantasy involving the use of a pointed cutting instrument, and calls on her father for protective reassurance. (That he has indeed been so available to her as comforter and protector is the basis of her consistent self-representations, and of her predictable capacity to move on past her current impulse-control concerns. This is an example of young children's continued need in changing modes of expression, for a "protective shield" or auxiliary ego to facilitate their psychological growth.)

On another level, one may note J.'s advance in utilizing causality concepts in thought. Though at this time the consequences she describes reflect more her affective than objective realities, the capacity for explicit anticipation of consequences opens the way to establishing viable connections between superego imperatives and anxieties about or-else consequences, and ego functions of judgment and reality testing, which in turn make possible superego schema modifications, and strengthen functional superego constancy.

The affective content in these records may be said to signal a change in the nature of her anxiety, as well as an increasing self-alignment with the protective aspects of her parent's injunctions, as interpreted by her. Viewed in psychoanalytic terms, this type of fantasy content reveals the influence of castration anxiety, replacing the earlier dominance of separation and loss-of-love-anxiety forms. Evidence that anxiety related to sexual-aggressive fantasy is a significant affect-organizer at this time, is found in Piaget's records of affect-laden observations of sex differences (penis envy and urethral focus in his two girls) around this age, followed by a concentrated phase centered on oedipal symbols and questions about birth of babies (e.g., obs. 116). The potential facilitating influence of these multiply motivated interests on a child's cognitive pursuits and expressions is illustrated in a number of Piaget's concurrent fantasy, play, and dream records (pp. 171–78, and obs. 117).

Record XXII

1. "At 4;6 (23), J. was walking on a steep mountain road: 'Mind that loose stone,' I said. J.: 'Marécage once trod on a stone, you know, and didn't care, and she slipped and hurt herself badly' " (obs. 87a).

2. "At 4;6 (26), on another precipitous path, I pointed out to J. the rushing stream at the foot of the mountain and told her to be careful. (She replied): 'Do you know what my little negress friend did? She rolled right to the bottom of the mountain into the lake. She rolled for four nights. She scraped her knee and her leg terribly. She did not even cry. [The old J. spirit.] They picked her up afterwards. She was in the lake, and she couldn't swim and was nearly drowned. At first they couldn't find her and

then they did.' 'How do you know all that?' I asked. 'She told me on the boat' (where J. first saw a Negro woman)" (obs. 87a).[38]

3. "At 4;7 (2), we were walking close to some nettles and I told her to be careful. She then pretended to be a little girl who had been stung.

The same day she played at scything with a thin, pointed stick. She then said to me of her own accord: 'Daddy, say "You won't cut yourself, Jacqueline, will you?" ' Then she told a story similar to the preceding ones" (obs. 87a).

4. At 4;6 J. "reproduced in detail, with Marécage as the character," two scenes, one in which she had been humiliated when laughed at, and the other following her "being frightened when she thought she was lost. On the same day I knocked against J.'s hands with a rake and made her cry. I said how sorry I was, and blamed my clumsiness. At first she didn't believe me, and went on being angry as though I had done it deliberately. Then she suddenly said, half appeased: 'You're Jacqueline and I'm daddy. There! (she hit my fingers). Now say: 'You've hurt me' —(I said it). 'I'm sorry, darling. I didn't do it on purpose. You know how clumsy I am,' etc." (obs. 86), repeating exactly her father's words.

[38] Piaget's view of these fantasy expressions, which he describes as games reproducing reality "but with the addition of exact or slightly exaggerated anticipation of the consequences of the action," is in accord with his theoretical interest in these materials as stepping stones to deductive reasoning. Hence, he claims: "J. is not concerned by the thought that stepping on a stone will make her slip, since this represents an unreal future which she finds difficult to image, but it is a vivid, tangible reality for her that Marécage fell to the bottom of the slope . . ." (p. 135). Does this mean that J.'s "game" is understandable as a reflection of the unreality to her of the dangers of herself falling, etc., down the mountain? How does it happen that the real dangers her daddy warns about appear unreal to her, yet she can depict the dangers to the defiant Marécage in such vivid detail? The present orientation is towards an analysis more cognizant of conflict and defense—as offering an expanded basis for understanding J.'s projection of punishment onto Marécage, for defiance of parental warnings.

5. "At about 6;0 there was little evidence of animism, except in *affective reactions* [my italics]. For example, at 6;6 she screamed with fright when the door of the hen-house, blown by the wind, hit her in the back. Then, crying, she said: 'The wind's horrid, it frightens us.'—But not on purpose?—'Yes, on purpose. It's horrid. It said we were naughty' . . ." (obs. 119).

Finally, there is some suggestion that past the middle of her fourth year, J. began to develop a greater sense of safety, with respect to the relation between her core-self aggressive impulses and superego ideals. She displays a greater flexibility of defense resources.[39] For the first time J. represents herself in fantasy as an "aggressive lady." Her free-flinging act of throwing the other lady's "husband and child through the window," reflects a phase-appropriate level of aggressive imagery. She is able to utilize simple distance-defense devices, without her former exclusive reliance on defenses of restitution, reaction-formation, or variants of identification with the nurturer.

"At 4;7 J. did her utmost to stage a scene with a car ride. L., age 2;3, was in the process of constructing a bed, and said 'Brr' to show that she was taking part . . . but did not stop her own game . . . J. *perseveringly* arranged the parts . . . came off victorious, and made L. the wife of

[39] Some idea of the type of individual differences in attitude and mode of dealing with aggressive impulses, in children with inferrable superego constancy, may be briefly gathered from these two fantasy records of J.'s sister L., the likes of which are not found among J.'s far more voluminous records. The first has no parallel in L.'s other records either.

"At 3;1 (0) her father had died, her mother and J. had been run over by a car, and an aunt was in charge. At about 3;1 (17), everybody in the games was naughty, which led to a distortion of the usual scenes" (obs. 82).

"After 3;7 her pillow 'Ali' became the essential character who was the centre of everything . . . 'Ali is very rough (like a real friend of hers). He's got lots of faults you know. I shall keep Ali until I'm married.' Sometimes he is the husband helping to look after his two or three children: 'My husband is helping me, but he's rather clumsy, you know' (an allusion to her father)" (obs. 82).

a doll: 'You're the wife of this husband—Yes,' —and made herself another lady. "We're two ladies in a car.' L.: 'Are you in the car, madame?'—J.: *'Yes, and I'm throwing your husband and your child through the window!'—and she threw the doll away* . . ." (obs. 90; my italics).

Jono

Jono's records, beginning shortly after his third birthday, encompass his first year in nursery school. In the early months of school he was often angry and ready to hit out when he was. There are differences in his behavior compared to the acting-out children described earlier, which in combination are significantly related to the earlier emergence and character of his superego manifestations: (1) His active expressions of aggression are limited to hitting (never biting or scratching), and are rarely without apparent cause in the immediate situation; (2) he displays wider interests in materials and pleasure in skill achievements; (3) more often than not, he is receptive to group rules or routines, and from the start he is very responsive to his teacher's overtures and regard. Signs of his internalized struggle and limited self-condemnation of angry hitting appear in his records after several months in school, followed by indicators of progressive changes in the character and mode of dealing with his conflicted aggressive impulses, in succeeding records. The basis for regarding these indicators as presumptive evidence of an evolving superego component of his personality organization will be specified.

Jono is quite articulate, engages readily in fantasy expression, characterized by a capacity for distance-forms of self-representation. Revealed in his self-representations and fantasy activity are identificatory strivings that embrace conflicted needs for power and affection in ways that promise positive resolution. For example, "I'm a daddy. Kiss me," he tells Marya (record XXIII-1), while his personified strivings for powerful strength are at times in support of dreams of glory (to be "very strong . . . like Hercules"), and at times expressive of his angry-destructive feelings ("Roar! Roar! I'm a tiger!").

Internalized conflict and anxiety at this phase of his development are seen in his efforts of containment or "undoing," sometimes following aggressive impulse expression even in fantasy. For example: (1) He chooses to make up a song about a monster during a circle-time songfest in his group, but he ends it with, "and I shoot him with the dark"; (2) He begins as a roaring tiger in two recorded episodes (#3, #4), but ends one as a lamb, so to speak (" . . . Get me my coffee") and the other, on the side of the law, when he "locks the tiger's door." [40] (3) As the doctor he sits on top of the struggling baby threatening, "I'm gonna cut your head open!"—but then adds, "Here, I'm gonna put'm back together."

Congruent with these signs of internalized struggle with his aggressive impulse thoughts is his projective condemnation of others (as in #5 and #6), followed shortly by specific self-condemnation (#10 and #11). The emergence of the defense, identification with the victim, is the next clear step in his conflicted struggle between core-self aggressive urges and presumed superego-core.

Let me note here that in contrast to Dori, whose "monster" expressions appear unmitigated, Jono can be both a roaring and a loving tiger. Moreover, Jono can also "shoot the monster." That is, he appears not to feel helpless to fight it or his fears of it (whether it be the bad part of his self or of his father), nor need to protect himself by intimidating others as a monster. In like vein, he is prepared to "lock up the tiger," in contrast to Gerry, who needs to

[40] Similarly, Lois Murphy (1956) notes that Colin's creating of "safe constructions to deal with animals," represents a type of response "often used by four-year-old children to express their acceptance of limits, structures, and patterns which can help curb dangerous impulses" (II, p. 221ff).

"lock the door" against external authority, to gain internal freedom to "shoot shoot people." To recapitulate, Gerry's internalized basis for self-condemnation (and related fluctuating certainty about the distinction between pretend and real) is less firmly established by the nature of his superego-core identifications, compared to Jono's. Gerry is relatively more liable to projection of conflict, which in turn recreates an earlier developmental state of concern and reliance on external sources of control or condemnation.

Early Conflict Manifestations

Record XXIII

Jono
(Limited Self-Condemnation)

A

1. 10/12 (Triggered by an earlier group discussion this morning about daddies)

Jono (to Marya): I'm a daddy. (He is wearing an old brown fedora from the doll corner and "driving" a red plastic car.) Kiss me!
Marya: Huh?
Jono: Kiss me! I gotta go to work!
Marya: O.K. (Kisses him.)
Jono: So long. (And he drives off in his car.)[41]

2. 10/24 (Begins the make-up songfest with one about a cow and a buffalo who open a door and find marshmallows, but ends it with a Halloween song about a monster)

Jono (very softly): Monster song! And the monster says,

[41] A related indication of his family atmosphere is found in this exchange (2/11/65): "Teacher: Jonathan brought something special foı each person. It's called a valentine. Do you know what a valentine is? Kate (very assuredly): A valentine—it's for Christmas! Jono: No! It's for a surprise when you're sitting watching television and your mommy brings you a valentine and candy."

"Boo!" And the monster says, "Boo! Boo!" And I shoot him with the dark.

3. 10/28

Jono: Roar! Roar! I'm a tiger.

Marya (delighted): Hello, tiger!

Jono (crawling around the yard): Roar! Roar! (He slides into his "cage" under the bars of the slide.)

Teacher (to Marya): Maybe the tiger is hungry.

Jono: Roar! Roar! Get me my coffee.

4. 10/29

Jono (coming over to Helen, Amanda, and Marya on the parallel bars): What's your trouble, girls?

Girls: Help! Help!

Amanda (getting Helen to join her): Let's make Jono cry. Ha! Ha! Ha!

Jono: I'm a tiger! ROAR! (Amanda continues her aggressive lead with suggestions of "Let's shoot the boys!" to which Helen responds with, "Tie him up! Tie him up!" The teacher intervenes with, "Where do tigers stay?" at which point the girls, stirred by the arousal of their own aggressive impulses, themselves become the tigers. Two other boys join them, one becoming their feeder who throws them each "a nice piece of juicy." Jono, however, has withdrawn from his role as a tiger. Carrying a big block, he says): *Here's a tiger door. I'm gonna lock them up.* You can't see the tigers now. It's closed up.

B

5. 12/7

Amanda: One, two, three, let's spit. (They are just about to spit at Jono when teacher enters.)

Teacher: Now why are you going to spit at Jono?

Amanda: 'Cause he spit at us!

Teacher: Jono, did you spit at these girls?

Jono (very emphatically, no defense offered): Yes, I did.

Teacher: But why, Jono?
Jono: 'Cause I'm angry.
Teacher: Why are you angry?
Jono: 'Cause *they're stupid!*

6. 12/9 (Two days later, a related conversation takes place between Jono and his teacher. His comments, as indicators of his attempt to deal with his own and others' aggressive impulses at this time, compared to his subsequent efforts, are best compared to episodes in record XXIV-9, 10, 11, to follow.)

Jono (in bathroom geting band-aid for his sore toe): I'm angry!
Teacher: You're angry again today, Jono?
Jono: Yes! (And he bangs his sore toe. Asked why he is angry, Jono claims): 'Cause they're stupid.
Teacher: Who?
Jono: The children.
Teacher: The children in our class? Stupid?
Jono: YES!
Teacher: But why?
Jono: 'Cause *they hit!*
Teacher: They're learning about talking instead of hitting. Sometimes they forget but they're learning just like you, Jono.
Jono: They're stupid!

7. (Jono also tried to be big and strong in ways that everyone can admire, but even in his fantasy play he does not always succeed in being his own hero.)

Jono (wearing a fireman's hat): I was an angry fireman. I was picking up things—like a big turtle.
Teacher: But why were you angry?
Jono: 'Cause I couldn't lift the big turtle. I was angry. (Several other children who have been listening now break in.)
Amanda (characteristically aggressively): Where is the angry turtle?

Others (with a dramatic show of strength to tell him *they* can lift that turtle): UP! UP! UP!

(Jono does not take up the challenge, and instead continues the dialogue with his teacher. Only now he is inspired to do something "big" and "good" in her terms, and asks her for a piece of paper to write as she was writing.)

Jono (writes on the paper): This says it's Jono's turn to pass the basket. (The meaning of his efforts to lift the big turtle becomes clear a week later, when climbing on the jungle gym he calls over to the teacher): I'm Hercules. I'm very strong.

Teacher: Who's Hercules?

Jono: He's a strong man on television. He lifts heavy things like turtles and animals. I watch Astro Boy at night. He flies from outer space. He has planets. (But he never attempted to "feel like" Astro Boy in his fantasy.)[42]

8. 12/18 (Note ready responsiveness to be good when felt supported by teacher. In the yard, Helen gets into green box; Jono runs over screaming): Get out! Get out! (Teacher comes over and suggests they both can fit into the big box. Jono continues to scream and scream. Helen gets out and goes over to the other green box next to it, containing John and Amanda. Tommy comes over and joins the three in the box. Jono is watching with a fierce look on his face as the four laugh and play. He screams at them. They yell back. He shouts enraged): Stop that yelling! It hurts my ears! Stop it! Stop it! (He becomes frantic and teacher comes over and tries to calm him. He then gets out of the box and says): Helen, you use it! (Helen an-

[42] It is instructive to note the individuality of the identification strivings aroused by the same TV characters in different children. One other child in the group several months earlier spontaneously expressed his admiration of Hercules to the teacher in these words: "Hercules is stronger than Superman. I can turn into Hercules and FLY. He can kill the drunk man stealing cars—and he can kill the police! He doesn't even need a cape!"

swers): No! (Jono looks at me angrily): She's being fresh (and goes away).

Signs of Developmental Changes in Internalization of Conflict

After the first of the year, Jono's records suggest steps in a child's progressive morality struggle with its aggressive (and related psychosexual) impulses, when these have already been modified by a stable superego-core in preceding phases. The most manifest changes are in his increased behavior controls, and in his expressions of identification with the victim,[43] which appear to replace his earlier, explicit experiences of self-condemnation. Jono's behavior helps to clarify aspects of a defensive-victim representation in this developmental phase: It need not represent a retreat to a passive or to a masochistic position, nor be an expression of aggression turned inward. Jono succinctly put it at one point, "I say to daddy, 'Don't spank me—I spank myself!' " (XXIV-11). His position is essentially to achieve control of the aggressor's action against him. To the extent that a defensive identification with victim rests on the premise of deserved punishment for one's aggressive intent, it is a special form of turning a passive into an active experience, an advanced offshoot of a primitive talion concept, and a contribution to as well as an expression of a capacity for empathy which serves as a most solid deterrent to aggressive acting out. As a transiently prominent mode of defense, identification with victim is in

[43] Even during this phase, however, Jono can express identification with comforter (XXIV-16 and 17), and following on his experience of tremendous pride in a reality achievement ("I'm a GENIUS!" #16), he can adopt a phallic-aggressive stance, without blurring anxiety about guilt-arousing aggression. In contrast, George's identification with the victim continued unrelieved throughout his fourth year, without any sign of possible spontaneous subsequent change. The difference between the two boys strongly suggests that when early identification expressions include, as Jono's, definite affectional provider qualities, identification with victim may be only a transient manifestation of normal internalization processes of self-alignment.

the line of a child's progress towards "owning" parental proscriptions and morality ideals.

Some features of Jono's records that signify the presumed intrapsychic changes are: (1) A spate of new fantasy expressions beginning in January in which he uses *direct "I" self-representation* to depict himself *as a victim* in a variety of ways, from getting "stung" to being "runned over" (#12 through #15). (2) On the other hand, when an aggressor during this phase, he (like George when an aggressor) employs the most extreme form of distance-defense, attacking non-human objects (he "spanks" the "bad fish" who "bite," or he gets a gun "to shoot the jungle"). (3) One may also note the consistent transformations of aggressive imagery (#13); e.g., he makes a snake, but then "they don't have heads" and really just look "like silly putty." Or he makes a monster which he then flattens into a rug and invites the teacher to walk on it. (4) Though still on occasions hitting or spitting in anger, he can now experience concern (#16), indeed excessively, for another child's hurt at his hands.[44] (5) Most striking as evidence of his internalized conflict and a functional superego is the sequence in #15. His expression of concern for Johnny's "hurting himself," and his quick reversal of position from aggressor to Johnny's victim both occur in response to the arousal of *angry impulses to hurt* Johnny, not to *his actual hurting* of Johnny.

[44] The sequence of events in #16 points to significant behavior dynamics that are capable of creating characterological features. When he felt a sense of pride and power through mastery of a real skill, he was enabled to take an aggressive stance suggestive of "phallic assertion," and somewhat separate from his aggression-anxiety. Feeling good in the sense of mastery, in his and his teacher's eyes, he was freed of negative aggressive affects both for genuine concern about hurting another child, and for cognitive clarity between accidental and intentional damage. At the same time, it is evident that at this stage a child continues to look for and need the adult's confirming or affirming distinction between motivation and behavioral outcome. In this respect, Jono called on his teacher in the same way as J. called on her father, to validate a distinction between her anxiety-fantasy of hurting herself and reality.

These behavioral indicators of intrapsychic changes in Jono meet some criteria of a superego system in psychoanalytic theory. E.g., (1) He expresses concern and remorse for his aggressive intents, as well as aggressive acts; (2) his defense form of identification with victim in part signifies his capacity for guilt-anxiety, in part his self-alignment with (separate from identification with) composite provider-aggressor ideal representations. It is this internalized core-self alignment which serves to foster and to distinguish guilt-anxiety from shame-anxiety, or from simply an ego-directed fear of punitive consequences.

Implicit in his behavior are (1) a strong need-desire for affective closeness with his primary objects; (2) a firm identification with provider (with differentiated maternal and paternal representations), which as cause and effect modifies aggressive impulse derivatives, enables early formation of superego schemas, and constitutes the template for empathy and for defense aims of restoration and reunion (e.g., #17). (1) and (2) give rise to (3), a wish-to-please, and a sensitivity to *actual* condemnation, which can become internalized to create sensitivity to *anticipated* rejection, and to (4) self-alignment with parental condemnation of particular behaviors, rather than global self-condemnation.

It is to be understood that the continued evolution of morality standards rests not only on the nature of the child's subsequent experiences of justice in his personal world, but also on the opportunities his environment offers him to "feel good" and admired for his ego-achievements, which have no connection with being good in a moral sense.

Record XXIV

Jono: Growth Changes

C

9. 1/6/65 (Jono hit and pushed another child. Teacher tried to talk to him about it but he walked away to the

fence, saying half to himself and half to her): I'm going to climb up here and fall off. (He spent the rest of the outdoor period sad and dejected, refusing any comfort from a teacher.)

10. 1/7

Jono (on toy telephone): Ah, shut up!

Teacher: Who are you talking to on the telephone, Jono?

Jono: To a stupid Jono! (Repeats in a loud, angry voice): AH, SHUT UP!

Teacher: Why are you saying that?

Jono: Because Jono is stupid.

11. (It was not until a month later that Jono spontaneously provided the background for his wrath against his bad-stupid self. He was watching other children build in the block-corner at the time. Presumably his recorded monologue below was in response to the teacher's suggestion that he build something too. It is also likely that he was recalling an incident or composite that occurred some time before, though the conflict situation was still an ongoing one.)

Jono: I'm a stranger that knocks down buildings. My sister called me "stupid." She called me "stupid" and she pinched me and I cried. I spanked her on the tooshie and then she cried too. My daddy spanked me on the tooshie and I fell down and broke my building. And I spanked me on the tooshie. *I say to daddy, "Don't spank me—I spank myself!"*

D

12. 2/3 (Identification with the victim.)

Jono (in the yard): I'm killed. (He lies down on the ground.) I'm dead. (He stays on the ground motionless. A few children come over and say to him that he is not dead. He becomes very angry.) I AM dead! I'm NOT alive!

Teacher: Who killed you?

Jono: A gun shoot me.
Teacher: Who shot the gun?
Jono: A car runned me down. (He lies down again.)

13. 2/3 (Some time during the day, while working with plasticene for the first time; note alternation of threatening and non-threatening content)

Jono: It's red dough. It matches the board. Look, teacher, look! Red like the board. (Continues working.) I'm making a ghost! Here's his eyes. (Then he rolls it up into a ball and sticks it on his nose.) Look! A nose! A cat nose! (Laughs, takes it off, puts it back on the clay board and pokes his finger into it.) My finger's caught. It's locked inside. (Places plasticene back on his nose.) Ouch! A bumblebee on my nose. Now I'm making a tunnel. (Now shapes the ball sticking his finger through it, then rolls it.) LOOK! A snake! They press their belly up. They don't have heads. Hey, this looks like silly putty. Now I'm making a monster. (Then he flattens it.) Teacher, it's a rug. You can walk on it. (He walks two fingers over it.)

14. 2/8

Jono (playing with boats in a basin of water next to Johnny, who is doing the same): It's deep water. (He is very excited.) Deeper and deeper and deeper. (Pushing boat down, he sticks his finger into the water.) The fish are biting. They can't bite my boat.

Johnny: The fish are biting my boat.

Jono: Well, take it out then! The people are in my boat. There's a gate, a gate so they don't fall out. You *bad fish*. Spank, spank. (He slaps the water.) The lifeguard saved the people and the captain. (Note that he does not represent himself as the hero-rescuer.)

15. 2/10 (Example of aggressive action, then aggressive intent, succeeded by identification with the victim)

Jono: Johnny can't catch me. Ha, ha, ha (tauntingly).

(Johnny tries to climb up after him on the jungle gym; Jono pushes him.) He can't come up. *I don't like him. He might fall off and hurt hisself.* I'm a pussycat. Meow, meow. (He has come down himself and lies on the ground.) I'm dead. I'm a dead pussycat.

Teacher: How did you get dead?

Jono: I got shooted.

Teacher: Who shot you?

Jono: Johnny did.

E

16. 2/5 (The one exception to the above episodes, which proves that the capacity for pride in a genuine achievement has at least temporary healing power)

Jono (building with blocks, suddenly exclaims with surprise): Look, teacher! I build a building! (Jumps up and down excitedly.) Genius! (Leaps.) Genius! (Leaps again, then continues to build carefully with satisfaction, the teacher sometimes handing him blocks or helping him to balance his building.) I need a gun—to shoot the jungle! This is where you shoot the gun. (He points to the top of building.) Abracadabra, abra—I knock down the people. (He knocks down the wedgie people.) Look, teacher! A pretty thing! Here! (He gives her a piece of colored paper he has just found and returns to building, but then notices an unsteady block and begins to get upset.) I don't want it to break! (When he has finished the building, he starts to play with a plastic airplane, throwing it around the room. It hits Helen accidentally. Jono runs up to Helen and rubs her arm, *saying anxiously to teacher*): It's just a little accident. (He rubs again. Helen is very pleased.)

17. 2/11

Jono: Candea's late today? (Candea is one of his two regular teachers.)

Teacher: She doesn't feel well today.

Jono: I have a doctor book to make Candea better. My mother bought me a doctor book.
Teacher: Does it tell you how doctors do things?
Jono: Yes, I get some pills and make her better.

Summary of Fantasy-Reality Data

The study records may be easily summarized in the manner of the paleontologist who recreates entire creatures from a few essential bones. The following findings have been strongly indicated by my key data, and they have the further merit of lending themselves to concise formulation.

(1) A pre-eminent identification with provider reflects continuity of appropriately changing "protective shield" experiences in the first two years. As cause and effect, it moderates the child's aggressive impulse experiences, facilitates an early, relatively unconflicted germination of superego schemas, and furthers core-self alignment with ideals as well as drive-controls. Identification with provider can evolve as a composite of both paternal and maternal representations. Other things being equal in subsequent experiences, children so equipped will manifest changes in their struggle to be good, reflecting progressive developmental-phase conflicts and associated changes in imagery content of prohibitions, level of anxiety about consequences, and morality directives—in rough accord with general cognitive, affective, and coping advances. Moreover, it would appear that the marked prominence of identification with provider represents experiences which produce a sense of entitlement in the child, as well as foster its wish-to-please. In such good-enough circumstances, the sense of entitlement sharpens the child's experiences of internalized conflict, and aids resolution based on integrative connections with ego and core-self components, rather than on compliance based mainly on inhibiting-type defenses. In brief, children whose experiences enable them to identify strongly with the provider are likely to develop superego schemas early, and with a far more protective than punitive cast; hence, their struggle to be good will

reflect more their wish-to-please than their fear of punitive consequences. Such an identification core, with its concomitant intrapsychic ramifications, founds a superego constancy, wherein a stability of basic morality injunctions and values remains, in the midst of developmental modifications and accruals in particular content, as a directive force on behavior choices in conflict-stress situations.

(2) Even in optimal relationship experiences a superego system includes aggressively infused attributes (e.g., in the "or-else" or "enforcement" imagery), and the study records illustrate that the intensity or globality of self-condemnation and imagery of anticipated consequences varies significantly in individual children. The struggle to be good in children who manifest a predominant identification with aggressor is discernibly different than in those with a predominant identification with provider. Within limits, the aggressor-identification core may serve to bind the separate strands of do's and don't's experiences, and play a major role in governing the child's good behavior in reality. But the intrapsychic resultant is, in effect, the installation of an internalized opposition, and at the extreme a persecutory enemy of one's me-self, rather than its guardian. As such, it will tend to be more subject to projection (or re-projection), and as a directive influence on behavior, relatively inconstant. One may consider a prominent identification with aggressor (within the normal range of checks and balances) to be an indicator of "cumulative trauma" (Khan, 1963).[45] Several interrelated cognitive affective features have

[45] According to Khan's formulation, the mother's empathic adaptation to her infant's sensory-motor and instinctual sensitivities functions as a "protective shield." The infant is thus enabled "not to become precociously aware of his dependence on [her] . . . , hence does not have to exploit whatever mental functions are emergent and available toward self-defense . . ." As a protective shield, the mother sustains "the illusion of omnipotence of well-being in the infant. Erikson (1950) has defined this sense of well-being as 'trust,' Benedek (1952) as 'confidence,' and Kris (1962) as 'comfort.'" Relative (not gross) failures in the mother's empathic adaptations during the child's critical psychosexual ascendancies (oral-sadistic, anal-sadistic and -erotic, and phallic-oedipal), constitute "cumulative trauma" experiences, which affect particularly the

been noted, as consequences, in some of the study children manifesting prominent (but not unmitigated) identification with aggressor: (a) self-condemnation tends to be global rather than limited to the specific bad act, and to be an unreliable deterrent *before* an act; (b) magical thinking, in areas apperceptively associated with aggression and power by the child, tends to persist despite other developmental advances in thought and reasoning; (c) a relative sense of unsafety or fluctuating certainty is arousable in such circumstances, beyond expectable developmental limitations; (d) both the creative range and defensive utility of fantasy appear constricted thereby, as is also the child's ability to develop some trust in his own impulses as good or controllable. In brief, a child with a relatively prominent identification with aggressor is one who also tends to be more preoccupied with aggressive impulse imagery, and whose good behavior or strivings tends to vary more in response to internal pressures, or the presence of external controls—compared to children with a relatively prominent identification with provider.

(3) At the extreme of the nursery school sample are the aggressive acting-out children, whose records suggest that internalization of conflict and the formation of a functional superego are delayed by a relative insufficiency of gratifying dependency-attachment experiences. The acting-out child behaves as though it felt precociously on its own for gratifications and safety against the physical harm it anticipates, or plans, and in any case fears. Primary signs associated with a precariously delayed superego in the young child include a marked preoccupation with primitive aggressive impulse imagery, *in conjunction with* an apparent *absence of empathy and of a wish-to-please.* In such circumstances, a child may learn specific do's and don'ts, and even comply more or less with them, but will do so largely according

---

"vicissitudes of body-ego development in the infant and the child, which over time form the substratum of the psychological personality" (1963, 293–94). "Cumulative trauma" thus refers to the creation of weak spots (akin to the influence of "fixation points"), which later stress periods in development will exacerbate and reveal.

to its conception of the rules of the game required to defend itself against a feeling of helplessness and possible attack, rather than out of identificatory strivings and struggle to be good. Cognizance of rules in itself is of course an ego, not a superego, resource of behavior controls. As such, it does not provide a foundation for moral directives of behavior beyond "expedient morality." The consequences of a delayed formation of the superego are thus to be found not merely in a child's relative unreliability in its aggressive impulse controls, but also in its continued pervasive sense of unsafety, and related recourse to magical causality thinking centered on the powers of its own or of others to control or attack.

6

Basic Concepts in Understanding Morality Development

A systematic outline of affective-cognitive features in development associated with the formation and function of a superego, however preliminary, is not warranted on the basis of the present fantasy data analysis. Nonetheless, it may be of interest to see how the proffered inferences and concepts, in combination with some current knowledge of child development, fit in as rudiments of such an outline.

To begin with, and having no intrinsic connections with moral development, there are organismic features and individual patterns of experiences in being cared for that provide the ground from which a superego system may evolve. Among the organismic features are the child's built-in capacities for discharge-delay, inhibitions of impulses, and detour responses (Anna Freud, 1966). Some individual differences—in sensitivity-arousal thresholds, in patterns of recovery from stimulus stress, in pre-eminence of motoric discharge of impulses—influence the ease with which an infant may elicit positive interactions with caretakers and establish impulse controls. Also relevant but non-specific to the superego are an infant's experiences in "being"—i.e., the balance and contrast of pleasure and pain in its recurrent experiences. The infant's capacity to feel and respond differently to these is accompanied by an equally given capacity to register such experiences in cause-effect sequences as it perceives them.

Primary Orientation to Causality in Thought

In Piaget's terminology, the infant's sense of self is an aspect of its evolving intelligence, emerging as the child can distinguish its person as a separate object *and* causality agent among the other objects. The idea that a child spontaneously wishes and attempts to be a causal agent is implicit in Rapaport's (1951) emphasis that the ubiquitous reaction of turning passive into active represents a general process of mental growth, not simply a defense device, which it can become. That is, not only may all happenings be perceived by the very young in some sense as outcomes of personal and intentional causality, but in the child's inherent readiness to experience events as causally related is the organismic cognitive basis for its perception of its self, or of its caretaker, as *making* pain or pleasure things happen.

Veridical ideas about causal sequences and about the powers of the agents of happenings are dependent on growth experiences, and are acquired slowly and with difficulty. The ease or difficulty in part is a function of the actual sense inherent in the child's reality experiences, which will invite or discourage valid expectations in the child of event connections. In part, however, some difficulty is inescapable. For the human child is endowed with an intrinsically adaptive intolerance of its early helplessness to make something happen which it intends, or just wishes, or to avoid events that are painful. In the cumulative balance of these experiences, and as these are attributed by the child to caretakers or to its own efforts, self and object representations are etched out and the first notions of good and bad are seeded.

What I have been describing may be considered an aspect of the "synthetic function" of the ego. What I wish to emphasize, however, is more an intrinsic aspect of reality orientation or reality testing. As I see it, one may speak of and study a spontaneous seeking in the child "to make sense" of happenings, especially of those which arouse concern, pleasure, or curiosity. The content of magical explanations of events, then, may be largely attributed to the predominating affects in the child at the time, but the functional foundation for such reasoning (when objective causes are uncomprehended) lies in its organismic orientation towards *causal linkage*. This inherent capacity and orientation, though unrelated to moral ends, may be considered a functional foundation for the human readiness to perceive painful occurrences within a blaming-causality frame, and for its related propensity to experience shame or guilt anxieties.

When a child's negative caretaking experiences are not sufficiently counterbalanced by positive ones, one may expect the child to continue to cognize these as the intentional acts of punitive, depriving agents, experience itself as not-good, not-entitled, hence, possesses little affective basis for modification of its original impulse-urgency and fulfillment-seeking. Internally, identification precipitates will be shaped primarily by defensive needs to avert negative consequences, such as are threatened by the arousal of rage, and related experiences of inner loss. On the other hand, a marked positive balance creates conditions for the establishment in an infant of connections between feeling a "good person" (while being so treated) and a motivation to be good in ways specified by its significant caretakers. One may regard the relative balance and pattern of aggressive/libidinal experiences as determining whether a child's compliant behaviors will be based more on submission to an aggressor (external or internalized), or more related to its self-connected, active strivings to be good. The latter represent reflections of a *wish-to-please,* some measure of which appears necessary for the evolution in a child of a readiness for internalization of conflict.

Wish-to-Please, Sense of Entitlement, and Pride

Another fundament in the formation of superego schemas is what may be regarded as a "survival given," in the same sense as the proposed human propensity towards causal linkage.

I refer to a primordial wish-to-be-pleasing which is implicit in Spitz's discussion of the infant's smile, for example. The early records of J. suggest that a child's internal readiness to assimilate parental standards and prohibitions may establish a functional superego before the age of two, and that such readiness is facilitated by caretaking experiences which enable a strong identification with provider, through which the primordial wish-to-be-pleasing is expanded to include the wish-to-please-the-other.

In the sense of a personality state or affective organizer, a wish-to-please may be described as varying in individuals and at different developmental phases or crises, in the characteristic primacy of its influence in interactions with the other, and in the extent of anxiety-imagery of consequences to not pleasing, either before or after the fact. Just as a child's pleasure in being pleasing (admired) is a priming source of its capacity for socialization, the wish-to-please may be seen as a priming source of superego formation. The toddler's discovery that he is expected to do certain things to gain approval fits in with his earlier dim awareness of a connection between his feeling good, lovable, and loving when his wishes are met, and the reverse when they are not. His wish to please is readily incorporated into compliance as a means of showing his love. Conversely, defiance, "not listening," or sheer opposition, become means of expressing anger and revenge. When a young child is moved to promise "I'll be good," it often means only "I will do what you want me to." Depending on the mutuality experienced in doing things that please, and in the opportunities of being admired for behaviors other than compliance, the child can begin to feel that it *should want to do* what the loving parent wishes, and that it is good and lovable insofar as the parental figure is pleased with it.

Whether the wish to please becomes connected with the specifics required of the child to be pleasing, and whether the specific standards and prohibitions become the child's "owned" morality guidelines, not only knowledge of means of avoiding punishment or contempt, are in part outcomes of a child's broader interrelated problems of living. Past the infancy phase of nurture-trust, a child's potential evolution of ideas of good and bad, beyond reliance on pleasing the other, is largely determined by its relative freedom from two types of hindering experiences: (1) the sense of constant struggle to please, or an abrupt loss between the ages of two–three, of prior experiences of closeness and unconflicted ability to please significant caretakers, or (2) parental confinement of notions of good to simple obedience. It appears that particularly during the phase-crises taking place between ages two–five, the parents' ability to function as an ego ally is tested; also, differences related to the child's experiences of being protected, intimidated, or involved in a power struggle in relation to prohibitions and standards, are forged. Among the internal background states generally emerging from a child's early "patterns of experiences" (Escalona and Corman, 1970) in pleasing, are pride in one's being, "basic trust" (Erikson), "sense of safety" (Sandler), "sense of competency" (White).

It will be recalled that the acting-out children gave little evidence in their behavior of any wish-to-please, empathy, or remorse for hurtful acts, nor of expectation of comfort or help from adults or peers, nor of spontaneous pride, nor even of much interest in their own achievements. Indeed, at least in some at times, one was struck by a particular kind of unawareness or heedlessness about own person and possessions. The patterning of these features, though somewhat different in each of the acting-out children, suggested a delayed superego. Only when a markedly positive relationship was established with a caretaking authority (teacher), which seeded a wish-to-please that adult, were the acting-out child's resources released for more synchronous growth. As newly won drive-deterrent resources opened the way to periods of "alert activity," the child's ego interests began to expand. As in much younger children developing in more optimal circumstances, the acting-out child needed the actual, immediate contact with his loved teacher for a considerable period of time, to sustain his self-involvement in new-found interests. In the dependency-attachment relationship he developed with his teacher, the child was able to respond to her as an ego ally in discoveries of his competencies, as well as a superego ally with respect to drive-deterrence. The emergence of the acting-out child's wish-to-please was manifested in behaviors suggestive of beginning internalization of conflict, and a transformation of its cognized do's and don'ts into "prohibitory schemas" allied with a superego introjection. These behavioral changes suggest a reciprocal relationship between the wish-to-please, and impulse controls associated with being good (superego formation), as well as point to a pervasive relationship between impulse controls and a child's potential freedom to expand attentional capacities necessary for learning (cf. Lustman, 1966).

Manda in the Threes did not seek nor ever gain a positive attachment to her teacher. She appeared impervious to adults, and correspondingly her aggressive acting-out behavior was without any evidence of remorse or scruple. She responded to the teacher only to the extent of ceasing unacceptable behavior when requested; there were no self-initiated changes in accord with her teacher's standards of good and bad. That is, unlike the changes that were observable to some extent in Mike and Scot, Manda's behavior revealed no apparent wish or strivings to be "good."

> . . . hitting, poking, pushing, are everyday occurrences with Manda; the immediate cause is seldom evident. If someone pushes her, she is likely to wait and then poke an entirely different child. There were days when she was full of amazing threats, such as one day in November: "I'll poke your eye out! I'll take your head off! I'll pull all your bones apart and tear your heart out . . ." (cf. Adam).

In the course of time Manda did develop an intense yearning relationship—but with another child, Reed, with whom she spent as much time as possible. In response to this attachment, her wish-to-please was stirred. The teacher overheard this poignant expression of it:

Reed (to another boy): That's a good boy!

Manda (quickly): And am I a good boy?

Junia provides a simple illustration of how a child's wish-to-please not only reflects a positive balance of relationship experiences (which he had with his primary family) and engenders internalization of conflict, but is the basis of self-alignment, hence pride, in being good as defined. Junia's marked decrease in impetuous, aggressive reactions to frustration, and such, was in nowise experienced by him as submission; the changes in his behavior could be said to have become a part of *his* code of honor.

Junia arrived in the United States one day, and went to school the next. His command of English was limited, but the language of hitting is universal. He was big and strong for his four years, with a naturally loud voice twice his size. In anger or frustration he hit out often in the first two months of school. The children were alternately fascinated and intimidated by him. Despite it all, as the teachers were able to see it and build on it, Junia was basically a good-natured and appealing child. About two months after school began, he was invited to visit with Josh after school. The next morning he burst into the classroom, booming with joy: "Teacher! Mrs. A.! I good! I no hit Josh!"

The relative stability of his internalized code (where school represented a continuity of prior good experiences) is reflected in the following incident where his behavior contrasts sharply with Josh's—a child who was virtually never physically aggressive, but whose conflict and anxiety about aggressive impulses were most evident in his preoccupation with whether his peers liked him. Also, in his responses of fluctuating certainty in several fantasy episodes, Josh displays a type of variable superego. Junia was part of a group of boys who were beginning to work out some dramatic play about robbers. Josh came by and hearing this burst out with, "But you've *got* to have some *good* guys!" He then assigned to himself the role of a good guy, and with no difficulty Junia agreed to be one of the bad guys. The fantasy activities got under way only briefly when Josh, in his protective coloration of a good guy, *really* hit Junia. Junia accepted the blow as fitting, though it did not fit the fantasy context, and made no move to hit back, though he could have as the bad guy.

Pride is an affective evaluation of "me" which, unlike shame and guilt, appears in its pristine spontaneity to be intrinsic in the infant's perception of its making something happen that feels good. (In this sense pride experiences are the active counterparts of pleasure in "passive gratifications.") Early experiences of being looked at beamingly for doing nothing but being, initially feed this basis of a state of well-being. When the infant begins to experience its own intentionality of efforts to do or to get something, then the responses of its caretaker audience to these will alter its initial sources of pride feelings, in accord with these new perceptions of how to be pleasing and admired. A sense of pride gained in relation to intentionality and real end-product, evolves into a "sense of competency," which is an essence of personal autonomy. And as Erikson has movingly described it (1950), when a child's efforts to "stand on its own feet" and be pleasing instead meet with disapproval, contempt or indifference, shame and doubt beset it. Shame experiences intensify a child's reliance on the reactions of others for self-regard as good or bad, which interfere with its potentiality for modifying early grandiose "ideal self" and "ideal object" constituents of a superego. Hence shame experiences (premature, excessive) will serve to impede the development and specificity of the experience of guilt.

Superego constancy will be more assured in development when pride has become an affective source of support of superego schemas. The positive defense efforts (Sandler, 1967) to maintain or recover a minimal state of pride in being one's self also support expansion of ego resources, whereas vulnerability to shame-anxiety may hinder both persistent pursuit of ego strivings and evolution of superego constancy. One may postulate that a concurrent basis for the development of pride in being (as a background state and a striving) consists in the child's appropriate experiences of sense of entitlement with respect to its strivings. Such experiences grow out of the balance of benign refusals as well as gratifications by significant caretakers (cf. J.'s experiences with her parents, and Mike's experiences with his teacher).

Too, analysis of the children's fantasy suggests that progressive steps toward superego ownership are contingent on experiences which enable a child to develop trust in its basically good impulses and a sense of safety in its ability to control or mitigate bad-aggressive impulses. As conceptualized, a child's *sense of entitlement* with respect to its core-impulse gratifications is, for several confluent reasons, a perquisite in the evolution of such self-trust. In a vital way the relative prominence and vicissitudes of the wish-to-please in a child's motivational repertoire, its place in the child's total functioning, are interdependent in relationship to the developmental features of its sense of entitlement. J.'s pattern of experiences clearly produced both a strong sense of entitlement and positive responsiveness to parental standards.

The feelings and effortfulness generated in association with a sense of entitlement further the development in the child of cognitive differentiations of reality features (separate from personal intentionality), and thus also contribute to its sense of safety. For appropriate refusals and prohibitions can begin to be discerned by the young child as being protective, not only punitive or humiliating. In this way the core-me-self of a child, intimately bound up as it is with its impulse-derived wishes, may achieve differentiation in accord with cognized distinctions between "good-entitled" wishes and "bad-forbidden" impulses. Such distinctions, in turn, are a cornerstone of capacity for spontaneity in autonomy, and give impetus to development of a sense of separate identity. Dependency feelings, moreover, are freed in this way from an overload of primitive aggressive impulses, which contain their own source of unsafety. In the acting-out children no such distinctions (entitled-not entitled, expectable-not expectable) appear to have been achieved, and in their case relatively unmitigated aggressive reactions led to such interrelated psychic consequences as premature disengagement from dependency (pseudo-independence), delayed formation of a superego nexus, and a background sense of unsafety. While a child's sense of entitlement does not prevent experiences of "outraged narcissism," it does rest on and promote a child's feeling of potency, which in turn encourages the persistency necessary to find detour solutions and helps cushion discovery of limitations. In contrast, caretaking experiences which beget feelings of helpless rage in the child, as inferrable in the acting-out children, tend to sustain early omnipotence and control ideals, hence hinder differential learning of impersonal causality of limitations and disappointments.

In passing, it is important to recognize that differences between children (at any developmental phase) in the nature of their characteristic internal affective stances, are reflected in diverse ways in behavior, and thus influence the kind of spontaneous reactions invoked in others towards them. With respect to sense-of-entitlement, at the extreme the child who does not venture to demand, or does so timidly for fear of "no," has itself become an interference to gaining potential experiences of gratifying fulfillment.[1] Or at the other extreme, a child with a reac-

[1] In a preliminary observational study of behavior characteristics several years ago, a totally unexpected finding was the wide difference in frequency and range of contacts initiated by the two teachers of the group, towards the two children being observed. The nursery group, attached to an institution, was small in number (6–8 children), and staffed by teachers given special training in sensitivity to children's personality problems. One of the little girls observed was selected initially on the basis of her outgoing and "entitled" behavior, the other because she represented retiring behavior. The teachers made 11 to 1 contacts in favor of the former—while they often did not even hear the requests of the latter unless she repeated them. This was completely unconscious selectivity on the teachers' part.

tive or otherwise inappropriate sense-of-entitlement, who demands aggressively or incessantly, will not be as easily overlooked or ignored as the first child, but invites spontaneous anger and refusal. In both extremes, the child's behavior in circular fashion reinforces its initial experiences and expectations of disappointment and rejection.

My discussion of the wish-to-please has been largely concerned with its relevance in the etching of a conscience; in itself, it is not an attribute of morality but rather a prerequisite to it and also a major factor in shaping subsequent growth trends. The wish-to-please may be conceived as a significant background motivational state which functions as an organizer of apperceptions and behavioral choice points in the evolution of personality generally, and morality specifically.

The wish-to-please may be a positive adjunct in the development of morality in selectively facilitating identifications and self-alignment with parental and later social values, provided the child is also relatively free of anxiety duress (not of concern) when confronted with or anticipating not pleasing the significant other. On the other hand, a wish-to-please orientation may become transformed by anxiety to an extent that the child's sense of having a choice or entitlement is sharply curtailed by an over-determined *need* to please. This is a source of constrictive, pathogenic defense devices in which pleasing becomes merely a means of safety, indistinguishable from placating. The *need* to please is also likely to perpetuate morality behavior in accord with "moral realism" (Piaget) in the service of defense, and to shortcircuit the child's core-self alignment with its moral structure. The need to please militates against developing clarity or distinctiveness of wishes and owned values; hence it is a hindrance to a person's sense of intentionality and moral choices, on which the maintenance of a superego constancy beyond early childhood is assumed to rest. Moreover, in effecting a kind of global vulnerability to the evaluative responses of others, the need to please constitutes a dynamic source of resentment, and as such is an integral cause of defensive chain reactions leading to aggressive, amoral thought, if not behavior also.

Developmental Views of a Superego

The time of onset of superego formation continues to be a debatable problem wherein distinctions between philosophical ideas of morality, psychological theories or constructs, and psychological "facts" are rather easily blurred in the relative absence of systematic developmental information. Freud presented his far-reaching construct of a superego structure and genesis, which embodied his cumulative clinical insights about the manifestations of "conscience" and guilt, in the framework of the prevailing position of primacy given to identifications generated in the child by its experiences of conflicted sexual-aggressive strivings and dissolution, in the oedipal phase of its relationship to parental figures.[2] Currently, Freud's classical formulation is being maintained within a more eclectic and detailed developmental orientation, by designating pre-oedipal manifestations of superego formation as precursors of a final or formed superego (e.g., Hartmann and Loewenstein, 1962; Jacobson, 1964; Nagera, 1966). The precursor formulation remains essentially a remnant of the pre-ego psychology orientation to factors in personality evolution, and may even be considered a deterrent to systematic developmental investigations, a hindrance to cohesive formulations.

In my view, the identifications (introjections) and functions which appear to "stand apart" from others, and "remind one of the superego" during the pre-oedipal period, as Hartmann and Loewenstein put it (1962), already constitute a distinctively functioning superego "system," though it is still open to changes along similar lines of structural advance as other psychic sys-

[2] In the classical orientation of psychoanalysts to the oedipal-phase crisis, I may note, the influence on guilt-anxiety or superego identifications of the child's destructive-aggressive impulses against his rival tends to be subsumed to that of guilt about his incestuous sexual longings, as in Freud's classic Little Hans (1909). A similar treatment is notable in the usual references to aggressive-impulse arousal and influence in the pre-oedipal phases, as tied in a hyphenated position to the psychosexual aspects.

tems. Though the superego is a more reflective repository and determinant of drive-control, ideal aims, and conflict in a person's psychic equipment than the ego, there appears to be no more heuristic value or validity in regarding the pre-oedipal superego format as "pre-superego" than in regarding the early forms and content of thought processes, memory, etc., as precursors of the mature ego. As is widely recognized, the post-oedipal-phase superego in its hierarchical and conflictual influence and ideal-enforcing imagery often undergoes changes during adolescence and even during later drive-related crisis periods. Insofar as the structure of a superego is open to evolutionary changes (not only more or less transitory dedifferentiation) with respect to its viable connections with ego resources of judgment and in its compelling ideal or enforcement constituents, one may of course consider all prior superego shapes as precursors of succeeding ones.

Two other points often offered in support of the traditional view of the superego as heir of the oedipal complex may be briefly commented on. For one, it is evident that in characterizing a child's early internalizations of good and bad criteria as "sphincter morality" (Ferenczi), scorn is implicit. And there is sophistry in claiming that a superego is "formed" only when the concept of evil has superseded that of danger (Loewenstein, 1966). Basically, these are value judgments of a mature superego, not evidence for or against a pre-oedipal-pre-superego structural theory. Moral value judgments of this nature may instead be considered useful, valid criteria in investigating the developmental steps and facilitating interexperiences in childhood, which enable a child to internalize as superego-ego accruals progressively ideal evaluative directives.

The discussion that follows represents an extrapolation from the data analysis of superego manifestations to these theoretical propositions: (a) In some children, the superego may be construed as formed and functioning by age two. (b) The content of internalized conflict and prohibitory schemas, and some of the attributes imbuing ideal child and ideal object representations, insofar as they reflect distinctive apperceptions and aims at given developmental phases, will manifest progressive changes in successive phase-crises. (c) But at each phase-crisis when such changes may be generated, the child may experience and draw on a relative constancy of affective orientation to its internalized ideal-authority imagos, and hence to the evaluative, drive-deterrent criteria embodied in or radiating out from its core-introjects. A child's relative stability of responsiveness to its introjects in conflicted behavior-choices, and evolution of a superego constancy toward reliable potency of internal morality-evaluative influence, will be governed by the child's early identifications with its primary caretaker-authority figures.

Identifications and Superego Constancy

While the "heir of the oedipal complex" may be questioned as the only genuine claimant to the title "superego proper," the essence of Freud's conceptualizations of the genesis and component functions of an internal morality system remains the most sound and seminal foundation for understanding and meaningful emendations. Within his framework, I should like to focus only on describing the attributes of superego introjection,[3] which in my view provide the child with the aim and raison d'être of drive-deterrence and engender firm, elemental morality, i.e., affective superego constancy.

To state my thesis baldly, an authority figure will be internalized by a child as a superego introject and serve to generate identificatory strivings with ideal child and ideal object attributes (as perceived), in response, and as a measure of its prior positive attachment-dependency feelings, to the parental figure as a provider-protector. When the caretaker-authority figure is, in the balance, feared more, or even predominantly admired, for its power to control and punish, a child may still internalize the authority's dicta, but functionally as expedient knowledge, not as grounding for moral aims or decisions derived from moral

[3] I am using the term "introjection" in the sense proposed by Sandler (1960): "Introjection is regarded as a transfer of authority from the real object to its internal representation."

ideals. With respect to *when* is a superego, the study data offer not proof but certainly support the idea that a child who experiences essentially positive nurturing in its first year of life will acquire, all other things being equal, distinctively associated schemas of a "conscience," by about age two.

In the study records, individual differences are found in the relatively protective or aggressive qualities characterizing presumptive superego demands. The differences appear to emerge out of and reflect the child's balance of libidinal/aggressive experiences of caretaking on the one hand, and the child's reactions to parental-authority do's and don'ts on the other. At one extreme, the study records of the acting-out children point up that not-good-enough attachment-dependency experiences tend to foster preoccupation with rage fantasies, maintain an early level of wishful strivings for absolutism of *own* powers and invulnerability, and interfere with internalization of conflict about aggressive impulse expression, along with the affects associated with a superego agency, remorse, guilt, and such.

Further, there appears to be a connection between a child's relative stability of internal (aggressive) drive-controls, or persistence of struggle to attain such controls within the context of good and bad evaluations, and the prominence of its self-representations (in fantasy expressions and behavior) reflective of identification with provider or protector. Conversely, children whose predominant self-representations reflect identification with the aggressor manifest less stability and struggle, greater reliance on external figures or particular situations for maintaining good behavior.

These connections between a child's provider-protector self-representations, relative stability of acquired impulse-controls, and importantly, the affectional pull implicit in its struggle to meet criteria of good, represent the basis in the data for formulating the concept of superego constancy.

While the child's dependence on its caretaker-authority figures for protection, direction, and approval continues throughout early childhood, a pervasive quality of its attachment-dependency as reflected in the selectivity of provider or aggressor representations appears to be causally related to the child's readiness or capacity for self-alignment with its superego introjections. A major reason for a fundamental relation between positively charged protector-provider experiences in infancy and superego constancy is that these generate an elemental capacity for empathy and remorse-anxiety in the child for the primitive destructive impulses which, as illustrated in the children's records, are not uncommon in early human development. These affective capacities are important fundaments in early formation of superego schema, and will ordinarily continue as significant personality attributes in the maintenance of obdurate limits to the person's enactment of destructive-aggressive impulses. The study data offer some evidence for the assumption of relationship between an early (relative) superego constancy, positively charged provider-protector experience in the first two years, the child's sense of a good "me" and its me-self alignment with related introjections. In optimally good-enough circumstances, early superego constancy is a significant influence on growth patterns, progressing developmentally in intertwined ways with and through the child's graduated experiences of separation-individuation, autonomy, entitlement, an increasing network of connection with various ego advances and I-representational acquisition, toward the attainment of the constancy of "ownership" of the internalized accruals of moral dicta and values.

The evidence of individual differences in the extent and form of behavioral expressions of variability of a superego influence (cathexis), as in drive-control indicators, strivings to be good, condemnation of bad, suggests that a key mediating or governing feature, on a conceptual level, is the child's me-self alignment with its superego introjections. One could describe the differences in the correspondent variabilities roughly on a four-point scale, beginning at the extreme: (1) The acting-out children described as delayed in formed superego schema. (2) Children manifesting preeminent identification with the aggressor introjection. (3) Children whose initial relationship founded and funded early superego schema, but who experienced a grievous discontinuity and loss of their relatively blissful attachment-dependency feelings to the "lost" good parents. The concomitant effects on separation-individuation processes, means of coping with or strangulating the reactive arousal of the child's own primitive rage-revenge feelings and acquired harsh-punitive mien of an authority introjection, and finally, the effects on its I-self achievements related to parental expectations and (ego) ideals, will differ in pattern and extent depending on the developmental attainments at the time (e.g., Tim and Evin, compared to Davi), as well as subsequent affectional circumstances. In ordinary circumstances, the interrelated combination of psychological events set in motion by sharp affectional discontinuities with the good parent provider-protector and resultant devaluation of "me" in the child also sets a psychic stage for recurrent feeling sequences in the child of mad-bad-sad and corresponding variability of superego constancy in thought and behavior. In the extreme, however, such children may be distinguished by their prepotent defensive stance congruent with identification with the victim, rather than with the aggressor. (4) Continuity of superego constancy in the midst of developmental variations as exemplified in J. and Jono, and more inferentially in Rondi.

In some respects, there is a similarity between the conceptualization of the affective essentials and developmental sequences in the evolution of object constancy, and that of the genesis and stabilization of a superego constancy. One may speculate that while the original superego introjection might optimally take place *prior* to the stable achievement of object constancy (considered by Mahler to be around age three), and if so, also entwined in that process, the firm achievement of object constancy is likely a necessary condition for the evolutionary attainment of a superego constancy. One may further speculate that insofar as the superego introjection provides a relatively constant affective source of internal self-evaluation and drive-related directives on behavior choices in successive developmental phases, it is also a potent factor facilitating the establishment of the experience of self-constancy in the midst of developmental and experiential changes.

It is evident that I have presented the concept of superego constancy in a developmental context which is not free of value judgments. One may employ the term "constancy" simply in the sense of a child's consistency of internal stance towards, and defenses mobilized in relation to the superego part of its psychic resources in drive-value conflict situations. A child may experience and manifest frequent ambivalence with respect to aspects of internalized drive-deterrent standards, and "lock the door" on this part of its behavior decisions when in conflict, in particular circumstances. However, in the functional sense, a superego constancy has not been founded.

Internalization of Conflict

A child's developing physical, mental, and emotional resources bring to the fore new strivings, apperceptions and opportunities for conflict crises at successive periods of confluence. I have previously discussed and presented evidences of internalization of conflict in a child's behavior, as reflecting the potency of its evaluative criteria of good and bad. It is true that a child may experience internal conflict primarily in response to anticipation of feared consequences to acting on its aggressive or sexual impulses. One could then conceptualize only an ego-id conflict. Indeed, it is on this ground that some of the acting-out children were considered to be delayed in forming a superego nexus. However, where internalization of conflict, as defined, is accompanied by evidences of identification of strivings with ideal-enforcing imagos (as indicated in relatively consistent self-representations), and by defenses or coping resources aimed to make the child feel good, one can regard it as a hallmark of a functioning superego.

A child's specific notions of good and bad in early childhood are honed in the course of its recurrent experiences of conflict with parental authority figures, and the particular do's and don'ts it encounters at different drive-conflict phases in the course of its developmental strides. The specific conflictual issues may be internalized by the child as a transitional step in the process of their assimilation as superego accruals, or they may remain fixated as conflictual content in direct or derivative form. In accordance with the attributes of superego constancy, a child's alignment of his me-self with his standard-bearer introjection as new conflictual content is experienced, fosters dissolution or signal guilt versus propensity for successive act-guilt sequences. Nagera (1966) states a comparable formulation of optimal superego development in terms of successive phases of internalization of conflict around psychosexual issues: "Developmental conflicts may start at one end of the scale as an admixture of different elements of 'external' and 'internalized' conflicts, while at the other end they are fully internalized" (p. 43).

In brief, if one may characterize the superego as a drive-deterrent agency with ideal self and ideal object representations at the helm, then it follows that at each critical phase of drive-conflict and resolution there will be new or modifying accruals of affective-cognitive schemas (rendered cohesive insofar as they may become crystallizations of enduring good and bad criteria). In this view, the oedipal conflict and its relative dissolution represents the last major drive-crisis in childhood, and one that comes at a time when the child's experience and modes of dissolution of it will not only reflect and further influence the superego system but also its advances in mental and social resources.

My hypothesis about superego development, with respect to the role of internalization of conflict and schema accruals at successive phase-crises (with individual variations in duration and intensity of drive-conflict derivatives), though originally stirred by analysis of the nursery records, found support in Piaget's records of "secondary symbolism." [4] This group is composed of some fantasy records and concurrent dreams centering on three main affect-laden themes, which Piaget describes as: (1) "interests connected with the child's body

[4] The category "secondary symbolism" represents essentially what is more typically considered symbolic expressions, with latent and manifest meanings generated by drive-related content.

(sucking, excretion), (2) those related to elementary family feelings (love, jealousy, aggression), and (3) those related to anxieties centered on the birth of babies" (p. 173). The creators of these records are mainly two little girls. The nature of their content led Piaget to render them anonymous, and to call the girls "X" and "Y". (There are presumptive links to J. and L. respectively.) He notes that in their fantasy expressions they conveyed their special involvement in these themes by "a state of slight excitement," by "a special way of laughing," "embarrassment at being heard," and the like.

Most frustrating for my purposes is Piaget's reticence in reporting these records as fully as the more affectively neutral ones representing, in his terms, "primary symbolism." (The records of J. quoted earlier in the text are culled from this group.) Nonetheless, despite the limitations in the relatively small number of "secondary symbolism" records, and his summarizing of some of these, when I reorganized the concurrent fantasy and dream records according to age, certain clear trends emerged. Sequential changes could be noted in the prominence of affective drive-related concerns, with the particular sequences following the psychoanalytic description of the progression and peaking in a child's psychosexual lines of development.[5]

Analysis of these sequential changes leads to a subsidiary hypothesis about steps in internalization of conflict within each phase of psychosexual prominence—i.e., there may be changes in conflict-anxiety, beginning with little, peaking, then subsiding. The character of these changes suggests a normal-curve type of movement from internalization to relative dissolution within a superego system. Actually, what I am proposing is that an

[5] Since the available data indicative of such changes are of the child's spoken communications, it is not surprising to find both oral and anal referents present in the earliest recorded themes (around sixteen months). Actually, one finds oral and anal imagery employed in fantasy expressions from ages two–six, but the later ones reflect individual differences akin to "fixation" or "sublimation," and also developmental changes in complexity of symbolic meanings or cognitive and affective contexts—e.g., there are sequential shifts in family play content, from caretaking to oedipal and/or pregnancy themes; shifts in oral imagery are from simple feeding contexts—to biting or cutting up—to notions of oral impregnation.

analysis of children's fantasy and concurrent dream records, with this focus, may reveal significant individual differences in the conflict-intensity and character of drive-deterrent achievements in successive developmental phases, hence also fresh insights into different patterns of superego evolution and effectiveness of morality directives.

Piaget's records lend themselves most readily to using the children's expressions of "excretory involvement" as a model of this thesis. As will be seen in the outline below, the children start off with considerably more pleasure than pain about the whole business. Their rather unconflicted pleasure and wide-ranging curiosity begins to change as they experience conflict with external sources; more intense conflict becomes manifest more or less rapidly, with indications of internalization of conflict, and subsidence of anxiety. Though the evidence is more implicit than explicit, one may suppose that equilibration of the specific phase-conflict issues took place in these children in the internal context of a superego constancy, in which there was an alignment of their "me" core self with their introjection, with respect to these superego schema accruals, and consequently ownership of the related dictums. It may be noted, as the subsequent pleasurable excretory observations suggest, that ownership not only minimizes internal conflict and situational variability, but also (in good-enough circumstances) frees the child from the anxiety that would otherwise maintain any initial tendency toward categorical-imperative compliance and obsessive defenses against "dirty-bad."

The developmental tale that unfolds in the excerpts that follow is clearly created in a non-punitive atmosphere, but one with firm training goals. In less favored circumstances (e.g., Scot's, p. 142), where the child's interexperiences foster reactions of anger, shame, and resistance, the nature of the child's struggle will involve its self differently, to the hindrance of attainment of ownership.

Initially the records denote (1) *mild, pleasurable excitement,* budding curiosity, and an eye for excretory imagery, or symbolic generalizations of "sitting on the pot." At age 1;4, for example, "X, after simulating certain needs, burst into laughter . . ." (obs. 95). "At 2;0, she expressed herself in terms that can easily be imagined when she saw water spurting from a fountain . . ." (obs. 115). The first signs of an internal change, in the illustrations available, appear at age 2;1, when J. indicates (2) *a partial alignment* with the pre-eminent drive-control values.[6] In this period "scenes connected with the toilet were frequently reproduced," but now the play sequences include ones in which first the dolls "dirtied" themselves, then are admonished with, "But you must ask for pot." From age 2–2;6, the little girls' sharp perceptions are often shaped by their prominent drive focus at the time; now their observations of phenomena like "water spouts, mountain torrents, etc." bring urethral imagery to the fore. (3) *Signs of internalized conflict and anxiety* about aggression and control centered in "dirtying" impulses appear after age 2;6. From 2;6–3;6 one finds both expressions with anxiety, and deliberate allusions to urethral and fecal imagery, with pleasurable excitement. Unfortunately for present purposes, Piaget prefers to summarize these data. One can glimpse the children's varied involvement, however, in the following excerpts:

> Many "symbolic fantasies and games" openly featured excretory interests— ". . . all sorts of objects had excretory organs, not only animal toys, but little cars, planes, cups, sticks, etc." (obs. 95). At 2;7 X. "laughed at an adult with a biscuit sticking out of his mouth and indulged in pleasantries it would be difficult to quote" (ibid). At 3;6

[6] It will be recalled that J. indicated her internalized alignment with oral-sadistic drive-control values in her "biting bear" fantasy when she was 1;8; the vicissitudes of oral-sadistic imagery in later drive-conflict contexts are evident in the children's dreams and fantasy. Consider, e.g., this rather complex, punitive dream at 3;8: ". . . when she was trying to overcome a tendency to bite her nails, she said when she woke, but was still half asleep: 'When I was little, a dog bit my fingers,' and showed the finger she most often put in her mouth, as she had probably been doing in her sleep" (obs. 98).

"her faeces were compared to a finger, a mouse, . . . or were even personified and given ladies' names."

Evidence of aggression-anxiety linkage: At 2;8 (11) "X. woke with a loud scream—'It was all dark, and I saw a lady over there' (pointing to her bed). 'That's why I screamed.' Then she explained that it was a horrid lady who stood with her legs apart and played with her feces" (obs. 98). "At 2;8 (4) she was wakened by a cock crowing, and said, still half-asleep: 'I'm afraid of the lady who's singing. She's singing very loud. She's scolding me.' " Y. in a dream at 3;10: "The horrid lady didn't make the beds or tidy the room and she broke a chair!" In a "symbolic game" on one of the following days the "horrid lady" was "the cause of all misdeameanors and unkindness, from wetting one's self to scolding . . ." (obs. 99).

It will be noted that in the reign of the horrid lady during this anal phase, she is an elastic representation. She may reflect either an externalization of a bad me-self image, or a conflicted internalized image of a "bad" parent. Either or both reflections in conjunction are indicative of a child's internalized struggle to be good, in the face of drive-connected impulses felt to be bad. The heyday of Piaget's children's involvement in this morality struggle, centering on sphincter control content and associated valuative strivings, appears to be over by age 3;6.

Oral and excretory imagery continue to be manifest in fantasy expressions and dreams in succeeding phases, but as impulse derivatives they are not storm centers. Rather, they appear to have become assimilated affective cognitive resources,[7] which now in fantasy expressions and dreams serve the later developmental drive-value focuses and dilemmas as more or

[7] I am clearly bypassing discussion of possible individual differences in experiences within early developmental phases, and the resultant proliferating patterns of differences evolving in subsequent phase-crises.

less unconscious bridging or adjunct imagery. The same kind of peaking and subsidence changes in affective and cognitive spheres may be noted in the successive, but overlapping phases (from age 3;6 to 6) governed by "phallic," "oedipal," and "birth" interests, strivings, and conflict anxieties. For example, the initial surge of the phallic phase is marked by the children's onset of questions and remarks about the anatomical differences between the sexes, and by heightened perceptions of phallic-imagery allusions in their surrounds, beginning around age 3;6.

> X at 3;6 (2): "I think the mountain hanging here grows and turns into a little long thing with a hole at the end for water to come out, like boys have" (obs. 95).

Remarks "sometimes serious and sometimes playful" follow "as to the possibility of making anatomical characteristics uniform," suggesting, Piaget adds, their "masculine protest." There are a number of dramatically suggestive indicators of heightened intensity of conflicted feelings affecting self-delineation and family feelings.[8] The manifest expressions of X. (J.) that follow will most simply illustrate the point I am making about "curvilinear" changes and internalization processes, when one compares those with her cited comment at age 3;6:

> At 5;8 (0): "Why do boys need a long thing for that? They could do it through their navel. Zoubab (current imaginative character) makes water through her navel."

[8] It is important, in terms of research in this area, that around age three, the two little girls differ considerably in their apparent feelings about their sexual identity. After age 3;3 Y. often played at being a boy, spoke of her baby Nicholas inside her (her mother had had a boy baby about a year earlier), and in one (age 3;11) proposed to her father that she go back inside him "and then I'll be a little baby again. I'll be called Y. (the masculine form of her name) because I'll be a boy." X., in contrast, never played at being a boy, nor expressed a wish to be one.

But the next day: ". . . after saying that boys could do it through a gate, X. played at nursing Zoubab who was ill: 'I'm making her make water through the bars' " (obs. 95)—an ability which appears would assure her recovery.

It goes without saying that this phase-focus offers different opportunities for prohibitory schemas, and for feelings, thoughts, or acts leading to shame or guilt arousal, compared to the earlier oral and anal phase conflicts. What I have suggested remains a constant, however, in the course of general developmental expansion of psychic resources, and specific accruals or modifications of prohibitory schemas is the child's basic orientation to evaluating its me-self in terms of designates of good and bad, which in turn is derived from the nature of its attachment to its actual and introjected nurturant-authority figures.

Patterns of Provider-Aggressor Experiences Affecting Internalization and Superego Genesis

A potentially testable hypothesis emerges from data on early mother-child interaction patterns reported by Escalona and Corman (1970), which expands my thesis of the pre-eminent role of identification with provider in the genesis of a superego introjection and the founding of superego constancy. That is, within the bounds of everyday interactions with attentive loving parents, children's pattern of experiences is constituted of differing balances of libidinal/aggressive (and entitlement-competency) experiences, at designated developmental phases from birth. The aggressive ("displeasurable") components, with respect to proportionate frequency, intensity, and chronicity in crucial phases of the first two years, will determine whether the initial generation of a superego formation is relatively "premature" or "optimal." As described by the authors, one subject's pattern of experiences stimulated intense dependency-attachment, early processes of individuation and separation problems, and early onset of ambivalence in a highly charged loving and conflictual interaction context. Behavioral manifestations of beginning internalization of conflict appeared quite early (10½ months), and somewhat later came articulated self-condemnation ("bad girl"); one may infer a superego introjection with Janus-type features, the relative prominence of its protector or aggressor shape being dependent on the later course of conflict stress periods. In contrast, the boy subject's first twelve months were relatively "blissful," presumably inducing a more unalloyed identification with provider, and for several reasons a less affectively intense, albeit highly positive dependency-attachment to his mother. In his behavior, there is no evidence of internalization of conflict or a superego formation during this period, though he encountered prohibitions which, "after first ignoring, he good-naturedly obeyed." One may surmise that internalization of conflict with intensity may not be initiated in him before the peaking of the anal phase.

I shall present the authors' descriptive comments about the little girl (G.) and the little boy (B.) in parallel columns, for ready comparison of their reported similarities and differences. More specific information, relevant to my focus, is provided for the little girl, but as will be seen this is related to the nature of their differences in frequency and intensity of conflict experiences. I have italicized items which appear pertinent in the light of my study data inferences, for understanding the apparent differences between them in the genesis and character of their superego.

Girl	*Boy*
First born	Ditto
Taken care of by own mother (M)	Ditto
Family income close to poverty line	Ditto
Caucasian	Black

Girl	*Boy*
Parents: "straightlaced, conservative, virtually unaffected by modern child-rearing principles, culturally relatively impoverished."	"Highly educated, child-centered, liberal."
"Attentive, loving parents"	Ditto
Delicate, moderately active, not especially sensitive.	Robust, intense, very active, yet also contained.
"*Comfortable early infancy, but thereafter plagued* by frequent respiratory infections, gastric troubles, and skin rashes." (I.e., had frequent negative physical caretaking experiences, in the sense that *possibly M's presence more than her ministrations* could provide comfort or a bulwark against anxiety.)	Colic in the early months, but *thereafter exceedingly healthy,* and turned out to be exceptionally large.
Showed intense, early stranger anxiety around 6.8 months.	He sobered at sight of strangers at 6.2 months but his *"peak* consisted of *brief whimper* and aversion, and did not occur until *10 months."*
She followed M "relentlessly from 7 months throughout second year."	Severe distress when M left came comparatively late. Following M all about room (at first in a walker), started later for him, and at no time was very prominent.

Girl	*Boy*
Visual discrimination of M's face earlier (4.5–7.6 mos.)	—7.1–8.5 months (on standard tests)
After the age of 8½ months her interpersonal experience was complex and distinctly stressful.	". . . blissfully unaware of such complexities well into the second year."
Strong evidence of ambivalence, as early as 9 mos. E.g., cried when M left, but if M returned soon afterwards, she screamed angrily at her (enraged at having been left).	Was transiently upset when M left, but content to play with toys as long as he knew she was accessible.
Prohibitions, teasing, conflict, internalization: She obeyed prohibitions, but not without protest. Having desisted from the forbidden act, she turned on M and loudly jabbered at her in unmistakable protest, as it were *"talking back."*	*Both parents adept at providing substitutes and diversions so he was rarely thwarted. Prohibitions were uttered not infrequently but were first ignored, later good-naturedly obeyed.*
She teased and was teased . . .	Not observed.
She and M had head-on collisions involving anger and distress for both, *followed by loving reunions* that soon led to *excited joyous play.*	*He and M shared a wide range of activities,* exploring everything in sight and reach.

Girl	*Boy*
"She understood the frequent warnings, scolding, and prohibitions that came her way (beginning comprehension at 8.5 mos.) so thoroughly, that *beginning at 10½ mos. she had internalized something like a conscience."* Internalization began with, e.g., her doing something she had previously been forbidden (like touching TV) and while doing so shaking her head and saying, "No, no."	Comprehended prohibitions at 11.0 mos. Not observed.
Later (age not specified) she *called herself "bad child,"* on appropriate occasions.	*Never observed to call himself "bad boy."* (With respect to the apparently little evidence of intensity of conflict entering into his "good-natured" acquiescence or alignment with the prohibitions he encountered in the first 12–14 mos., his initiating processes of internalization appear similar to those in J. before she was 20 mos.)
Incidental notes on cognitive and social development: She had relatively little interest in play with	Socially speaking, he was a baby while she was a little girl.

Girl	*Boy*
toys, but sought out people and showed high zest and animation, as well as what was often described as a kind of sophistication in that context.	
Developed normally and test results always placed her in the average range.	Cognitive development, zest and enterprise far exceeded average standards . . . persistence in pursuit of goals was striking.

As Escalona and Corman characterize G.'s relationship with her mother, "Her existence was focused on a mother to whom she was deeply attached, and from whom she derived joys and satisfactions, but also stress and conflict." It is a relationship in which the components of her "patterns of experience" in generating intense dependency-attachment, early onset of individuation processes, ambivalence, and separation anxiety, also foster early internalization of conflict, and affects of remorse and guilt-equivalents (as in persistent separation-anxiety) for rage feelings towards the mother.

One may infer that her superego introjection will be marked from the beginning by her identification with both provider and aggressor attributes, though the former is likely to be distinctly more prominent (cf. "bad girl" comments below). The aggressor qualities of her introjection can be related both to the nature of her actual experiences (for instance, the unavoidable frequency of non-comfort physical happenings, the recurrent teasing, scolding, manipulating), and to the reactive instigation in her of defiant, manipulative, rage-induced impulses against her mother. Because of the prominence of her "attentive, loving" experiences and relative freedom to "talk back" (which reduces humiliation-fury), her aggressive impulses and concerns are not likely to become preoccupying interferences in her development of a wish-to-please (in contrast to the acting-out children).

I believe it was especially instrumental in facilitating an early, perhaps even premature superego, that while she had recurrent experiences of stressful conflict, she was able both to "talk back," and frequently to enjoy excited, joyful reunions following pain episodes. That is, G. had early frequent but sharply contrasting experiences associated with being good and bad in parental terms. (This pattern or balance of experiences, aside from the absolute frequency of good occasions, appears conspicuously absent in the acting-out children characterized as having a delayed superego.) Hence, it may be hypothesized that early internalization of conflict and prohibitory schemas are fostered by both the relative prominence of distinctly good experiences with mother (separate from non-mother experiences), and the possibility in the interaction for the child to connect these causally to its efforts to be good in defined ways.

It may also be noted that one consequence of the particular balance of her libidinal/aggressive experiences was the early evidence of her self-condemnation as "bad girl." Though this represents a global form of self-condemnation, it differs in its implications from those drawn from my data. There is no implication that it was as intensely self-attacking as, for example, Dori's, while her self-condemnation is also reported specifically as "appropriate to the occasion." In these circumstances, and considering the early age of its appearance, G.'s global self-condemnation at this time appears mainly reflective of her natural developmental limitations (i.e., little capacity for differentiation between external condemnation of a bad behavior and of her whole self), while its prominence in children past the age of three appears more reflective of affective interferences. One may also see her record as supporting some comments made earlier (cf. Jono) about limited self-condemnation in children past the age of three, i.e., that it represents both a child's strivings to turn passive into active, and is a measure of its internal readiness to align with its real and introjected imago(s), with the aim of maintaining vital links of *connection* (internally, of self and object representations) rather than to be self-punitive.

There may be some obstacle to optimal separation- individuation progression (cf. G.'s intense, persistent following behavior), and relatedly, to optimal connections between a child's me-self nexus and its evolving I-self affective core, associated with a child's premature engagement in bad child condemnation. (Other consequences are predictable if a child experiences such condemnation frequently and as only from external sources.) In any case, G.'s active fighting back-reunion pattern points up that neither introjection processes nor self-condemnation is likely to be initiated primarily by intimidation or punishment. Indeed, in particular circumstances, punishment itself may constitute a hindrance to internalization of conflict associated with a superego introjection. With respect to G.'s record and the concept of superego constancy, it is clear that only later observations can provide definitive evidence, though if so inclined one may see some supportive shreds in it.

Self-Condemnation, Judgment Resources, and Ownership

The single most significant outcome of superego formation is the attainment thereby of some measure of freedom from primary reliance on external controls and standards. Feeling oneself to be good or worthless at the early stages in response to the positive or negative reactions of significant others is difficult to modify, however. The oppositional child is as enmeshed in its original tie as the over-compliant one; in paranoia and suicide, the tie is pathologically distorted. As we have seen, the nature of the child's reactions to its real caretakers as authority-evaluative figures will shape the characteristics and function of its internalized self-condemnation. The extent of optimal distance from dependency on others for drive-related controls or for self-esteem that a person may potentially achieve, is related to the type of self-condemnation and its psychic consequences or correlates. It is evident that the achievement of such distance is a hallmark of superego maturity or a person's ownership of the values inherent in internalized drive-deterrent standards and ideals, and is necessarily a gradual developmental attainment.

It is also evident that while individual variations in such development involve personality-cognitive attributes beyond a morality system, a person's morality resources also exert an influence, circular or reciprocal, on these attributes. Ownership, for example, rests on a child's advances in reality testing and objective causality reasoning, as well as on its experiential opportunities to develop basic trust in its own good impulses and controls.

In the under-six age group studied, one can expect to find only the beginnings of objectified reasoning in personal affective situations, compared to their advances in dealing with impersonal realities. Yet one can already see in the study group individual differences in potentiality and progress towards it. For example, in its very nature global self-condemnation[9] represents a child's diffuse reaction to a negative outcome wherein its whole self appears to be on trial rather than the specific transgression. With such a focus, the child's capacity for cause-effect evaluation of specific happenings is hindered, as well as its readiness to think in terms of restitutive or other behavior alternatives. It may be recalled that Dori's expressions of intense self-condemnation were accompanied by behaviors that conveyed a sense of despair about her self, and that she tended to run away from, not seek "reunion" with her teacher.

Steps in the growth of objective causality understanding of means-end sequences, and probabilities in pain-laden situations are illustrated in part by the differences in reasoning between aggressive acting-out children and those who manifest fluctuating certainty.

[9] Some children may be observed who seem to have developed defense devices that "tune out" self-evaluative perceptions of their own behavior, and their knowledge of expectable consequences. They react with genuine amazement "Who me?" when confronted with their doing something they know is against the rules. In effect, they are reacting to self-other conflict, with the obverse of self-condemnation.

It is of conceptual interest to observe in passing that while in primitive cause-effect reasoning pain happenings to oneself are always ascribed to the intentionality of the other (in accord with omnipotence ideals and beliefs), one can also see in the reactions of some of the acting-out children prone to such apperceptions evidence of implicit justification of their attacker. It is as though built into the child's experience of pain, even in the midst of its hate-fury at the presumed aggressor, it is also feeling, and in some fashion figuring, how it deserved what happened. Naturally, since in such children magical thinking prevails in these circumstances, their veridical cause-effect conclusions are impeded. When Mike accidentally fell and hurt his head, he said that it hurt (maybe even that he fell) because his mother hit him that morning. Why? For hitting his little brother. It will also be recalled that even J. at age six, startled, pained, and furious when the door of the chicken house suddenly slammed against her, believed at the moment that the wind did it "on purpose" because she was "naughty."

The spontaneous relating of pain happenings to punishment, when these are not otherwise comprehensible for affective or developmental reasons, appear to express a fundamental human search for causal logic, beginning in a pre-logical personal format, as well as exemplifying a primordial form of or foundation for guilt-anxiety. (Like the adult's cry when harrowed by some blow of fate: "Why did this happen to *me?*" "What did I do to deserve this?") A young child depends on the adult to establish some clarity of distinction between intentionality (affecting self-valuation in relation to morality standards), actual behavior (as bad or good), and the consequences. This is the vital affective message to the child, for example, in the adult's distinction between accidental and intentional.

Freud described the genesis of these feelings in a highly personal, moving passage in which he commented that ". . . to people living means the same as being loved," and that the feeling of being loved derives in a penultimate sense from the relatively harmonious integration of impulse life, superego ideals and moral values, and ego achievements. The "good" superego intrapsychically

> fulfills the same function of protecting and saving that was fulfilled in earlier days by the father [and mother] and later by Providence or destiny. But, when the ego finds itself in overwhelming danger of a real order which it believes itself unable to overcome by its own strength, it is bound to draw the same conclusion. It sees itself deserted by all the forces of protection . . . Here . . . is once again the same situation as that which underlay . . . the infantile anxiety of longing for an absent person—the anxiety of separation from the protecting mother (1923, pp. 86–87).

Types of Affective Causality Reasoning

Piaget's concepts of "spatialized" and "objective" causality reasoning, referring to reality-adaptive steps in objective situations, may be utilized to describe requisite cognitive advances for optimal functioning in affective-reality situations, advances which also mediate a person's attainment of superego maturity. Without doing violence to Piaget's meanings, one can say that feelings of self-blame (guilt) become objectified when the person is able to distinguish effectively between his actions or intentions, and their consequences or effects on the other. For example, in "The Witches" Aries' reactions to David's tears, and the witch-children's reactions to their teacher's intervention, illustrate non-objectified responses. Their responses in this affect-laden situation are comparable to toddler reliance on the caretaker's reactions for self-definition as good or bad. On the other hand, objectified distinctions are embodied in Rondi's alternative proposals to the witch-children (who had chased her for their supper) that they be "neighbor witches" or "gorilla families."

Some features relevant in a child's movement toward objectified distinction between motivation and behavioral outcome, as it affects his self-evaluation (and ultimate ownership of compelling morality directives), is illustrated by Jono's reactions to hurting Helen with his airplane, which climaxed his self-acclamation of "Genius!" It will be recalled that he was just throwing the plane around in this spurt of feeling great about himself when it hit Helen. In this context, he was able to know with certainty that he had no wish or intention to hurt Helen, yet he could not be certain that he was good, or that all his being good was not lost now in his teacher's eyes because Helen was hit by him. He required and looked for his teacher's reaction of trust in him as good; her confirmation that the hurt he inflicted was an accident gave this to him. He did not have to feel guilt or reactive hate for Helen for causing his fall from grace. Instead, his wellsprings of sympathy could now flow freely, and he delighted Helen with his profuse concern. (It is also relevant, of course, that the pain he had caused was mild.) It can be seen that such circumstantial sequences exemplify developmental experiences which potentiate and enhance a child's feeling of trust in its good impulses.

Two factors may be noted in this connection. (1) "Objectified" does not mean uncaring; indeed, it may at times be a requisite for caring. That is, objectified distinctions between intention and outcome (in self or another) do not preclude and may facilitate feelings of empathy or sympathy because the self is not on trial. While such distinctions depend on developmental achievement of perception of own feelings and intentionality (potentially evident beginning at age three), circumstances may hinder or enhance such perceptions. Facilitating circumstances will contribute both to growth in self-awareness of feelings and to the child's adaptive efforts to consider behavioral expressions in relation to anticipation of consequences. Unless one can make such distinctions in relation to his own intentionality, he cannot make it to another's. The obstacles to growth in these respects are clear in the interlocking cognitive-affective relationships underlying reactions characteristic of the acting-out study children. Their orientation to intentionality in its derivative linkage to early omnipotent ideals inherently precludes distinctions between accidental and intentional; their experientially induced preoccupation with aggressive impulses (by or against them) creates a defensive adherence to notions of omnipotence, maintains magical thinking, which in turn renders them chronically uncertain or unaware of the distinction between objective and personal causality of displeasurable events. Similarly, these interrelated features impede the children's developmental capacity for anticipation of consequences which is anchored in reality testing.

(2) At least until age five or so, a child relies on and needs to trust adult standards and judgment of his goodness for him to achieve clarity about his own feelings and be oriented towards making moral judgments of his own behavior. Some children make this need clearer to adults than others do.

Causality thinking with respect to feelings can be described as spatialized when the individual recognizes (can tolerate) the distance or separateness of his thoughts and actions from those of the other person, or the eventual outcome. This is clearly the other side of the coin, complementary to objectified thought. The distinction between the two facets is in part related to the fact that theoretically it is easier to be clear about one's own feelings and intentionality than it is to be certain about another's.

Projection is a prime example of non-spatialized thinking. In early development, the study materials suggest that the child's capacity for projection is an indispensable form of thought to expand cognitive-affect comprehension of the other. But the chronic use of projection as a defense mechanism clearly impedes the development of spatialized-affective reasoning. Magical thought processes do not lend themselves to spatialized reasoning either. An experience of empathy may be considered an optimal expression of spatialized thought, in contrast to projection (over-identification) or experiences of melding with another.

Broadly speaking, the child (or adult) who continues primarily to be oriented to the reactions of outside sources for self-evaluation is less able to develop objectified or spatialized reasoning, in negative-outcome situations especially. Insofar as shame affects, more than guilt, are hinged to expectations of or actual exposure of one's self, a child's pattern of experiences which intensify its given vulnerability to shame thereby also interferes with its ability to draw on cognitive advances in affective situations. In similar vein, one may posit that a superego formation in a person characteristically vulnerable to frequent shame experiences will be less accessible to viable connections with the person's potential ego resources of evaluative reasoning, as modifying influences on primitive ideal constituents and categorical imperatives.

Shame and Guilt

Though shame reactions tend to rouse the most distinctive wish to hide (one can "die of shame"), while guilt reactions seek a level of confession or punishment and redemption, both affects derive their peremptory character from the person's accordant sense of deserving the opprobrium and loss of value. To my knowledge, no specific study of young children's shame and guilt vulnerability and differential modes of dealing with each has been made, but general consensus is that shame is an earlier experience in development. Since both affect responses may be manifested in a variety of direct and indirect ways, singly or commingled or successively, the task of finding reliable criteria of each in a child's behavior is certainly difficult. A broad rule of thumb, apart from the distinctive somatic manifestations of shame (e.g., blushing, special way of smiling), is that shame is more likely a reaction in situations of loss of drive-controls, loss of face, or being made a fool of, whereas guilt is more likely when one feels destructive, unloving, evil.

Susan Isaacs (1932) reports examples in a combined category of "shame and guilt," without attempting to distinguish between the two or to indicate beyond the cited content the criteria for either. The tenor of the child's quoted comments, and the presumptive likelihood of the situational context to arouse shame or guilt, give credence to her broad category without offering clarity about why one type of reaction occurs rather than the other. The present study offers no definitive criteria either, though I have made scattered references to some children's reactions as strongly suggesting guilt.

In one view, shame seems antithetical to, or the obverse of guilt, since shame tends to incite rage and revenge fantasies (sometimes cloaked in obsessive thinking)[10] which may or may not be the sources of guilt, but feelings of guilt do not evoke shame, and may, paradoxically, even be a source of pride. In clinical experience, one observes individual differences in vulnerability more to shame or to guilt reactions. Can this signify a difference in the character of the superego introjection? Can a superego be booted into being and spurred more by shame experiences than by the child's affective self-alignment with a provider-protector introject, which provides a basis and stimulates its capacity for remorse and guilt? Are the children prone to global self-condemnation (akin to self-hatred and linked to identification with aggressor) indicating a superego formation functionally activated by, and more conducive to experiences of shame than guilt—and vice-versa in the limited-self-condemnation children?

On the basis of the present study data, one can only point to some indicators of different superego formations (introjections) in young children, related to their different relationship experiences in conflict stress situations. One may hypothesize that children subject to global self-condemnation suffer psychic consequences (possibly including proneness to shame experiences) which militate against the evolution of functional integration of infantile superego constituents and modes of functioning with advances in other intrapsychic parts, hence impeding the child's attainment of ownership or superego maturity.

Piaget's Concepts of Moral Development in Relation to Ownership

The terms "moral realism" and "moral relativism" represent in the American literature Piaget's concepts of developmental

[10] Cf. Helen B. Lewis' original contribution in her book *Shame and Guilt in Neurosis.*

changes in cognitive characteristics of moral judgment. Moral realism, or "heteronomous" moral judgment, refers to a young child's code of morals, based largely on the constraints in social and legal definitions of right and wrong, which it has learned and more or less fears to overthrow. Leaving aside the generic role of identifications in the psychoanalytic construct of superego, Piaget's concept of moral realism appears kin to the morality of categorical imperatives, characteristic of early prohibitory schemas. Too, moral realism as a basis of judgment or behavior reflects early dichotomous, all-or-none thought formulations and unthinking reliance on internalized standards as mnemonics, and connotes little or no freedom for autonomous, ego-connected judgments.

Moral relativism, as the next step in moral judgment maturity, refers to moral judgments that take situational contingencies into account and thus obviously involve ego-connected thought. To this extent, it fits into the psychoanalytic description of a requisite condition of superego maturity. It is evident, however, that achievement of the internal freedom to question and weigh accepted moral values and designated specific practices does not guarantee a "moral" conclusion, in thought or deed. Piaget states: "Honesty, a sense of justice, and reciprocity, together form a rational [moral] system" (1968, p. 58). This is so, in the sense that one may have rationale for upholding particular value assignments. But to explain moral choices and behavior when these are neither categorical nor submissive to authority, one must look beyond this similarity to schemas of logical reasoning to something in the nature of an internal commitment, in which one's sense of well-being is weighed. In psychoanalytic theory, and as supported by these study data, a child's moral strivings (wish-to-be-good) and relative stability of congruent behavior depend on its internalization and identification with a superego introjection, reflective of its pattern of relationship experiences in early childhood. The child's internal commitment, which I have described as relative to its superego constancy, alone determines whether its "rational moral system" and behavior devolves from its development of a "moral ego," or is more an expression of and judgment based on moral expediency.

Piaget implicitly recognizes the potential gap between moral judgment (conscious "I-self" beliefs) and moral behavior, as well as that the highest expression of either is insufficiently explained by references to cognitive advances and expanding social interactions with peers (inducing "reciprocity" values). For he introduces the concept of "will" as the person's "affective equivalent of the operation of reason." Will is achieved at the point and "to the extent that the emotions become organized beyond the 'impulsivity' or 'intuitive' morality of early childhood." Like William James, he distinguishes will as a special instance of intentionality and regards it as the basis for a moral decision, when the person is in conflict, for example, between an act of pleasure ("inferior tendency") or of duty ("superior tendency"). Conceived as the regulator of moral decisions in conflict, "will" can obviously vary more or less widely in different individuals, with different circumstances, in strength to overcome the temptation to a dishonest or unjust act. Beyond stating that will is a later developmental emergent (middle childhood), Piaget is not concerned with its genesis, or antecedent experiences necessary for its emergence, or with those that may facilitate or hinder its effective operation in the creation of individual differences.

One may consider the proposed concept of a wish-to-please as an early form and foundation of will, as Piaget uses the term. However, the former is described only as an internal state or affective organizer which serves as catalyzer of internalization of conflict and prohibitory schemas, not as the decisive factor in a person's moral decisions when in conflict. In the psychoanalytic conceptions of the genesis and characteristics of a functioning superego, there is no need for a separate construct of will. The child's internalized sources of commitment, or extent of self-alignment and ownership, are the sources of strength and stability of will in moral behavior-decisions in conflict.

7

Summary and Suggestions for Further Research

I have described a qualitative, observational investigation of a sample of nursery school children's spontaneous fantasy, the analysis of which has been supplemented by selections from Piaget's records (1945), re-evaluated and reorganized to reveal individual and age trends. In general, I would like to think that this study has made clear that observational research of young children's spontaneous fantasy in natural settings is a feasible, exciting source of psychological insights, offering a royal road to some of the interrelations of affects and thought in developmental, individual, and cross-cultural perspectives. If it stimulates renewed appreciation and research investigations of fantasy, my broad aim will have been realized.

I have illustrated modes of analysis of selected individual children's records which bring into focus some of the dynamically interrelated aspects of their functioning that mediate or govern differences in their behavior. I then proposed certain hypotheses and formulations which are more broadly applicable to understanding particular features of affective cognitive development. Throughout, the study findings and extrapolations were placed in the framework of related psychoanalytic constructs and child development data, and used as a basis for confirming, expanding, or challenging aspects of this framework. The particular aims and means employed in the present analysis of the study records by no means exhaust the ways in which the psychological treasures in fantasy materials may be mined.

General Findings About Fantasy

As is known from previous investigators (especially Isaacs, Murphy, and Piaget) young children display different patterns of relationship between their fantasy and their reality-directed activities. Some children are reality-bound, unable for psychological reasons to engage in fantasy expression. My study materials suggest that a child's fantasy reflects its intellectual and emotional resources, and that its freedom for such expression (versus compulsion) is a valuable if not indispensable aid to optimal integration of affects and cognition. Since a child may begin to verbalize fantasy before age two, the potentiality for psychic gains, or conversely for being disadvantaged if unable to utilize this developmental capacity, is present early.

There is, of course, a relationship between language development and a flowering of fantasy expression. Some cognitive-social losses, resulting from a combined depression of language development and fantasy expression have been reported by Lovell, Hoyle, and Siddall. The positive converse has been described by some Head Start teachers, who reported that progress in their children is as much marked by an increase in their fantasy play as by a decrease in acting-out. The implication of some intimate relationship between the two, though the cause-effect connections are obviously complex, is also noted in my discussion of acting-out children. They, however, do not suffer from any psychophysical or psychosocial interferences in language development. "Too little" recourse to overt fantasy by age three appears to be a diagnostic indicator either of insufficiencies or inadequacies, affecting pleasure in imagination and playing with ideas. Or, as in the acting-out study children, some psychological impediments in development are related to aggressive impulse preoccupations.

Recently, too, some educators have specifically recognized, in contrast to teach-by-drill advocates, the need for greater use of a child's imagination and fantasy in the classroom, as a means of vitalizing the child's processes of learning and improving the calibre of teaching methods generally. Actually, there has not yet been a systematic investigation of the interrelated factors in early development, which may influence the quality, quantity, and role of fantasy in psychological growth. The findings of the Harvard Growth Studies group are certainly provocative, in demonstrating the frequency of fantasy in their highly "competent" subjects, and its relative dearth in the "low competence" children. The variables, however, are complicated, as evidenced in the predominance of "low competence" obtained by children from low SES families. It is not yet established whether fantasy activity reciprocally enhances aspects of a child's emotional and intellectual development, or reflects them and provides a means for utilizing them. I am inclined to opt for all three possibilities.

In any case, a systematic investigation of possible interrelationships would ideally incorporate the following methodological goals:

(a) To devise and assess methods of collection and analysis of fantasy in natural settings, across-time and across-age, in representative samples of cross-cultural groups.

(b) To collect concurrent dreams and make-up stories, to evaluate the significance of the affective and cognitive themes prominent in the children's fantasy, and to gain insight into the different modes of expressing and dealing with the same conflictual problems.

(c) To collect concurrent observations of the children's reality-directed behaviors, to evaluate the consistency, import, and interrelationships of designated affective and cognitive characteristics—as manifested in fantasy records and everyday behaviors. (In nursery school this would mean coverage of such situations as circle-discussion time, lunch table, work periods, yard time, doll corner, and the like.) One could, of course, also utilize the advantages of such an across-situation approach over a period of time in a single group of children, with a narrowed focus on a selected developmental theme—e.g., aggressive-theme imagery and self-representations in fantasy play, compared to the child's reactions to and aggressive behavioral expressions in real social and workaday situations.

One could also discover a great deal about the nature and meaning of fantasy in a child's functioning, as well as attributes of its inner world, by studying it in special groups of children. For instance: a comparison of fantasy expressions (frequency, thematic content, cognate structure, etc.) in blind versus sighted children; development, frequency, and type of fantasy in Head-Start-type groups that differ in educational procedures, in terms of individual and group characteristics and achievements. One could also utilize fantasy expressions both to understand differences in the inner world of children in therapy (through middle childhood and differing in clinical diagnoses) and to appraise or discover criteria of change and progress across-time of treatment.

As defined in the text, "fantasy expression" implies a child's ability to distinguish between pretend and real. This significant mental achievement is signaled by the infant as early as twelve months, according to Piaget's records. A more recent study (Tennes and Lampl, 1969) unexpectedly revealed an infant's capacity to use sensorimotor fantasy as an *adaptive defense* against its painful reality as early as nine months of age. This finding is in itself, I believe, a remarkable stimulant to advancing theoretical conceptualizations of possible mental complexities in infancy. It also demonstrates the surprisingly early potential utility of spontaneous fantasy as a research resource for learning more about individual and developmental affective cognitive evolution, in conflict and in adaptation.

Tennes and Lampl conducted a modest, thoughtful, longitudinal investigation of children's reactions to separation from their mothers, observing them at intervals from age six months to age three years. In the nine–twelve-month age session in the study room, the infant played with the observer for a given time in the mother's presence, and at a prearranged signal the mother left the room for ten to fifteen minutes. As soon as the infant began to cry, the observer put it on her lap. Five of the twelve infants in the study then stopped crying and assumed a posture—semi-sitting, or at her shoulder with arms around her neck "typical of earlier infancy," *but with the eyes averted* from her. When the observer (to test intentionality) put her face in their line of vision, each infant immediately turned away, or began to cry until it could again resume *not seeing* her. The infant's assumed kinesthetic-motor posture represents its restitution fantasy of comfort and safety with its "lost object," and on another level demonstrates that before one year of age a child may already have at its disposal a transitional mode of symbolic defense. Tennes and Lampl's observation may be related to a number of psychoanalytic developmental and clinical ideas, including individual differences in and potential psychological interferences or accretions to the functional use of vision. But at the simplest level, in noting how some children defended themselves (temporarily) against the pain induced by their external reality, by literally not facing reality, one is observing that before an infant has evolved symbolic representational capacities and object constancy, its defense resources rest on concrete sensorimotor activities, much as it requires "protective shield" experiences to be concrete. Furthermore, one may surmise that, whatever developmental interpersonal experiences stimulate a child's proclivities for fantasy formulations, its engagement in fantasy expression is likely to facilitate the evolution of symbolic modes of thought.

A child's understanding of distinction between pretend and real is initially limited to its own behavior. Certainty about the pretend or real behavior (intent) of an other is acquired later, and more or less gradually. As is known, affect states may introduce or intensify existing ambiguities in an objective situation. In the present study, since nursery school children's fantasy deals much with themes of death, destruction, and violence, particular opportunities were afforded to observe marked individual differences in the age a child achieves certainty and clarity of distinction between pretend and real. (Distinctions between pretend and real are related to later reality-testing in terms of possible and probable.) I found that a child's preoccupation and concerns with aggressive-impulse imagery engenders an affective state which interferes with its cognitive advances or operations in this respect.

The nursery children were found to differ in their preoccupation with aggressive fantasy themes, in their developmental level of aggressive anxiety-imagery, and in their mode of expression within the fantasy. Differences in mode of expression were analyzed as clues to differences in the anxiety levels or in the sources mediating the aggressive content. Overall, the prevalence of aggressive themes in fantasy (especially in the Fours), and the analysis of individual differences in involvement with aggressive impulses and derivatives, point up that in "good-enough" circumstances psychological growth occurs in part because of, not despite the anxiety and conflicts engendered by aggressive impulses. And overall, whether aggressive impulse conflicts are progressively dissolved (i.e., dealt with in a way salutory to growth in personal and social resources), or at the other extreme create islands of arrested cognitive-affect development, is seen as depending on the child's balance of libidinal/aggressive experiences of its world.

Fantasy content and structure may be utilized as a main or adjunct research resource, and their analysis geared to a variety of purposes. But the fundamental premise for spurring any type of research plan (and that sparked the present one) is that a child's spontaneous fantasy is an intrinsic response of its mental growth and creativity and a unique expression of its affective developmental dilemmas, as well as its comprehension at different ages of the significant features in its reality world. The relative lack of fantasy play may be as much a sign of internal duress or inadequately stimulated ego resources as the excessive recourse to it is a sign of pathology. In one, the potential enrichment of reality-directed thought by imaginative symbolism resources is lost to the child, as is a potentially adaptive means of working through conflicts and anxiety. In the other, the necessary nutrients of reality testing for coping in reality are less available, with a loss of potential enrichment of fantasy content as well. The present study concentrates on extracting from the fantasy content reflections of a child's inner world attributes, which influence its behavior and affective-cognitive patterns in development.

Study Findings and Future Research

My conceptualization of the types and modes of children's self-representations proved fruitful, and will be feasible to adopt in subsequent research. The highlight findings that invite further research and emerged from the pattern analyses may be briefly summarized.

In the fantasy records across time, children tend to be consistent in their fantasy characterizations both with respect to their preferred type of manifest identification (with provider-comforter-protector, or with victim, or with aggressor), and with respect to their expressing these in direct "I" or distance modes. Past the age of three in my data, a child unable to project its self in fantasy expressions as a person or animal, is signaling interferences in developing clarity of core-self delineation, as well as in positive experiences of other people, which underlie or mediate such delineation. I found this type of disturbance in some, not all of the aggressive acting-out children.

A child's use of direct "I" self-representation appears to precede its expressions of self-distancing devices, hence the following indicators are significantly revealing of interrelated affective-cognitive patterns in development. Children past the age of 3;6–4 years who consistently employ "I" forms of self-representation are those who manifest consistent identification either with victim or with aggressor, not with provider, and are also prone to states of fluctuating certainty. (It will be recalled that fluctuating certainty designates an ego state during which clarity of distinction between pretend and real or improbable and probable, is more or less transiently, more or less frequently blurred. Beyond a given age, fluctuating certainty points to a type of anxiety-arousal that constitutes a cognitive interference.) Children who represent themselves in identification with provider are also those who have achieved distancing devices. Thus children characteristically employing direct "I" forms also are manifesting a rigidity in their defensive deployment of victim or aggressor representations. In contrast, only (but not all) the children who deploy consistent distance-defense forms achieve some flexibility in their type of identification-representations; only the child who expresses identification with provider on occasion crosses the category-lines and employing distance-devices, assumes an aggressor role.

The analysis of the fantasy-reality records supports my thesis that a child's use of distance-representation in aggressive fantasy is an indicator of internalization of conflict about aggressive impulses, and as such a clue to individual differences in functional superego characteristics. Another indicator of the superego was the type of self-condemnation characteristically employed by a child—global or limited. Global self-condemnation is a virulent expression of identification with the aggressor, encouraging shame and despair reactions more than guilt, and typical of children who in their aggressive fantasy represent themselves as "I" in identification with aggressor. Limited self-condemnation is more typically expressed by children who employ distance forms of representation in aggressive fantasy and whose self-representations prominently manifest provider-protector identifications or strivings. The more consistent and successful struggle to achieve drive-deterrent ideals noted in these children compared to those prone to the global type, has significant self-evident implications for child rearing and education practices.

Schafer points out that an important implication of Freud's view about the relation between unsurmounted difficulties of oedipal dissolution and severity of a superego, is that "the severity of superego function testifies to the inadequacy of superego formation." It follows that this measure of inadequacy or superego malformation may be noted *prior* to the child's struggle with oedipal phase problems. In the present study analysis, global self-condemnation is such an expression of undue severity. Hence, too, global self-condemnation in early childhood may more broadly presage special difficulties in reaching or dissolving subsequent drive and ego (affective and cognitive) patterns of development.

Clearly only future research can validate the interrelationships I have summarized, between a child's adequacy of defense against aggressive impulses (direct versus distance forms) and the relative prominence of its provider-protector or aggressor self-representations (identifications). Children whose self-representations are in identification with victim may be expressing a transient or more enduring type of compromise formation, but in any case appear to represent a more advanced, potentially more stable self-alignment with moral dicta (superego constancy) than those with predominant aggressor representations. Moreover, insofar as a child's identifications reflect its significant experiences of and with its caretakers, its core me-self images will expectably be forged simultaneously *in relation to* these identifications. Hence, some significant attributes of a child's me-self nexus may be also inferred in studies of self-representational content in fantasy expressions. Investigation of the development and changes in the selective "imitations" appearing in young children's spontaneous fantasy may contribute some to the broad question of development of "self"—what helps a child to stretch its self through its capacity to take in and in some measure to become the other, and in this process to become its *own* rather than an *as if self*. Spitz (1958) commented that each individual child "obviously makes a selection of his own among the vast number of" imitation and identification "items which he could take over," but a study of the conditions which govern the selection is yet to be made (p. 395). Both points remain unchallenged.

Though the separate strands of evidence in the present study are not conclusive, it is of interest to see how they limn a psychologically meaningful pattern, and in so doing invite further research. Consider the portrait that may be drawn of a child who expresses a prominent identification with provider, in comparison to that of a child conveying a prominent identification with aggressor.

He is a child who (1) is more likely to have developed distance forms of defense (by age three) against his aggressive impulses, which represent a developmental advance over direct "I" forms, and are also more effective, more productive as a mode of defense; (2) is least likely to experience fluctuating certainty in comparable circumstances; (3) exhibits more reliable aggressive-drive controls in reality (related to superego constancy), or is more responsive to this ideal; (4) demonstrates more capacity for empathy, remorse, and felicitous efforts towards "reunion"; (5) is more likely to express a limited than a global type of self-condemnation, and (6) in his fantasy expressions reflects a greater freedom to utilize his aggressive energies for creative elaborations of his underlying conflicts.

Emphasized in different ways throughout is that a most significant factor inducing early internalization of conflict, creating the foundation for a superego constancy, and facilitating later developmental modifications in specific prohibitory schemas and functional integration productive of superego "maturity," is the child's affective orientation towards adults as provider-caretakers, *before* they emerge as authority drive-deterrent figures. The child's internal circumstances, based in part on the balance or pattern of its libidinal/aggressive experiences and the real character of the emergent authority figure, then become decisive, interlocking influences.

The connections found in the pattern analysis between a child's provider-protector self-representations, relative stability of its acquired impulse-controls, and importantly, of the affectional pull implicit in its struggle to meet criteria of "good," represent the basis in the data for formulating the concept of a superego constancy. The early development of a sense of entitlement in a child with respect to its core-self impulses, along with a somewhat later emergence of the wish-to-please have been described as major interrelated sources of individual differences in superego formation and functioning. Superego constancy, as conceptualized, refers to the stability and peremptory affective import (commensurate with the child's developmental capacities at different phases), which a child's superego introjection may generate, and which serves both as a relatively constant internal moral-ideal influence on the child's behavior choices and as a source of the child's sense of well-being or esteem.

I have suggested that this concept of superego constancy may have heuristic value for developmental investigations of individual differences in the evolution of "ownership" of early and later modifications of morality directives. Superego constancy derives from the child's largely *positive,* affectively synchronous involvement with its introjection(s), and functions in such wise that the child's self-value is inextricably connected with its heeding its internalized drive-deterrent guidelines and ideal representations. In the course of the child's advances in physical and mental resources, towards a functional independence of its actual relationships with its primary family figures, the earlier relative constancy of the superego as a source of drive-deterrence and me-self evaluation becomes stabilized, and may be said to function importantly as basis for the experience of self-constancy in the midst of developmental changes and situational variations throughout life.

Individual variations in the genesis of relative superego inconstancy in childhood, and in the behavioral manifestations resulting from the difficulties in a child's effecting functional integration of superego schemas with other components of its psychic system have been illustrated. That the difficulties in effecting functional integration in childhood years may continue to plague the person in adult years is evident in the following anguished description by a young professional woman of her internalized locked-in-battle state:

> I'm angry a lot and cry when I am . . . (feeling helpless to resolve conflict between "I want," "I should want," "I can"). I only want what I can't get—because as soon as I get it I don't want it. I am just a spoiled child (ineffectual global self-condemnation). . . . I am constantly aware of my not doing what I'm supposed to and I can't

> do what I want to. I am only able to want something wholeheartedly as long as I am stopped (by external sources) from getting or doing it.

Moreover, that unassimilated discontinuities in early childhood may embalm a devalued me-self core along with fear based on primitive aggressive imagery, which continues active in derivative ways while remaining severed from mainstream connections with I-self representation accruals and behaviors in reality, is poignantly clear in these words of an estimable man in a caretaking profession who, at a late point in therapy, exclaimed with horror and despair:

> When I come right down to it I see no way out. I have so much hate inside and greed. I can't let it out. I'm like one hungry monster . . . I'm a greedy, hungry, killing monster—and if I were to kill them off—so what'll be left—and I'll just die. Like there's nothing else and that's all I am. . . .

The conclusion drawn from the analysis of the superego materials is that the traditional psychoanalytic primacy given to the oedipal complex and dissolution, and the related assignment as "precursors" to pre-oedipal superego formations are not in accord with a consistent developmental orientation and represent a dispensable proposition in the essential framework of Freudian contributions.[1]

Hartmann and Lowenstein's point (1962) that it is a long way from the primitive imitative forms, and from role-playing, to the "highest expressions of superego formation" is well taken, but in no way supplies support to a definition of superego in terms only of its "highest expressions." With respect to role-playing in the study records, it is clearly no more a simple dram-

[1] One may wonder what kinds of differences in identifications and ideals, or modes of superego expression, may prevail in children whose primary affective relationships are established in an intact extended family (e.g., kibbutz), rather than in a typical "closed" middle-class family unit.

atized imitation than a child's inner representational world is a simple perceptual mirroring of its self and object transactions. In the same article, however, Hartmann and Loewenstein also note that the history of earliest aggressions likely enters into the formation of the superego as well as superego-ego relations, but that this idea unfortunately was not yet widely applied to clinical thinking or to direct observation of children (p. 54).

Anna Freud (1966) bypasses the precursor-oedipal issues in her presentation of a consistent developmental view. In enviable simplicity she points out that with growth, different ways of dealing with conflicts emerge, as well as different kinds of conflict to be dealt with. She suggests that these changes are concurrent with increasing differentiation of the superego, "which represents both particular means of dealing with as well as of solving conflicts with the external and the internal press." The details of the study findings offer support of her position—and vice versa.

I have occasionally observed in nursery-age children a superego indicator which is open to research investigation, though not noted in any of the teachers' recordings. I am referring to a child's unconscious recourse to a "directing voice," which is distinctive both from its normal one and from one it may deliberately assume in the course of role-playing. This "superego voice" is usually not "the voice of the turtle." It tends to be bossy or scolding. Sometimes, however, one hears a child use a protective parental voice, to give itself soothing guidance in a new or suddenly uncertain situation. The voice may be expressed to instruct, warn, or scold another child, or itself.[2] Of

[2] Especially in the therapy of persons characterized as borderline, one may hear the unconscious assumption of a condemnatory superego voice directed against one's self, sometimes against another. In either case, it is noteworthy that the behavior circumstances are treated as "unforgivable," and the unforgivable is often a "foolish" exposure of self in the person's eyes. This emphasis (of shame more than guilt) suggests the persistence of an early prominent aggressor superego introjection in the borderline, a tendency to global self-condemnation, and behavior consonant with a superego inconstancy. A sign of progress in treatment is the disappearance of this ferociously punitive voice, along with decreased vulnerability to shame and humiliation experiences.

course, not all children will manifest equal sensitivity to auditory imprinting of this type, but for those who do, a study of the circumstances that call it forth and the type of superego voice that emerges would be an informative adjunct to other sources of inference concerning a child's identificatory strivings, and relative functional integration of its "me" and "thou" representations.

Also open to research is a study of the types of punishments anticipated or prescribed by children at different ages, for particular transgressions. Notable in relation to content are individual and/or developmental differences in severity and in levels of psychosexual-aggressive imagery. One can see in Susan Isaacs' records of children's spontaneous comments a potential means of appraising the relationship between the manifest content of a child's concerns and its identification-representations, as well as between its actual impulse-transgressions and its projected or anticipated type of punishment in fantasy or reality-oriented behavior. Isaacs summarizes the types of punishment as ranging "in severity from being given hard tasks, being scorned, laughed at or reproached, to being put in prison, whipped, shut out from home and mother's love, deprived of food and starved, being attacked and eaten up, and done to death in various ways . . ." (1933, p. 370).

One may also investigate changes in the imagery level and influence of guilt-anxiety as developmental phenomena, and evaluate individual differences in accord with individual patterns of relationship experiences. It will be recalled that the reactions of the "witch-children" suggested that they experienced guilt-anxiety as "loneliness." This sense of internal emptiness is on a different level than other possible manifestations of early guilt-induced imagery—such as belly-emptiness, fear of starvation as in psychosomatic hunger, expectation of "losing" some relationship, or anxiety about physical damage. In Clara's monologues, for example, one could infer guilt-anxiety imagery which ran the gamut from a sense of total desolation, "I'm dead" (crying), "I want my Mommy," to variations on the theme of cutting off and losing parts of the body (in her case, the head was especially prominent). The different imagery levels of punishment suggested in children's spontaneous fantasy (as in Susan Isaacs' records), the points in the fantasy content which propel the child into a more primitive level of impulse-imagery (as in record I), are among the sources of data that could fill in some of the present gaps in the developmental scene, relevant to superego introjections, identificatory alignment with the introjections, and stability of superego functions.[3]

It is evident that much is still to be learned about the formation and constituents of internalized morality-evaluative directives in young children, which will serve them as compelling guidelines in conflict decisions, in short, that will lead them to choose to be good, not simply fear to be bad.

I have been describing my analysis of children's spontaneous fantasy as a means of elucidating patterns of cognitive-affective relationships that influence behavior and development. Let me conclude now with a general tribute to the meaning and function of fantasy expressions in early childhood. It is evident that the present study supports the position that fantasy activities have a vital place in the child's development, in expanding horizons of thoughts and feelings, and as a potential means of achieving some internal distance from affective dilemmas. Anna Freud (1936) spoke of the value of fantasy outlets in these words: "The real point at issue is how far it must be the task of education to induce children of even the tenderest years, to devote all their efforts to assimilating reality, and how far it is permissible to encourage them to turn away from reality and construct a world of phantasy" (p. 91).

Fantasy is powered by passionate basic impulses and by defenses aimed to deal with conflicts characteristic in psychological growth. Discouragement or impediments to its spontaneous emergence and evolution may constitute a deprivation of a path-

[3] Malmquist (1968) quotes a four-year-old's poignant expression of remorse and sadness after committing a transgression, which is remarkably similar to that conveyed in the witch-children's reactive behaviors. The child said that he felt "bad" and explained, "It's like I feel lonesome when Mommy is gone."

way to integration of affects and ego functions, in one sense similar to that exemplified in dream deprivation. Optimal development of ego functions depends on the flexibility and freedom of access a child has to its imagination as well as to reality knowledge. As the study data show, the child's internal wellsprings and external world experiences intermingle or oscillate in various ways in fantasy expressions, to the enrichment of both sources of knowledge. The two worlds of reality and imagination need never be as far apart as is often implied.

Bibliography

Ames, L. B. and J. Learned (1946), Imaginary companions and related phenomena, *J. Genet. Psychol. 69*

Apfelbaum, B. (1965), Ego psychology, psychic energy, and the hazards of quantitative explanation in psychoanalytic theory, *Internat. J. Psychoan. 46*

Aronson, E. and J. M. Carlsmith (1963), Effect of the severity of threat on the devaluation of forbidden behavior, *J. Abn. & Soc. Psychol. 66*

Axline, V. (1964), *Dibs.* New York: Ballantine Books

Bandura, A. and A. E. Hustin (1961), Identification and incidental learning, *J. Abn. & Soc. Psychol. 63*

Beres, D. (1958), Vicissitudes of superego functions and superego precursors in childhood, in *Psychoanalytic Study of the Child,* Vol. 13. New York: International Universities Press

——— (1968), The humaneness of human beings: Psychoanalytic considerations, *Psychoan. Quart. 37*

Bertini, M., H. B. Lewis, and H. A. Witkin (1964), Some preliminary observations with an experimental procedure for study of hypnogogic and related phenomena, *Arch Psicol. Neurol. 6*

Bowlby, J. (1969), *Attachment* (*Attachment and Loss,* Vol. I). New York: Basic Books

Brody, S. and S. Axelrad (1966), Anxiety, socialization, and ego functions, *Internat. J. Psychoan. 47*

Current Status of the Theory of the Superego (1964). Panel discussion reported by S. Goodman, *J. Amer. Psychoan. Assoc. 13.* The following papers present views of superego formation that are in some respect parallel or comparable to formulations I have derived from the fantasy-reality study materials: M. Furer, A developmental phenomenon: Concern for the object (empathy); D. Beres, Simultaneous development and relationships of ego and superego functions; H. Lichtenstein, Superego function and problems of identity maintenance; G. Piers, Shame and guilt.

Décarie, T. Gouin (1962), *Intelligence and Affectivity in Early Childhood,* tr. by E. P. & L. W. Brandt. New York: International Universities Press, 1966.

De la Mare, W. (1952), "Miss T.," in *Time for Poetry,* M. H. Arbuthnot, ed. New York: Scott, Foresman

Emmerich, W. (1966), Continuity and stability in early social development, *Child Develop. 37*

Erikson, E. H. (1940), Studies in interpretation of play: I. Clinical observation of play disruption in young children, *Genet. Psychol. Monogr. 22*

——— (1950), *Childhood and Society.* New York: W. W. Norton (Rev. ed., 1963)

Escalona, S. K. (1961), Patterns of infantile experiences and the developmental process, in *Psychoanalytic Study of the Child,* Vol. 16. New York: International Universities Press

——— and H. H. Corman (1970), Vicissitudes of mother-child interaction during the first two years. (Paper presented at annual meeting of the American Psychological Association.)

Fenichel, O. (1945), *Psychoanalytic Theory of Neurosis.* New York: W. W. Norton

Freud, A. (1936), *The Ego and the Mechanisms of Defense.* London: Hogarth Press. (My conceptualization of "ownership" encompasses the psychic changes that Anna Freud describes here as "true morality." It begins ". . . when the internalized criticism, now embodied in the standard exacted by the superego, coincides with the ego's perception of its own fault" (p. 128).

——— and D. Burlingham (1943), *War and Children.* New York: International Universities Press

——— and S. Dann (1951), An experiment in group upbringing, in

Psychoanalytic Study of the Child, Vol. 6. New York: International Universities Press

Freud, A. (1962), Assessment of childhood disturbances, ibid., Vol. 18

——— (1963), Regression in mental development, in *Modern Perspectives in Child Development,* S. Provence and A. J. Solnit, eds. New York: International Universities Press

——— (1965), *Normality and Pathology in Childhood.* New York: International Universities Press

——— (1966), Links between Hartmann's ego psychology and the child analyst's thinking, in *Psychoanalysis—A General Psychology,* R. M. Loewenstein *et al.,* eds. New York: International Universities Press

Freud, S. (1908), Creative writers and day-dreaming, in Standard Edition, Vol. 9. London: Hogarth Press

——— (1909), Analysis of a phobia in a five-year-old boy, ibid.

——— (1919), *Totem and Taboo.* Standard Edition, Vol. 15

——— (1920), *Beyond the Pleasure Principle.* Standard Edition, Vol. 18

——— (1923), *The Ego and the Id.* Standard Edition, Vol. 19

Glover, E. (1945), The Klein system of psychology, in *Psychoanalytic Study of the Child,* Vol. 1. New York: International Universities Press.

Gould, R. (1942), Repression experimentally analyzed, *Char. and Personal. 10*

——— (in progress), Piaget and affects

——— (in progress), "Morality" in studies of moral judgment, moral behavior, and superego in children

Greenacre, P. (1958), Early physical determinants in the development of the sense of identity, *J. Amer. Psychoan. Assoc. 6*

——— (1959), Play and creative imagination, in *Psychoanalytic Study of the Child,* Vol. 14. New York: International Universities Press

Griffiths, R. (1945), *Imagination in Early Childhood.* London: Kegan Paul

Hartmann, H. (1939), *Ego Psychology and the Problem of Adaptation.* New York: International Universities Press, 1958

——— and R. M. Loewenstein (1962), Notes on the superego, in *Psychoanalytic Study of the Child,* Vol. 17. New York: International Universities Press

Holt, R. R. (1961), The nature of TAT stories as cognitive products, in *Contemporary Issues in Thematic Apperception Methods,* J. Kagan, ed. Springfield, Ill.: C. C. Thomas

Hunt, F. McV. (1961), *Intelligence and Experience* (Ch. 5–8). New York: Ronald Press

I Never Saw a Butterfly—Children's Drawings and Poems, 1942–4. New York: McGraw-Hill, 1965

Internat. J. Psychiat. 31 (1967), Psychoanalysis and developmental psychology

Isaacs, S. (1930), *Intellectual Growth in Young Children.* London: Routledge & Kegan Paul

——— (1933), *Social Development in Young Children.* London: Routledge & Kegan Paul

Jacobson, E. (1964), *The Self and Object World.* New York: International Universities Press

Jersild, A. *et al.* (1933), Children's fears, dreams, wishes, daydreams, likes, dislikes, pleasant and unpleasant memories, *Child Dev. Monogr. 2*

Kardos, E. and A. Peto (1956), Contributions to the theory of play, *Brit. J. Med. Psychol. 29*

Khan, M. M. R. (1963), The concept of cumulative trauma, in *Psychoanalytic Study of the Child,* Vol. 18. New York: International Universities Press

Klein, M. (1933), *Contributions to Psychoanalysis.* New York: Hillary (1950). Her orientation to superego formation and constituents emphasizes aggression rather than libido as the pathogenic factor, and particularly the child's own destructive impulses. It is the child's "internal persecutors" that constitute the superego; he attempts to avert their expected reprisal, instigates the introjection, and with this the superego emerges as a distinct organization.

——— (1957), *Envy and Gratitude.* New York: Basic Books

Kohl, H. (1967), *36 Children.* New York: Signet Books

Kohlberg, L. (1963), The development of children's orientations toward a moral order, *Vita Humana 6*

Kramer, P. (1958), One of the preoedipal roots of the superego, *J. Amer. Psychoan. Assoc. 6.* Kramer relates a patient's pathogenic absence of "ownership" of morality standards to his primary identification with the aggressor and "developmental lack of the benign superego aspect."

Kris, E. (1952), *Psychoanalytic Explorations in Art.* New York: International Universities Press

——— (1955), Neutralization and sublimation, in *Psychoanalytic Study of the Child,* Vol. 10. New York: International Universities Press. Kris calls attention to the need for the investigation of aggressive energies for understanding normal as well as pathological development.

Laing, R. D. (1960), *The Divided Self.* Baltimore: Penguin Books (1965)

Lederer, W. (1969), Dragons, delinquents, and destiny, *Psychol. Issues.* Discusses the father's role in the development of a benevolent or harsh superego and also points to the different impact of each on the child's adaptation and "ego identity."

Lewin, K. (1935), *A Dynamic Theory of Personality.* New York: McGraw-Hill

Loewenstein, R. M. (1966), On the theory of superego, in *Psychoanalysis: A General Psychology,* R. M. Loewenstein *et al.,* eds. New York: International Universities Press

Lovell, K., H. W. Hoyle, and M. Q. Siddall (1968), Play and language of children with delayed speech, *J. Child Psychol. & Psychiat. 9*

Lustman, S. L. (1966), Impulse control, structure, and the synthetic function, in Loewenstein, *et al., op. cit.*

Mahler, M. S. (1963), Thoughts about development and individuation, in *Psychoanalytic Study of the Child,* Vol. 18. New York: International Universities Press

Malmquist, C. P. (1968), Conscience development, ibid., Vol. 23.

Malone, C. A. (1966), Some observations of children of disorganized families, in *Developmental Approach to Acting Out,* E. Rexford, ed. New York: International Universities Press

Mattick, I. (1965), Adaptation of nursery school techniques to deprived children, *J. Amer. Acad. Child Psychiat. 4.* Finds that "deprived" children engage little in symbolic as-if play and suggests the likelihood that symbolic play is a relevant precursor in the growth of language and logical thought.

Moore, T. and L. E. Ucko (1961), Four to six: constructiveness and conflict in meeting doll play problems, *J. Child Psychol. 2*

Moore, T. (1964), Realism and fantasy in children's play, *J. Child Psychol. & Psychiat. 5*

Murphy, L. B. (1956), *Personality Development in Young Children.* New York: Basic Books

——— and Associates (1962), *The Widening World of Childhood.* New York: Basic Books.

Nagera, H. (1966), Early childhood disturbances, Monogr. #2, *Psychoanalytic Study of the Child.* New York: International Universities Press

Nass, M. (1964), Development of conscience: a comparison of the moral judgment of deaf and hearing children, *Child Develop. 35*

——— (1966), The superego and moral development in the theories of Freud and Piaget, in *Psychoanalytic Study of the Child,* Vol. 21. New York: International Universities Press

Ostfeld, B. and P. A. Katz (1969), The effect of threat severity in children of varying socioeconomic levels, *Develop. Psychol. 1*

Peller, L. (1954), Libidinal phases, ego development, and play, in *Psychoanalytic Study of the Child,* Vol. 9. New York: International Universities Press

Piaget, J. (1932), *The Moral Judgement of the Child.* New York: Free Press Paperback Edition, 1965

——— . (1945), *Play, Dreams, and Imitation in Childhood.* New York: International Universities Press (2nd ed., 1956)

——— (1937), *The Construction of Reality in the Child.* New York: Basic Books, 1954

——— (1968), *Six Psychological Studies,* D. Elkind, ed. New York: Random House

Pines, M. (1969), A review of growth studies at Harvard, *New York Times Magazine,* July 6

Rapaport, D. (1951), *Organization and Pathology of Thought.* New York: Columbia University Press

Ritvo, S. and A. I. Solnit (1958), Influences of early mother-child interaction on identification processes, in *Psychoanalytic Study of the Child,* Vol. 13. New York: International Universities Press. In his comments on Ritvo and Solnit's presentation, R. P. Knight called attention to the possible significance of their material for understanding early, individual differences in superego formation and superego-ego relationships: ". . . could one say that in Evelyne the internalization of a well-attuned mother might postpone and mitigate the formation later of a punitive superego, while in Margaret the prototype of a harsh and tyrannical superego is already in evidence and almost undistinguishable from the process of ego identification?"

——— (1960), The relationship of early ego identifications to superego formation, *Internat. J. Psychoanal. 41*

Sandler, Joseph (1960), On the concept of the superego, in *Psychoanalytic Study of the Child,* Vol. 15.

Sandler, J. and H. Nagera (1963), Aspects of the metapsychology of fantasy, in *Psychoanalytic Study of the Child,* Vol. 18. New York: International Universities Press

———, A. Holder, and D. Meers (1963), The ego ideal and the ideal self, ibid.

——— and W. G. Joffe (1967), On the psychoanalytic theory of autonomy and the autonomy of psychoanalytic theory, *Internat. J. Psychiat. 3*

Schafer, R. (1960), The loving and beloved superego in Freud's structural theory, in *Psychoanalytic Study of the Child,* Vol. 15. New York: International Universities Press

Singer, J. L. and J. S. Antrobus (1962), Imagination and waiting ability in childhood, *J. Personal. 29*

Singer, J. L. (1966), *Daydreaming.* New York: Random House

Spitz, R. A. (1958), On the genesis of superego components, in *Psychoanalytic Study of the Child,* Vol. 13. New York: International Universities Press. Spitz agrees with Nunberg's thesis that the origin of the ego ideal is predominantly maternal and possibly initiated as early as the first half of the first year of life. Whereas Nunberg assumes that the ego ideal is formed only through renouncing instinct gratifications out of fear of losing the provider, Spitz believes that there are three primordia of the superego: (i) parental behaviors aimed at inhibiting the infant's physical movements; (ii) the child's strivings for mastery through imitations of parental actions and gestures; (iii) the child's identification with the aggressor, usually at the beginning of the second year. All three "have in common the (child's) wish to identify with the love object at any cost."

——— (1970), Talk at meetings of New York Clinical Psychologists describing current research.

Spock, B. (1965), Innate inhibition of aggressiveness in infancy, in *Psychoanalytic Study of the Child,* Vol. 20. New York: International Universities Press. Spock's observations of infants suggest that "their potential hostile aggressiveness toward other people is initially under a strong innate inhibition, and that they have to be taught (by the reactions of the parents when they do 'aggress' or by experiences of aggression against them) to release it."

Stein, M. (1969), The problem of character theory, *J. Amer. Psychoan. Assoc. 17*

Symposium on Clinical and Theoretical Aspects of the "As if" Characters (1965), *J. Amer. Psychoan. Assoc. 14*

Symposium on Fantasy (1964), *Internat. J. Psychoan. 45*

Tennes, K. H. and E. E. Lampl (1969), Defensive reactions to infantile separation anxiety, *J. Amer. Psychoan. Assoc. 17*

Werner, H. (1967), The concept of development from a comparative and organismic point of view, in *The Concept of Development*, D. B. Harris, ed. Minneapolis: University of Minnesota Press

White, R. W. (1963), Ego and reality in psychoanalytic theory, *Psychol. Issues 11*

Winnicott, D. W. (1953), Transitional objects and transitional phenomena, *Internat. J. Psychoan. 34*

——— (1960), Theory of the parent-infant relationship, *Internat. J. Psychoan. 41*

Witkin, H. A., H. B. Lewis, R. Dyk, and H. Faterson (1962), *Psychological Differentiation.* New York: Wiley

Wolff, P. H. (1960), The developmental psychologies of Jean Piaget and psychoanalysis, *Psychol. Issues 5*

Index

Index